SPORT IN
THE ANCIENT WORLD
FROM A TO Z

THE ANCIENT WORLD FROM A TO Z

What were the ancient fashions in men's shoes? How did you cook a tunny or spice a dormouse? What was the daily wage of a Syracusan builder? What did Romans use for contraception?

This new Routledge series will provide the answers to such questions, which are often overlooked by standard reference works. Volumes will cover key topics in ancient culture and society – from food, sex and sport to money, dress and domestic life.

Each author will be an acknowledged expert in their field, offering readers vivid, immediate and academically sound insights into the fascinating details of daily life in antiquity. The main focus will be on Greece and Rome, though some volumes will also encompass Egypt and the Near East.

The series will be suitable both as background for those studying classical subjects and as enjoyable reading for anyone with an interest in the ancient world.

Already published:

Food in the Ancient World from A to Z
Andrew Dalby

Sport in the Ancient World from A to Z
Mark Golden

Forthcoming titles:

Sex in the Ancient World from A to Z
John Younger

Birds in the Ancient World from A to Z
Geoffrey Arnott

Money in the Ancient World from A to Z
Andrew Meadows

Domestic Life in the Ancient World from A to Z
Ruth Westgate and Kate Gilliver

Dress in the Ancient World from A to Z
Lloyd Llewellyn Jones *et al.*

SPORT IN THE ANCIENT WORLD FROM A TO Z

Mark Golden

 Routledge
Taylor & Francis Group

LONDON AND NEW YORK

First published 2004
by Routledge
11 New Fetter Lane, London EC4P 4EE

Simultaneously published in the USA and Canada
by Routledge
29 West 35th Street, New York, NY 10001

Routledge is an imprint of the Taylor & Francis Group

© 2004 Mark Golden

Typeset in Sabon by Taylor and Francis Books Ltd
Printed and bound in Great Britain by
TJ International Ltd, Padstow, Cornwall

British Library Cataloguing in Publication Data
A catalogue record for this book is available from the British Library

Library of Congress Cataloging in Publication Data
A catalog record for this book has been requested

ISBN 0-415-24881-7

Contents

Introduction

As to Hercules and Theseus, they were nothing to me. They had sport, and
never learned to write a book-keeping hand.
(George Eliot, Middlemarch [New York 1910] 604)

Who knows what Fred Vincy would have made of a book combining ancient
athletes and their labours with a dictionary's dry detail? Certainly our time seems
ready. University classes in ancient sport are full to overflowing, new books
abound, Russell Crowe wins an Oscar for *Gladiator*. (He was Best Actor, a fitting
reward for a New Zealander who lived in Australia and affects a British accent to
play the Spaniard, a gladiator with an Italian-speaking son.) The modern
Olympics provide recurring reminders of their ancient origins, the legacy which
has helped create and justify their present-day prestige. Yet all this exposure to
ancient sport may raise interest more than understanding. So in just one
paragraph of a story on preparations for Athens's Olympics in 2004, a Canadian
news magazine referred to the ancient Olympic truce (wars were suspended), to
the first modern games of 1896, and to the messenger's run to report victory over
the Persians which inspired the modern marathon.[1] In fact, the ancient truce
involved only a safe passage for those travelling to the festival – the sanctuary
itself was the scene of a battle in 364 BCE; modern Greeks celebrated successful
Olympic revivals as early as 1859; and the messenger's run is as likely to be
legend as history. Accuracy (as Fred discovered) is hard work too, if not
necessarily Herculean.

The truth is, we may learn as much about ancient Greek sport by stressing the
differences between the ancient and modern Olympics as supposed similarities.
After all, today's games now come around every two years, a winter congregation
alternating with the original summer sports; even when they were quadrennial,
they were cancelled because of wars (1916, 1940, 1944) and compromised by
boycotts (1976, 1980, 1984); and they move from city to city, continent to
continent, like an exiled dictator, enticed by ever more lavish facilities for
athletes, officials and onlookers. Spectacular and secular, their celebration
ultimately encompasses nothing but themselves. By contrast, the ancient games

were part of the most revered of Greek religious rites, the festival of Zeus at Olympia, and so held there and there alone for over one thousand years. Sulla's games drew all except the boys' *stadion* competitors to Rome in 80 BCE; Nero had the festival rescheduled to suit his itinerary in 67 CE; the Eleians themselves excluded Sparta from Olympia for perhaps twenty years at the end of the fifth century BCE. But in general the Greeks could set their watches by the Olympics: Olympiads provided the common calendar for hundreds of city-states with years which began at various dates and were differently identified. Yet despite its panhellenic importance, and the throngs who made it the main meeting place of the Greek world, Olympia was simple, even stark, no match for Isthmia in its facilities for fans, or for Delphi in its setting – hot, dusty and hard to reach, without a steady supply of water until the second century of our era. Perhaps because of the cult context, the Olympics were also conservative in their programme. The athletic events were virtually fixed by 520 BCE – though many equestrian events were admitted later, in response to the hunger of the horse-racing elite for Olympic victory; and only male athletes competed and then solely in events for individuals. What is more, all competitors had to be Greek or at least accepted as Greek on the grounds of mastery of the Mediterranean world (the "Nero clause").

Now, of course, new events, for teams as well as solo competitors, are added almost every Olympics. Women take part. We have come a long way since sport was thought to threaten their femininity, sex appeal or capacity for motherhood. Some uniforms (such as speed-skaters' see-through sheaths) almost erase another distinction between modern athletes and the Greeks, who competed naked, not Niked. Part of the Olympics as they are, however, women are still separate and not quite equal. They almost always compete apart from men, and the programme includes very few events in which their performance might challenge or outdo men's – marathon swimming, for instance. (The Greeks insisted on age classes – at Olympia, boys under eighteen and men – from a similar concern that youth might be served more swiftly than their elders thought fit.) Such comparisons are facilitated by another modern phenomenon, the careful measurement of times and distances, with Olympic and world records much prized and their integrity assured by rigorous policing of the circumstances under which they are set. (Distances and equipment are of standard size, wind speed is monitored, altitude, though it does not invalidate records, may vitiate them.) Perhaps times for footraces were more difficult for the Greeks to establish – they couldn't really set their watches by the Olympics – but they could measure distances accurately enough to produce temples whose architectural sophistication is still the object of controversy and awe. They didn't. They didn't care to, any more than they worried that the foot (and so the footraces) at the Olympics was almost 10 per cent longer than that at the Pythian games. All that mattered was to defeat rivals and claim the victor's olive wreath. To be the fastest Olympic runner ever, to throw the discus further than at any games of the last decade, to achieve a personal best, was worth as much as finishing second or third: nothing at all. Modern athletes strive to compete at the Olympics, and modern nations collude with them to do so, since involvement in itself brings status; the Jamaican bob-sleighers were aiming for the bottom, and grateful just to get there in one piece. Greeks came to Olympia to win.

Specialists in Greek sport – and, I hope, readers of this book – will recognize simplifications and silences in this sketch. Some major festivals (like Athens's Panathenaea) did award second prizes. Women could win Olympic wreaths as owners of race horses and chariot teams. Some records – to be the first of a city or region to win at Olympia, or the first to repeat as champion, or to combine events – were eagerly sought and proclaimed with pride. (Today also, such milestones, distinctions which cannot be eclipsed by faster times or further distances, have become prevalent: accounts of the last soccer World Cup noted that Brazil's Ronaldo and Rivaldo had become the only duo from the same side to score in their team's first four games.) The point, however, remains valid: the modern Olympics are a poor guide to ancient Greek competitive ideals and practices. How much less reliable must they be for the Romans! From Augustus on, emperors fostered festival competitions in the Greek east of their realms, whether from philhellenism or the desire to give their subjects what they liked; the number reached 500 or even more.[2] Augustus founded the Actian games in Greece, reorganizing an old festival of Apollo to celebrate his victory over Antony and Cleopatra, and the Sebastan games at Naples in Greek-speaking southern Italy. Domitian's Capitoline games at Rome itself joined them in the expanded circuit of major competitive festivals. But unlike the Greek elite, who monopolized athletic success from the start and never lost their taste for it, their Roman counterparts disdained public displays of personal physical prowess – nudity was only one reason for this.

Even the equestrian events for which both peoples had a passion were conducted differently. Wealthy Greeks drove their own chariots on occasion and trumpeted their triumphs through the coins they struck (as magistrates, tyrants or kings) and the statues and poems they commissioned. At Rome, where chariots were so popular as to virtually exclude horse racing, teams were owned by entrepreneurs, on their own or in syndicates, and organized into four factions, racing stables much like modern motor sport teams, which regularly had two or three entries in a race. (Only the showiest Greeks, like Alcibiades of Athens, did that.) Their colours let spectators know which team had won, and the most successful drivers became celebrities, prosperous enough to leave us lavish monuments as well as their names. But while we can identify very few Greek charioteers (likewise usually hirelings or slaves), it is the owners of the Roman chariots who remain most obscure. For their part, Roman magistrates and rulers demonstrated distinction by organizing and presiding over chariot programmes instead of by competing in them.

Gladiatorial combat raises more fundamental questions for a book like this. Can it be considered sport at all? Such issues bedevil the modern Olympic movement: curlers – for all that they have the nerve, light touch and inner thigh muscles of porn stars – don't always look like athletes, and synchronized swimming has been slandered as "underwater smiling". The American weekly

Sports Illustrated periodically reviews the claims of activities such as crocodile hunting, noodling (catching catfish barehanded) and solo ballooning around the world to be considered sports; a case has been canvassed for Greek and Roman cock fighting.[3] This book excludes the musicians and other performers who competed at many of the festivals which also hosted athletic and equestrian events. Trumpeters and heralds are exceptions, not because I consider them athletes, but for the important role they played in athletic and equestrian programmes (signalling starts, proclaiming victors), one recognized by the inclusion of a competition for both at Olympia from 396 BCE. The categorization of gladiators is complex, involving both abstract definitions of "sport" and empirical issues such as the expectation of serious injury or death. (How likely were such misfortunes? Were they more prevalent than in Greek boxing or, say, modern motor sport? Where might we place them on a spectrum between essential elements – as in the noontime execution of convicts in the amphitheatre – and tragic contingencies?) I intend to take this up at greater length elsewhere. For the present, I offer a few considerations which have led me to incorporate gladiatorial combat in this book.

First, its outcome was unpredictable, as in other sporting activities. Make no mistake: this was real competition – efforts were made to prevent collusion – in a sense neither North American pro wrestling or crocodile hunting (where even victorious crocodiles get no prizes) can claim. Second, gladiators were trained and skilled in disciplines with recognized attributes and techniques and fought following conventions and rules. Third, despite their humble status as a group (gladiators were generally slaves, often foreign prisoners of war), gifted and fortunate combatants might gain admiration and significant rewards; they are known to us for much the same reasons as other successful competitors. Finally, in the Greek east of the Roman Empire at least, gladiatorial combat was assimilated to sport. It never played a part in regularly scheduled competitive festivals. But gladiators referred to themselves and their activities in the language of athletic competition ("athletes of Ares", they might boast to be *aleiptos*, "undefeated", or *paradoxos*, "an exceptional champion") and the provincial elite who sponsored gladiatorial spectacles was drawn from the same class (and were sometimes the same individuals) who presided over Greek games. It is, I hope, unnecessary to say that my decision to include this form of competition here does not signify approval, any more than the many entries under "W" imply support for the President of the United States or the frequent use of zero, for Tony Blair.

To categorize and annotate every aspect of the sporting life of two relatively well documented cultures stretching from Britain to Babylon, from the Bronze Age to the fifth century CE, is impossible in a short book. Michael Poliakoff's *Studies in the Terminology of the Greek Combat Sports* (1986) has thirty-eight entries under the Greek letter *alpha* alone. However desirable a work which covers the whole field on the same scale, this isn't it.[4] I have been selective; in fact, though my subject matter is Greek and Roman sport from A to Z, there is no entry under the letter Y. I have included only the most famous or best attested of the hundreds of Greek and Roman settings and sites for competition, privileged the lexicon of officials and events over technical terms, discussed only the most significant of the many ancient authors whose work touches on sport. Deciding which competitors – athletes, equestrian owners, charioteers, horses, gladiators – to discuss was especially daunting: we know over 700 Olympic champions and 200 Roman charioteers. I have opted to follow the lead of Pausanias, who faced the same problem with the profusion of victory statues at Olympia. ("I will mention only those Olympic victors who themselves gained some distinction, or whose statues happened to be better made than others", Pausanias 6.1.2.) There are entries for double winners at Olympia, others whose athletic careers there or elsewhere are noteworthy for the number or nature of their successes (for example, those who won Olympic events on their entry into the programme), still others for whom sport was a start or a supplement to distinction in other endeavours (such as the Greek commander Aratus). Cross-references are given in small capitals.

Greek names are given in their Latinate forms (Cleombrotus, not Kleombrotos), sometimes modified in the interests of familiarity (Cimon, Solon; not Cimo, Solo). Roman emperors appear as English readers are likely to recognize them (Augustus, Nero, Hadrian). Other Roman citizens are listed by their *nomen*, the name of their *gens*, with their personal name, the *praenomen*, given in full (*Cornelius* Sulla Felix, Lucius); (likely) non-citizens are listed under the name by which they are usually known (*Diocles*, Gaius Appuleius). All individuals are dated (when possible) by century, with more accurate chronological indications sometimes available later in the entry; only for dates CE is the era specified. For each entry, I have appended a list of the essential ancient evidence. This has been organized by genre, with Greek printed texts, inscriptions and papyri followed by Latin printed texts and inscriptions; each class of evidence is itself ordered (not always confidently) by date. English translations of much of this evidence are available in the sourcebooks by Mahoney (2001), Miller (1991), Robinson (1981) and Sweet (1987). I have also provided references to modern scholarship. These only rarely include standard sources familiar to scholars: Pauly's *Real-Encyclopädie der klassischen Altertumswissenschaft, Der Neue Pauly*, Moretti's original list of Olympic victors (1957 – but I have referred to its latest supplement [1987]), Jüthner's commentary on Philostratus (1909) or the massive compilations edited after his death by Brein (1965, 1968), general books by Gardiner (1910, 1930), Harris (1964, 1972), Patrucco (1972), Weiler (1981), Decker (1995). The more recent and more specialized work I cite will inevitably become outdated but may prove useful as a starting point for research backwards (since it normally includes references to earlier studies) and in the future (where the annual bibliographies in the journal *Nikephoros* will be invaluable). The reader should be aware throughout that this is a compilation, not a work of original scholarship, though (to be sure) some of the research I have relied on is my own.

Notes

1 B. Aubin, *Macleans* (26 April 2002) 27.
2 W. Leschhorn, "Die Verbreitung von Agonen in den östlichen Provinzen des römischen Reiches", in M. Lämmer (ed.) *Agonistik in der römischen Kaiserzeit. Colloquium Landhaus Rothenberge bei Münster 25–27 Oktober 1995* (Sankt Augustin 1998) 31–57, 31.
3 J. Dumont, "Les combats de coq furent-ils un sport?", *Pallas* 34 (1988) 33–44.
4 For this ideal and another book which does not match it, see the review of D. Matz, *Greek and Roman Sport. A Dictionary of Athletes and Events from the Eighth Century B.C. to the Third Century A.D.* (Jefferson NC 1991) by I. Weiler, *Nikephoros* 5 (1992) 249–257.

Acknowledgements and dedication

I am grateful to Richard Stoneman, who asked me to write this book when I needed the money, and to the colleagues who subsequently helped me in other ways: Michael Carter, Nigel Crowther, Don Kyle, Victor Matthews, Jenifer Neils, Pauline Ripat, Thomas Scanlon, William Slater, Peter Toohey and Robert Weir. Heather Mathieson and Lynne Schultz of the University of Winnipeg's Interlending and Document Supply Services brought books and articles into a library increasingly given over to computer screens; Paul Nielson showed me how useful those screens can be. Lou Lépine typed every word and my students listened to some. My debt of longest standing is owed to my parents: to my father, who shared with me his love of baseball, and to my mother, who has allowed us to indulge it. This book is dedicated to them.

Mark Golden
University of Winnipeg
January 2003

Abbreviations and short titles

AAntHung	*Acta Antiqua Academiae Scientiarum Hungaricae*
ABSA	*Annual of the British School at Athens*
AC	*Antiquité classique*
AHB	*Ancient History Bulletin*
AJA	*American Journal of Archaeology*
AJAH	*American Journal of Ancient History*
AJP	*American Journal of Philology*
AncW	*Ancient World*
ANRW	H. Temporini (ed.) *Aufstieg und Niedergang der römischen Welt* (Berlin and New York 1972–)
APF	*Archiv für Papyrusforschung*
ASNP	*Annali della Scuola Normale Superiore di Pisa*
BCH	*Bulletin de correspondance hellénique*
BE	*Bulletin épigraphique*
BICS	*Bulletin of the Institute of Classical Studies of the University of London*
CA	*Classical Antiquity*
Caldelli (1993)	M. L. Caldelli, *L'agon Capitolinus: storia e protagonisti dall'istituzione domizianea al IV secolo* (Rome 1993)
CEA	*Cahiers des études anciennes*
CID	*Corpus des inscriptions de Delphes* (Paris 1977–)
CIG	A. Boeckh, *Corpus Inscriptionum Graecarum* (Berlin 1828–1877)
CIL	*Corpus Inscriptionum Latinarum* (Berlin 1863–)
CJ	*Classical Journal*
CP	*Classical Philology*
CR	*Classical Review*
CRAI	*Comptes rendus de l'Académie des Inscriptions et Belles-lettres*
CSCA	*California Studies in Classical Antiquity*
CW	*Classical World*

Decker (1995)	W. Decker, *Sport in der griechischen Antike. Von minoischen Wettkampf bis zu den Olympischen Spielen* (Munich 1995)
Delph.	*Fouilles de Delphes* (Paris 1909–)
DK	H. Diels and W. Kranz, *Die Fragmente der Vorsokratiker* (Berlin 1952)
EA	*Epigraphica Anatolica*
Ebert (1972)	J. Ebert, *Griechische Epigramme auf Sieger an gymnischen und hippischen Agonen* (Berlin 1972) *Abhandlungen der sächsischen Akademie der Wissenschaften zu Leipzig, Philologisch-historische Klasse* 63.2
EMC	*Échos du monde classique* (now *Mouseion*)
FGrH	F. Jacoby, *Die Fragmente der griechischen Historiker* (Leiden 1957)
Fontenrose (1968)	J. Fontenrose, "The hero as athlete", *CSCA* 1 (1968) 73–104
G&R	*Greece and Rome*
García Romero (1992)	F. García Romero, "Sobre algunos términos del léxico del deporte: pruebas hípicas menores", *Cuadernos de Filología Clásica (Estudios griegos e indoeuropeos)* 2 (1992) 187–193
Gardiner (1910)	E. N. Gardiner, *Greek Athletic Sports and Festivals* (London 1910)
Gardiner (1930)	E. N. Gardiner, *Athletics of the Ancient World* (Oxford 1930)
Golden (1998)	M. Golden, *Sport and Society in Ancient Greece* (Cambridge 1998)
GRBS	*Greek, Roman and Byzantine Studies*
Harris (1964)	H. A. Harris, *Greek Athletes and Athletics* (London 1964)
Harris (1972)	H. A. Harris, *Sport in Greece and Rome* (London and Ithaca NY 1972)
Horsmann (1998)	G. Horsmann, *Die Wagenlenker der römischen Kaiserzeit* (Stuttgart 1998)
HSCP	*Harvard Studies in Classical Philology*
ICS	*Illinois Classical Studies*
ID	F. Durrbach, *Inscriptions de Délos* (Paris 1926–)
IDidyma	A. Rehm, *Die Inschriften. Milet 3* (Berlin 1914)
IG	*Inscriptiones Graecae* (Berlin 1873–)
IGL Syrie	L. Jalabert and R. Mouterde, *Inscriptions grecques et latines de la Syrie* (Paris 1929–)
IGRom.	*Inscriptiones Graecae ad res Romanas pertinentes* (Paris 1906–)
ILindos	C. Blinkenberg, *Lindos 2. Inscriptions 1–2* (Berlin and Copenhagen 1941)
ILS	H. Dessau, *Inscriptiones Latinae Selectae* (Berlin 1892–1916)

IMagn.	O. Kern, *Die Inschriften von Magnesia am Maeander* (Berlin 1900)
Inscr. Perg.	M. Fränkel, *Die Altertümer von Pergamon* 8.1–2. *Die Inschriften* (Berlin 1895–1900)
Inscr. Prien.	F. Hiller von Gaertringen, *Die Inschriften von Priene* (Berlin 1906)
ISardis	W. H. Buckler and D. M. Robinson, *Sardis 7. Greek and Latin Inscriptions* (Leiden 1932)
IvO	W. Dittenberger and K. Purgold, *Inschriften von Olympia* (Berlin 1896)
JHS	*Journal of Hellenic Studies*
JNG	*Jahrbuch für Numismatik und Geldgeschichte*
JRA	*Journal of Roman Archaeology*
JRS	*Journal of Roman Studies*
JSH	*Journal of Sport History*
Jüthner (1909)	J. Jüthner, *Philostratos, Über Gymnastik* (Berlin 1909)
Jüthner (1965)	J. Jüthner, *Die Athletischen Leibesübungen der Griechen 1. Geschichte der Leibesübungen* ed. F. Brein (Vienna 1965)
Jüthner (1968)	J. Jüthner, *Die Athletischen Leibesübungen der Griechen 2.1. Einzelne Sportarten. Lauf-, Sprung-und Wurfbewerbe* ed. F. Brein (Vienna 1968)
Klee (1918)	T. Klee, *Zur Geschichte der gymnischen Agone an griechischen Festen* (Leipzig 1918)
Kyle (1987)	D. G. Kyle, *Athletics in Ancient Athens* (Leiden 1987)
Mahoney (2001)	A. Mahoney, *Roman Sports and Spectacles. A Sourcebook* (Newburyport MA 2001)
MDAI(A)	*Mitteilungen des deutschen archäologischen Instituts. Athenische Abteilung*
MDAI(R)	*Mitteilungen des deutschen archäologischen Instituts. Römische Abteilung*
MEFRA	*Mélanges d'archéologie et d'histoire de l'École française de Rome. Antiquité*
MGR	*Miscellanea greca e romana*
MH	*Museum Helveticum*
Miller (1991)	Stephen G. Miller, *Arete. Greek Sports from Ancient Sources* (2nd edn, Berkeley and Los Angeles 1991)
Moretti (1953)	L. Moretti, *Iscrizioni agonistiche greche* (Rome 1953)
Moretti (1987)	L. Moretti, "Nuovo supplemento al catalogo degli Olympionikai", *MGR* 12 (1987) 67–91
Mosci Sassi (1992)	M. G. Mosci Sassi, *Il linguaggio gladiatorio* (Bologna 1992)
N^2	A. Nauck, *Tragicorum Graecorum Fragmenta* (2nd edn, Leipzig 1889)
OGI	W. Dittenberger, *Orientis Graeci Inscriptiones Selectae* (Leipzig 1903–1905)
P. London	*Greek Papyri in the British Museum* (London 1893–)

P.Mil.Vogl. 8 309	G. Bastianini and C. Gallazzi (with C. Austin), *Papiri dell'Università degli Studi di Milano 8. Posidippo di Pella, Epigrammi (P.Mil.Vogl.* VIIII 309) (Milan 2001)
Patrucco (1972)	R. Patrucco, *Lo sport nella grecia antica* (Florence 1972)
PdP	*La Parola del Passato*
PMG	D. L. Page, *Poetae Melici Graeci* (Oxford 1962)
Poliakoff (1986)	M. B. Poliakoff, *Studies in the Terminology of the Greek Combat Sports* (2nd edn, Königstein 1986)
Poliakoff (1987)	M. B. Poliakoff, *Combat Sports in the Ancient World. Competition, Violence and Culture* (New Haven 1987)
PRyl	*Catalogue of the Greek Papyri in the John Rylands Library at Manchester* (Manchester 1911–1952)
PSI	*Papiri greci e latini. Pubblicazioni della Società italiana per la ricerca dei papiri greci e latini in Egitto*
QUCC	*Quaderni Urbinati di cultura classica*
Raschke (1988)	W. J. Raschke (ed.) *The Archaeology of the Olympics. The Olympics and Other Festivals in Antiquity* (Madison WI 1988)
RE	A. Pauly, G. Wissowa and W. Kroll (eds) *Real Encyclopädie der klassischen Altertumswissenschaft* (Stuttgart 1893–)
REA	*Revue des études anciennes*
Reed (1998)	N. B. Reed, *More than Just a Game: the Military Nature of Greek Athletic Contests* (Chicago 1998)
REG	*Revue des études grecques*
REL	*Revue des études latines*
RFIC	*Rivista di filologia e di istruzione classica*
Robert (1940)	L. Robert, *Les gladiateurs dans l'Orient grec* (Paris 1940)
Robinson (1981)	R. S. Robinson, *Sources for the History of Greek Athletics* (Chicago 1981)
RPh	*Revue de philologie*
Scanlon (2002)	T. F. Scanlon, *Eros and Greek Athletics* (New York 2002)
SEG	*Supplementum Epigraphicum Graecum* (Leiden 1923–)
SIFC	*Studi italiani di filologia classica*
*SIG*³	W. Dittenberger, *Sylloge Inscriptionum Graecarum* (3rd edn, Leipzig 1915–1924)
Sweet (1987)	W. E. Sweet, *Sport and Recreation in Ancient Greece. A Soucebook with Translations* (Oxford 1987)
TAPA	*Transactions of the American Philological Association*
Tzachou-Alexandri (1989)	O. Tzachou-Alexandri (ed.) *Mind and Body: Athletic Contests in Ancient Greece* (Athens 1989)
Weiler (1981)	I. Weiler, *Der Sport bei den Völkern der Alten Welt* (Darmstadt 1981)
Young (1984)	D. C. Young, *The Olympic Myth of Greek Amateur Athletics* (Chicago 1984)
ZPE	*Zeitschrift für Papyrologie und Epigraphik*

Some important dates

note: Many dates are approximate or conjectural.

Bronze age
1500 BCE   Bull-leaping on Crete
1200 BCE   Chariot races and funeral games (?) on Mycenaean artefacts

Dark ages
1000–500 BCE Etruscans dominate central Italy
884 BCE   Olympic games (Eratosthenes's date)
776 BCE   Olympic games (Hippias's date)
756 BCE   Oebotas
753 BCE   Founding of Rome

Archaic period (Greece)/Regal period and Republican period (Rome)

750 BCE   Homer, *Iliad*: Achilles, funeral games of Patroclus
724 BCE   Orsippus
704 BCE   Olympic games (Mallwitz's date)
668 BCE   Pheidon
660 BCE   Chionis
632 BCE   Boys' events at Olympia (Hippias's date)
            Cylon
596 BCE   Boys' events at Olympia (Philostratus's date)
594 BCE   Solon
586/582 BCE Pythian games
582 BCE   Isthmian games
580 BCE   Heraea at Olympia
573 BCE   Nemean games
566 BCE   Greater Panathenaea
564 BCE   Arrichion
560 BCE   Earliest evidence for gymnasium
            Ibycus

	Circus Maximus
544 BCE	Praxidamas
536 BCE	Milo
	Cimon
520 BCE	Race in armour at Olympia
	Glaucus
510 BCE	*Perizoma* (loincloth) vases
509 BCE	Establishment of Roman Republic
500 BCE	*Apēnē* at Olympia
	Simonides
	Xenophanes
498–446 BCE	Pindar's poems
496 BCE	*Kalpē* at Olympia
492 BCE	Cleomedes
	Tisamenus
490 BCE	Persians invade Greece (Marathon):
	Pheidippides
484 BCE	Astylus
	Euthymus
480 BCE	Persians invade Greece (Salamis)
	Phaÿllus
	Theogenes

Classical period (Greece)/Republican period (Rome)

480–450 BCE	Bacchylides's poems
479 BCE	Eleutheria at Plataea
476 BCE	Hieron
470 BCE	Temple of Zeus at Olympia
464 BCE	Diagoras
	Xenophon
460 BCE	Melesias
450 BCE	Stadium III at Olympia
444 BCE	*Apēnē* and *kalpē* dropped from programme at Olympia
	Iccus
425 BCE	Nemea destroyed by warfare
421 BCE	Autolycus
420 BCE	Lichas
416 BCE	Alcibiades
408 BCE	*Synōris* (two-horse chariot race) at Olympia
	Eubatas of Cyrene
	Pulydamas
404 BCE	Pherenice
400 BCE	Hippias of Elis compiles list of Olympic victors
	Damonon
399 BCE	Socrates executed
396 BCE	Heralds (*kērykes*) and trumpeters (*salpinktai*) at Olympia
	Cynisca

384 BCE	Colts (*pōloi*) at Olympia
380 BCE	Prize-list from Greater Panathenaea
372 BCE	Troilus
371 BCE	Basileia at Lebadeia
364 BCE	Arcadians and Eleians wage war at Olympia
356 BCE	Philip II of Macedon
336 BCE	Dioxippus
332 BCE	Calippus
328 BCE	Demades
323 BCE	Alexander the Great dies

Hellenistic period (Greece)/Republican period (Rome)

282 BCE	Ptolemaieia at Alexandria
279 BCE	Soteria at Delphi
268 BCE	Bilistiche
264 BCE	First gladiatorial *munus* at Rome
250 BCE	Nemean games at Argos
248 BCE	Berenice II
242 BCE	Asclepieia on Cos
240 BCE	Callimachus
216 BCE	Clitomachus
200 BCE	*Pankration* for boys at Olympia
198 BCE	Polycrates
196 BCE	Eleutheria at Larisa
186 BCE	Fulvius Nobilior presents Greek athletes at Rome
167 BCE	Theseia reorganized at Athens
164 BCE	Leonidas
146 BCE	Greece becomes a Roman province (Achaea)
	Isthmian games at Sicyon
80 BCE	Cornelius Sulla's Greek games at Rome
73 BCE	Revolt of Spartacus

Imperial period

27 BCE	Augustus becomes first Roman emperor
	Actian games
4 BCE	Tiberius wins at Olympia
2 CE	Sebastan games at Naples
37 CE	Nicostratus
40 CE	Isthmian games return to Isthmia
47 CE	Hermesianax's daughters
66–67 CE	Nero competes in Greece
69 CE	Polites
80 CE	Colosseum dedicated
81 CE	Flavius Hermogenes
85 CE	Flavius Artemidorus
86 CE	Capitoline games at Rome

	Flavius Metrobius
117–138 CE	Hadrian
125 CE	Demostheneia at Oenoanda
	Diocles the charioteer
129 CE	Ulpius Domesticus
142 CE	Eusebeia at Puteoli
150 CE	Herodes Atticus
173 CE	Aurelius Demostratus Damas
175 CE	Pausanias
180 CE	Commodus
181 CE	Aurelius Asclepiades "Hermodorus"
200 CE	Calpurnianus Gutta
220 CE	Sextus Julius Africanus compiles list of Olympic victors
229 CE	Demetrius
240 CE	Philostratus
267 CE	Herulians overrun Olympia
385 CE	Aurelius Zopyrus, latest known Olympic victor
393 CE	Theodosius I bans pagan festivals
520 CE	Last Olympic games at Antioch

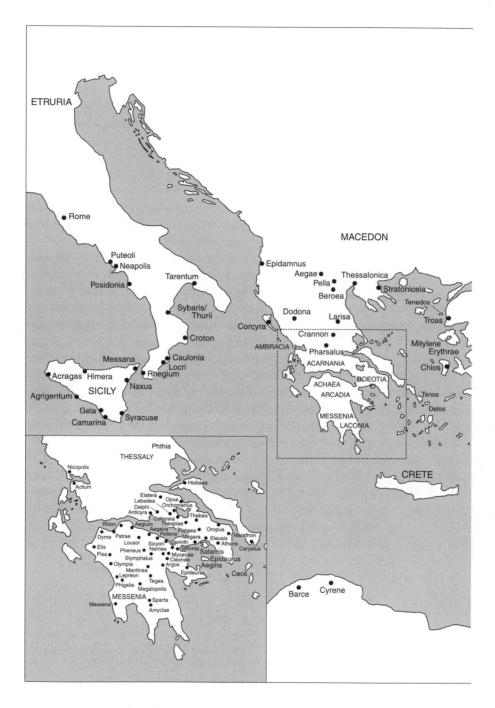

Figure 1 The Greek and Roman world
Source: Adapted from H. A. Harris, *Greek Athletes and Athletics* (London 1964) map 4.

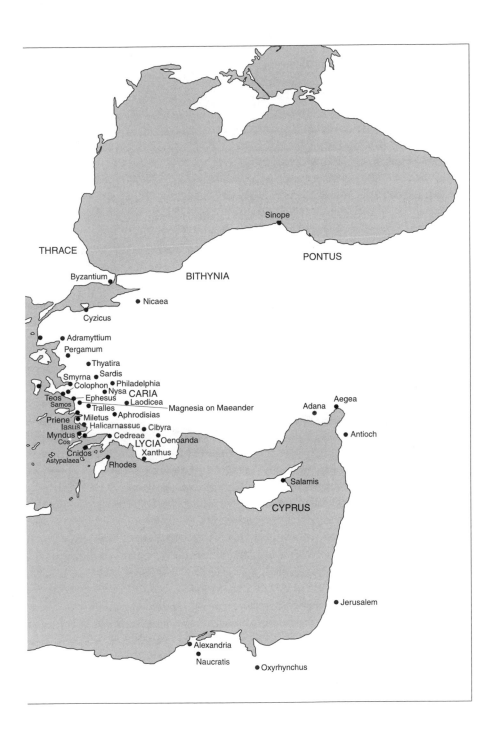

THRACE

PONTUS

Sinope

Byzantium

BITHYNIA

Nicaea

Cyzicus

Adramyttium

Pergamum

Thyatira

Smyrna Sardis

Colophon Philadelphia

Teos Nysa CARIA

Ephesus Laodicea

Samos Tralles Magnesia on Maeander

Priene Miletus Aphrodisias

Iasus Halicarnassus Cibyra

Myndus Cedreae

Cos Oenoanda

Astypalaea Cnidos LYCIA

Xanthus

Rhodes

Adana Aegea

Antioch

Salamis

CYPRUS

Jerusalem

Alexandria

Naucratis

Oxyrhynchus

A

Abigeius, Roman chariot horse, early second century CE. Abigeius was part of teams DIOCLES drove to 445 victories, including 103 in one year.

ILS 5287.

Academy, Athenian GYMNASIUM. Located in the grove sacred to the hero Hecademus in Athens's northwest suburbs, the Academy was likely a place for exercise from the sixth century BCE. (Traditions link it with the sons of the tyrant Pisistratus.) Its development as Athens's first major athletic facility was owed to the largesse of the fifth-century political leader Cimon, its fame in the history of culture to Plato's choice of it as a place to meet students. A house he built nearby became the centre of his famous school, the Academy. Most extant archaeological remains – a PALAESTRA, baths, dressing rooms – are of Hellenistic or Roman date. Aside from exercise, the Academy's grounds served as a site for equestrian processions and exercise (including the ANTHIPPASIA) and as the starting-point for torch races at the PANATHENAEA and other festivals.

Aristophanes, *Clouds* 1005, 1008; Xenophon, *Hipparchicus* 3.1, 14; Plutarch, *Cimon* 13.8; Pausanias 1.30.2.

Kyle (1987) 71–77; M.-F. Billot, "Académie (topographie et archéologie)", in R. Goulet (ed.) *Dictionnaire des philosophes antiques* (Paris 1989) 1.693–789.

Acanthus, of SPARTA, first Olympic champion in DOLICHOS (720 BCE) and sometimes said to have been the first athlete to compete naked (see NUDITY).

Pausanias 5.8.6; Dionysius of Halicarnassus, *Roman Antiquities* 7.72.2–3.

Acastidas, son of Cleomnestus, Theban athlete, second century. Acastidas won the STADION race and pentathlon for AGENEIOI at the Panathenaea of 182. He was famous enough that the historian Polybius identifies Pytheas, a leader of the Boeotian resistance to the Romans in the mid-second century, as the brother of "Acastides the *stadion*-runner".

Polybius 38.14.1; *IG* 2² 2314.

Accendo (plural *accendones*), "instigator", perhaps an attendant who urged GLADIATORS on or one who accompanied their combat with music.

Tertullian, *On the Pallium* 6.2.

Mosci Sassi (1992) 65–68.

Acestorides, son of Hermocreon, Trojan chariot victor, third century. The first native of the Troad to win at Olympia, in a chariot race for PŌLOI about 212, Acestorides triumphed at Nemea, Epidaurus, Lousoi and Pheneus too.

IvO 184.

Ebert (1972) 201–203.

Achilles, of Phthia in Thessaly, Greek epic hero. Son of the mortal Peleus and the sea-goddess Thetis, Achilles (like many other heroes) was educated on Mt Pelion by the centaur Chiron. There he ate the entrails of boars, lions and bears, caught deer on foot and ran on thin ice (to foster lightness of foot), earning in the end the distinctive epithet "swift-footed". The most feared of Greek fighters, Achilles used his great speed to pursue the Trojan champion Hector around the walls of Troy and slew him in single combat. He later presided over FUNERAL GAMES for his friend Patroclus, one of Hector's victims. His feet betrayed him in the end, however, when an arrow from the bow of Paris (guided by Apollo) struck him on the heel – the only vulnerable part of his body. Achilles too was honoured with funeral games.

Homer, *Iliad* 22, 23; Pindar, *Nemeans* 3.43–63.

V. J. Matthews, "Swift-footed Achilles", *EMC* 19 (1975) 37–43.

Acmatidas, of Sparta, pentathlete, fifth century. Acmatidas won the Olympic pentathlon (perhaps in 500) unopposed (AKONITI), the first such victory we know of. Anaxandrus, winner of the Olympic chariot race (perhaps in 428), was likely his grandson.

Pausanias 6.1.7, 2.1; *SEG* 11.1215.

Actia, "Actian games", name given to several competitive festivals meant to mark AUGUSTUS's victory over Antony and Cleopatra at the Battle of Actium in 31. The most prominent, at the new city of Nicopolis across the Ambracian Gulf from Actium, developed an old biennial festival for Apollo at nearby Anactorium into a quadrennial games originally under the supervision of the Spartans, who had joined Augustus's forces. It included athletic, equestrian and musical contests as well as a less common boat race. (Actium was a naval battle and the festival's prizes were wreaths of reeds, linked to Posei-don.) Athletes competed in three age-classes (boys, AGENEIOI, men). The first celebration, in 27, was thought to open a new era, to be reckoned in Actiads (on the model of Olympiads); later festivals were held on the anniversary of the battle, 2 September. These Actian Games joined the PERIODOS; Nero thought a victory there worth winning (66 CE). They are attested until the late third century CE, and were perhaps later briefly revived by the emperor Julian (361–363 CE).

Strabo 7.7.6; Josephus, *Jewish War* 1.20.4; Suetonius, *Augustus* 18; Cassius Dio 51.1, 53.1; *IvO* 231.

Th. Sarikakis, "Aktia ta en Nikopolei", *Archaiologikē Ephēmeris* (1965) 145–162; M. Lämmer, "Die Aktischen Spiele von Nikopolis", *Stadion* 12/13 (1986–1987) 27–38; Caldelli (1993) 24–28; D. O. A. Klose, "Zur Entstehung der Preiskronen. Das Beispiel der Aktischen Spiele", *JNG* 47 (1997) 29–45.

Acusilaus *see* DIAGORAS

Aegyptus *see* TIMON (2)

Aelius Alcandridas, Publius, son of Damocratidas, Spartan runner, third century CE. Twice PERIODONIKĒS some time after AFRICANUS's list ends in 217 CE, Alcandridas won the STADION race for boys twice at Isthmia and Nemea, for adults twice at Olympia, and DIAULOS twice at the Pythian games. Like his son P. Aelius Democratidas, he earned the title "best of the Greeks" in the race in armour at the Plataean ELEUTHERIA (1).

IG 5.1 305, 556; *IvO* 238; *SEG* 11.802, 831.

A. J. S. Spawforth, "Notes on the third century AD in Spartan epigraphy", *ABSA* 79 (1984) 263–288 (273–274).

Aristomachus, Aelius Publius, of Magnesia on Maeander, pancratiast, second century CE. Winner of the boys' *pankration* at Olympia in 117 CE, Aristomachus went on to enough other triumphs at major festivals to style himself PERIODONIKĒS (though he had no Pythian crowns). Later in life he served as envoy to HADRIAN and as head of the athletes' GUILD at Cyzicus, where he must have had a hand in organizing the emperor's Olympic games; he, his parents and his brother earned Roman citizenship in return.

IMagn. 180, 181.

Ebert (1972) 232–237.

Aelius Aurelius Maron, Titus, of Seleucia on Calycadnus, wrestler, second century CE. An honorary citizen of Athens, Alexandria and many other cities, and XYS-TARCHĒS of an athletes' GUILD, Maron was successful not only at Olympia, Delphi (twice), Isthmia and Nemea (three times each), but at all the other major festivals – at Athens no less than five times as well as in forty-four lesser games. He claimed the distinction of being a *teleios* PERIODONIKĒS, a full circuit champion.

Philostratus, *On Athletic Exercise* 36; *SEG* 41.1407.

S. Şahin, "Inschriften aus Seleukia am Kaly-kadnos (Silifke)", *EA* 17 (1991) 139–166 (141–149); P. Herz, "Seltsame Kaisergentilizien. Beobachtungen zur kaiserzeitlichen Nomenklatur", in F. Blakolmer, K. R. Krierer, A. Landskron-Dinstl, H. D. Szemethy and K. Zhuber-Okrog (eds) *Fremde Zeiten. Festschrift für Jürgen Borchhardt* ... (Vienna 1996) 2.253–259; P. Grossardt, "Der Ringer Maron und der Pankratiast 'Halter' in epigraphischen und literarischen Quellen", *EA* 34 (2002) 170-172.

Aelius Aurelius Menander, Marcus, of Aphrodisias, pancratiast, second century CE. The first athlete to win in all three main AGE-CLASSES (as *PAIS*, *AGENEIOS* and adult) in a period of two years, Menander claimed many triumphs, including three at Nemea (once as a boy, twice as an adult), and others at the Pythian, Nemean and CAPITOLINE games in the third quarter of the second century CE.

Moretti (1953) 206–211.

Aelius Aurelius Metrodorus, Titus, of Philadelphia (Lydia), athlete, second century CE. Metrodorus is listed as a PERIODONIKĒS in an inscription from Philadelphia.

L. Robert, *Bulletin épigraphique* (1958) 223.

Aelius Granianus, of Sicyon, runner, second century CE. A multiple winner at Olympia, Granianus was crowned for the boys' *STADION* (? 133), for *DIAULOS* and the race in armour (? 137) and twice for pentathlon (? 137, 141).

Pausanias 2.11.8; *SEG* 11.838.

Aelius Granianus Fanius Artemidorus, Publius, of Miletus, athlete, second/third century CE. Artemidorus was a PERIOD-ONIKĒS in an unknown event at the end of the second century CE.

IDidyma 81, 182, 188, 189, 243, 244.

Moretti (1987) 79.

Aemilius Scaurus, Marcus, Roman politician, first century. As aedile in 58, Aemilius put on games featuring athletic competitions, extravagant enough to leave the impression that they were the first at Rome. See FULVIUS.

Valerius Maximus 2.4.7.

Aenetus, of Amyclae, pentathlete, undated. Aenetus won at Olympia but died while the wreath was being placed on his head. Pausanias saw his statue at Amyclae but we know nothing more about him.

Pausanias 3.18.7.

Aeschines, of Elis, pentathlete, undated. PAUSANIAS saw two statues of Aeschines at Olympia, one for each of his pentathlon victories.

Pausanias 6.14.13.

Africanus, Julius *see* IULIUS AFRICANUS

Agathoclea, daughter of Numenius, of Alexandria, chariot victor, second century. The daughter of a leading figure in the court of the Ptolemies, a governor of the

Thebais and ambassador to Rome, Agathoclea was one of several female victors at the PANATHENAEA in the mid-second century, winning the colts' chariot race in 162.

Hesperia 60 (1991) 188–189.

Agathos Daimon, "Good Luck", Alexandrian boxer, undated. A victor at the NEMEAN games, he died at thirty-five in competition at Olympia, sometime early in the present era.

SEG 22. 354.

Age-class (Greek *krisis*, plural *kriseis*), division into which competitors at Greek games were grouped. The most common divisions were between ANDRES, "men" and PAIDES, "boys" (as at the Olympic and, at least originally, the Pythian Games and the many modelled on them); and between ANDRES, AGENEIOI, "beardless youths", and *paides* (as at other games of the PERIODOS and the greater PANATHENAEA). Other attested age-classes include *paides Pythikoi*, "Pythian boys", and *paides Isthmiakoi*, "Isthmian boys"; still others are known from local festivals. Age-classes became more numerous over time, perhaps as a means to give more competitors (drawn in the main from the same circles as those in charge of the festivals) a chance to win; this seems most likely in the case of equestrian events, where races for PŌLOI, "colts", enter the main festivals only in the fourth century. It is unclear whether the criteria for age-classes involved exact chronological age (on which we only rarely have any information) or subjective judgements based on physical development. In either case, the use of age-classes as an organizing principle is especially remarkable in combat sports, since it allowed athletes of very different sizes and weights to fight.

W. Petermandl, "Überlegungen zur Funktion der Altersklassen bei den griechischen Agonen", *Nikephoros* 10 (1997) 135–147; Golden (1998) 104–116; I. L. Pfeijffer, "Athletic age categories in victory odes", *Nikephoros* 11 (1998) 21–38.

Ageneioi, "beardless youths", AGE-CLASS for athletes at the ISTHMIAN and NEMEAN and other Greek games (perhaps including the PYTHIAN Games from the third century). *Ageneioi* were between PAIDES and ANDRES in age, likely in their late teens. Their prizes at the PANATHENAEA were a little higher than those for *paides*, markedly less than *andres*.

IG 2² 2311.

Golden (1998) 104–116.

Agesarchus, son of (?) Amestratus, of Trileia (Arcadia), boxer, second century. A PERIODONIKĒS in boxing, Agesarchus's Olympic victory may date to 120.

Pausanias 6.12.8.

Agesilaus, king of Sparta, 445–359. Agesilaus is said to have disdained chariot competition – despite Sparta's long list of victors at Olympia – and preferred to reach renown through nobler contests: standing first in his people's affections, serving his country and comrades best, outstripping others in punishing his enemies. Indeed, one tradition ascribes his sister CYNISCA's unprecedented victory in an Olympic chariot race (396) to Agesilaus; he wished to show that such distinctions are owed to wealth rather than merit. Agesilaus was not always so disengaged, however. He intervened for the son of the Athenian Eualces, to ensure that he was allowed to compete among the PAIDES in the STADION race at Olympia despite his unusual height.

Xenophon, *Greek History* 4.1.40; *Agesilaus* 9.6–7; Plutarch, *Agesilaus* 13.3, 20.1; *Moral Essays* 212B.

Ageus, son of Aristocles, Argive runner, fourth century. Ageus won the Olympic DOLICHOS (328) and ran to ARGOS, 110km (sixty-eight miles) away on the same day to announce his victory. He likely won at the Lycaea around 315 as well.

Eusebius, *Chronicon* 1.206 Schoene; *SIG*³ 314.

Agitator (plural *agitatores*), Roman charioteer. The term was usually applied to an
experienced and successful driver who
had moved from two-horse to four-horse
teams. Cf. AURIGA.

Pliny, *Natural History* 36.5.43.

J.-P. Thuillier, *"Auriga/agitator*: de simples synonymes?", *RPh* 61 (1987) 233–237.

Agōn (plural *agōnes*), "contest", the regular Greek word for athletic and equestrian competition. The word's root
meaning ("gathering") and its associations
with everything from doctors' disagree-
ments to beauty contests to war give it
much different overtones than our
"sport". Personified, a statue of Agon
joined Ares, god of war, on the table used
to set out winners' wreaths at Olympia.
Greek competitive festivals were divided
into two groups, those which awarded
only a crown or wreath (*agōnes hieroi,
stephanitai, phyllinai*) and those which
offered money prizes (*themides, agōnes
argyritai, chrēmatitai, thematikoi, thema-
titai*). These might be further distinguished. Some crown games were
eiselastikoi (from *eiselaunein*, "drive inside"). Among other privileges, winners
could enter their home cities in a chariot
(perhaps driving through a breach in the
walls, a practice which may have originated with NERO); money games might be
talantiaioi or *hēmitalantiaioi*, "with prizes
of a talent/half-talent" in value. These
distinctions were sometimes ignored or
manipulated, however, and festivals could
change their status; like the foundation of
a new crown games, this required the
emperor's approval in later antiquity.
Becoming a crown games represented an
increase in prestige. Honorary inscriptions
generally list victories in crown games by
name and simply provide the number of
the others.

Diodorus 13.82.7; Pollux 3.153; *IG* 14 739,
1102; *IGRom.* 3.319, 1012.

H. W. Pleket, "Games, prizes, athletes and
ideology", *Arena* (now *Stadion*) 1 (1975) 49–
89 (54–71); T. F. Scanlon, "The vocabulary of
competition: *agon* and *aethlos*, Greek terms for
contest", *Arete. The Journal of Sport Literature*
(now *Aethlon*) 1.1 (1983) 147–162.

Agōnothetēs (plural *agōnothetai*), Greek
term for the sponsor or supervisor of a
contest or competitive programme. *Agōnothetai* (who might be women) might act
on their own initiative but were most
often magistrates, ex-magistrates or
wealthy citizens nominated by magistrates. They were generally responsible
for some or all of a festival's costs as well
as its conduct. Most served for one
festival only, but we also hear of *agōnothetai* who held this honour for life. In
some cities, *agōnothetai* earned special
honours – the wearing of purple clothing
and golden ornaments at ARGOS.

Herodotus 6.127.3.

H. W. Pleket, "Three epigraphic notes", *Mnemosyne* 10 (1957) 141–146 (141–143); K.
Mantas, "Women and athletics in the Roman
East", *Nikephoros* 8 (1995) 125–144 (136–
140).

Agora (plural *agorai*), "meeting place",
the Greek city centre. An open area with
public administrative buildings and religious shrines, the *agora* was also a site for
competition; the word is related to AGŌN.
Legendary examples include the games of
the Phaeacians in Homer, historical ones
the SPARTAN Gymnopaediae and, perhaps,
chariot races at Corinth. At Athens, torch
races at the PANATHENAEA and other
festivals ran through the *agora* and equestrian events for the Athenian cavalry took
place there, in the Hellenistic period at
least. At this time too, GYMNASIA were
built in and around the *agora*.

Homer, *Odyssey* 8.109; Pausanias 3.11.9.

Kyle (1987) 57–64.

Aianteia, competitive festivals for two
legendary local heroes, both named Ajax
(Greek Aias) – the son of Oileus (in Opus
in Locris) and the son of Telamon (on
Salamis). The Salaminian festival was also

held in Athens, as part of the Athenian claim to the offshore island of Salamis. It became more important after the naval victory over the Persians off Salamis (480 BCE) – the inspiration for a boat race for EPHEBES. This Aianteia was still celebrated in Roman times. Ironically, neither Ajax was a successful competitor in Patroclus's FUNERAL GAMES. The son of Oileus (despite his speed) finished second in the footrace when Athena tripped him up in a pile of dung; the son of Telamon (despite his size and strength) lost out in the weight throw and armed combat and drew with Odysseus in the wrestling.

Homer, *Iliad* 23.700–849.

Aisymnētēs (plural *aisymnētai*), judge of a Greek contest.

Homer, *Odyssey* 8.258; Hesychius α 2143.

Akampion, "unbending", horse or chariot race of one length of the HIPPODROME.

IG 2² 2316.

Akōn see JAVELIN

Akoniti, "dustlessly", used of a walkover, a victory won without competition. Such testaments to prestige were much prized. The term may refer to the DUST athletes sprinkled on their oiled bodies before competition or to that stirred up in its course. In a famous anecdote, MILON was the only entrant at a festival but slipped on his way to get his wreath. The crowd reacted – he was no longer dustless – but Milon wittily responded that no-one had given him the other two falls needed for a wrestling win. Most winners *akoniti* were HEAVY athletes like Milon, but others triumphed in DIAULOS, DOLICHOS and even PENTATHLON (in this case perhaps when remaining competitors withdrew before wrestling).

Philostratus, *On Athletic Exercise* 11; *Greek Anthology* 11.316; *Suda* α 923; *SEG* 11.1227.

E. Klingenberg, "*Diakōlyein antagōnistēn*. Eine platonische Bestimmung des Griechische Wett-kampfrechts: Pl. Lg. 955A2-B4", in *Studi in onore di Arnaldo Biscardi* 6 (Milan 1987) 435–470 (452–459); R. Wachter, "Lakonisch *asskonitei*", *MH* 52 (1995) 155–169.

Akrocheiria, akrocheirisis, akrocheirismos, "finger-tipping", sparring or shadow boxing.

Plato, *Alcibiades* 1 107E; Lucian, *Lexiphanes* 5; Philostratus, *On Athletic Exercise* 50.

Alcaenetus, son of Theantus, of Lepreon, boxer, fifth century. Alcaenetus won the boys' event at Olympia (?) 456, the men's perhaps twelve years later. His sons Hellanicus (424) and Theantus (420) were also champion boxers at Olympia as boys.

Pausanias 6.7.8; *IvO* 155 (*ISS*; *Oxyrhynchus Papyri* 222.

Alcibiades, Athenian politician, commander and competitor, 451/0–404/3. Adept like other youths among the Athenian elite at wrestling – he is said to have sparred with the philosopher Socrates – Alcibiades later won chariot races at the PYTHIAN, NEMEAN and PANATHENAIC Games. At the Olympic festival of 416, he entered an unprecedented seven chariots (one defrauded from a friend) and finished first, second and fourth, an extravagance and an achievement which later buttressed his (successful) claim to lead the Athenian armada to Sicily in 415.

Thucydides 6.16; Euripides 755, 756, *PMG*; Isocrates 16.32–34; Plutarch, *Alcibiades* 2.2, 4.4, 11, 16.7.

Kyle (1987) 195–196, W. M. Ellis, *Alcibiades* (London and New York 1989) 50–52.

Alcimedon, son of Iphion, of Aegina, wrestler, fifth century. Defeating four rivals, Alcimedon won the boys' wrestling at Olympia in 460, the sixth panhellenic victory wreath for his family and the thirtieth for his trainer, MELESIAS.

Pindar, *Olympians* 8.

Alcmaeon *see* MEGACLES

Aleiptēs (plural *aleiptai*), "anointer", a masseur and, more generally, a TRAINER, Latin *aliptes*.

Aristotle, *Nicomachean Ethics* 2.1106b1–5; Plutarch, *Pericles* 4.1; Juvenal 6.422.

Alexander I, king of Macedon *c*.498–454. Despite protests, Alexander was allowed to compete at Olympia (? 476) on the grounds of the descent he claimed from the legendary Greek hero Perseus – an early instance of the flexibility which led later HELLANODIKAI to admit entrants from the Roman imperial family. He may (the evidence is unclear) have run a dead heat with the eventual winner of the STADION race before losing a rematch (see DRAW).

Herodotus 5.22.

P. Roos, "Alexander I in Olympia", *Eranos* 83 (1985) 162–168.

Alexander III ("The Great"), king of Macedon 336–323. Alexander's birth in 356 was reported to his father PHILIP II the same day as news of his victories over the Illyrians and in the horse race at Olympia. The synchronism suggests that Philip had achieved all a man, even a king, could hope for. His son proved still more successful, disdaining to run at Olympia (unless other kings were in the field) but destined, through his conquests, to spread the gymnasium, physical training and festival competition, three hallmarks of Hellenism, throughout the eastern Mediterranean and beyond. The FUNERAL GAMES which marked Alexander's death had the same self-consciously Homeric echoes as much of his life.

Plutarch, *Alexander* 3.8, 4.10–11.

S. Slowikowski, "Alexander the Great and sport history: a commentary on scholarship", *JSH* 18 (1989) 70–78.

Alindēsis, "rolling" on the ground, a part of many wrestling and *pankration* matches and a training for those who competed in them. Contact with DUST and mud was thought to be beneficial; the physician Rufus of Ephesus recommends *alindēsis* for girls at puberty.

Hippocrates, *Regimen* 2.64, 3.68, 3.76, 3.81, 4.89; Oribasius, *Liber Incertus* 18 (2).11 R.

Poliakoff (1986) 20–27.

Alseia, competitive festival for Zeus on the island of Cos. It included TORCH races for individuals and teams (boys and youths), each preceded by preliminary HEATS a few days before. Teams also competed in *EUEXIA*.

P. Gauthier, "Du nouveau sur les courses aux flambeaux d'après deux inscriptions de Kos", *REG* 108 (1995) 576–585.

Altis, the sacred grove of Zeus at OLYMPIA. The *Altis* included the Temples of Zeus and Hera, the Pelopion (shrine of Pelops), Zeus's altar and sacred olive tree, STATUES of Olympic victors, and (in the fourth century) the Philippeion (erected by PHILIP II of Macedon or his son, ALEXANDER III the Great) and the Metroön (Temple of the Mother of the Gods). A vaulted tunnel brought athletes and officials from the *Altis* to the stadium. The *Altis* was the most sacred sector at Olympia. Nevertheless, when the Arcadians and their allies ousted the Eleians from Olympia and were celebrating the festival of 364, an Eleian army marched against them and a battle broke out in the *Altis*, with fighters hurling missiles from temple roofs. Pentathletes were wrestling in the *Altis* at the time, but this is likely to have been as exceptional as other occurrences at that festival.

Xenophon, *Greek History* 7.4.28–32; Pausanias 5.10, 13, 20.

Alytarchēs (plural *alytarchai*) "leader of the *alytai*", Greek festival official. At Olympia, the *alytarchēs* (and his underlings: ALYTAI, MASTIGOPHOROI, RHABDOPHOROI) was responsible for crowd control, overseeing the drawing of lots by competitors, and disciplining rulebreakers. In later antiquity, he took on more responsibility (some previously exercised by HELLANODIKAI) and holders of the office were as a consequence drawn from the elite. At ANTIOCH, the *alytarchēs* was the chief magistrate of the local Olympic festival, Zeus's representative. He slept on a rush mat in the open air, wore a white robe with gold ornaments, a gem-studded crown, and white sandals, and carried an ebony rod.

Lucian, *Hermotimus* 40; John Malalas, *Chronicle* 286.12–287.7; *Etymologicum Magnum* 72.14; *IvO* 240.

Alytēs (plural *alytai*), minor Greek festival official. *Alytai*, like MASTIGOPHOROI and RHABDOPHOROI, used lashes (if necessary) to restrain and punish spectators and competitors.

Etymologicum Magnum 72.14; *IvO* 483.

Amentum see ANKYLĒ

Amertas, of Elis, wrestler, (?) fifth century. Amertas won boys' wrestling at Olympia (perhaps in 420) and later men's in the Pythian games at Delphi.

Pausanias 6.8.1.

Amesinas, or Alesias, of Barce, wrestler, fifth century. A cowherd, Amesinas is said to have trained by fighting with a bull before winning the wrestling crown at Olympia in 460.

Eusebius, *Chronicon* 1.203 Schoene.

Amphiaraeia, panhellenic competitive festival at Oropus, on the border of Boeotia and Attica. Held every four years to honour the Argive hero Amphiaraüs, it is remarkable for its full and varied programme. Athletes at the earliest attested festival (in the fourth century) included competitors *apo gymnasiōn*, "from the gymnasia", as well as ANDRES, AGENEIOI and PAIDES; though *ageneioi* had relatively few events, the programme for *paides* matched that for men (with the exception of the race in armour), and both ran the HIPPIOS in addition to the more common STADION, DIAULOS and DOLICHOS. There were also musical and equestrian contests and one for panegyric. Programmes in the Roman period were still more ambitious, with contests for trumpeters and heralds, rhetorical and epic recitation, and drama. Early and late festivals were held under Athenian auspices, but Oropus was often disputed territory, and management of the Amphiaraeia shifted accordingly.

IG 7 414, 416–420.

B. Petrakos, *O Oropos kai to Hieron tou Amphiaraou* (Athens 1968); M. B. Walbank, "Regulations for an Athenian festival", in *Studies in Attic Epigraphy, History and Topography Presented to Eugene Vanderpool* (*Hesperia* Supplement 19: Princeton 1982) 173–182.

Amphitheatre, the usual site of GLADIATORIAL shows. Derived from two Greek words, the amphitheatre, "theatre-in-the-round", is nevertheless a distinctively Roman structure, an oval in which spectators sat and stood in banked rows around a central sandy stage, the HARENA. The earliest surviving permanent examples were built in Campania in the earlier first century. At Rome, gladiators fought in the Forum, equipped for each occasion with temporary wooden stands, before the first permanent amphitheatre was built for AUGUSTUS by Statilius Taurus in the Campus Martius in 29 BCE. The Flavian Amphitheatre, or COLOSSEUM, dedicated in 80 CE, set the standard for later amphitheatres, a monumental building able to hold as many as 55,000 seated spectators and many more standees, and embellished with elaborate facades and much sculptural adornment. Cities in the Roman west vied to build impressive amphitheatres as expressions of civic pride. In the Greek east, however, theatres were often modified for gladiatorial shows and the amphitheatre long remained a visible sign, not always welcome, of Roman cultural influence.

J.-C. Golvin, *L'amphithéâtre romain. Essai sur la théorisation de sa forme et de ses fonctions* (Paris 1988); K. Welch, "The Roman arena in late Republican Italy: a new interpretation", *JRA* 7 (1994) 59–80; D. L. Bomgardner, *The Story of the Roman Amphitheatre* (London and New York 2000).

Amphoritēs (also *amphiphoritēs*, *hydrophoria*), "water-jug-carry", a race at Aegina. Competitors ran from the harbour to a spring, filled and shouldered a pot of water, and ran back to the coast. The first are said to have been Jason's Argonauts, near the end of their voyage home.

Apollonius of Rhodes 4.1765–1772.

Amphōtis (plural *amphōtides*), "ear-guards", used by Greek boxers.

Plutarch, *Moral Essays* 38B.

Amycus, legendary king of the Bebryces. Colossal and cruel, Amycus forced visitors to box with him and killed many. However, when the Argonauts called in on their quest for the Golden Fleece, his brute strength was no match for POLLUX's skill. In defeat Amycus swore to honour guests in future.

Apollonius of Rhodes 2.1–97; Theocritus 22.27–134.

Anabatēs (plural *anabatai*), "mounter, cavalryman", equestrian competitor in Greek festivals. It is uncertain whether or how to distinguish the *anabatēs* from the better-known APOBATĒS. Perhaps the *anabatēs* wore military equipment, rode on a horse, dismounted before the end of a race and finished on foot, leading his mount at a trot (cf. KALPĒ).

Pausanias 5.9.2.

García Romero (1992).

Anacharsis, largely legendary Scythian prince who figures as a sage outsider in Greek sources. Lucian's *Anacharsis* (written about 170 CE) presents him in conversation with the Athenian statesman Solon (early sixth century), who explains the important role of athletic competition in Greek culture. Whether Lucian himself shares Solon's enthusiasm more than Anacharsis's puzzlement is unclear.

P. Angeli Bernardini, *Luciano. Anacarsi o sull'atletica* (Pordenone 1995).

Anankophagia, "forced feeding", an athlete's training DIET.

Aristotle, *Politics* 8.1339a6.

Anapalē, dance in which participants moved their feet to music while miming wrestling and *pankration* with their hands. SPARTAN boys performed something similar at the Gymnopaediae.

Athenaeus 14.631B.

Anauchidas, son of Philys, Eleian wrestler, undated. Anauchidas won twice as a wrestler at Olympia, as a boy and as an adult.

Pausanias 5.27.12, 6.14.11, 16.1.

Anaxilas, tyrant of Rhegium and winner in the APĒNĒ at Olympia, 484 or 480. Anaxilas marked his triumph by issuing coins and commissioning a poem from SIMONIDES. Insulted by the fee or the subject matter – mule-racing may have been the sport of kings, but not of poets – Simonides found inspiration after Anaxilas upped his offer.

Aristotle, *Rhetoric* 3.1405b24; Heraclides Ponticus, *Politics* 25.5 (*FHG* 2.219).

J. H. Molyneux, *Simonides. A Historical Study* (Wauconda 1992) 211–214.

Andabata (plural *andabatae*), type of GLADIATOR. Their visors had no eye-openings and so they fought blind.

Cicero, *Letters to Friends* 7.10.2.

Mosci Sassi (1992) 74–75.

Andraemo, "Brave Blood", Roman chariot horse, late first century CE. Owned by the Green CIRCUS FACTION and driven by the CHARIOTEER Flavius SCORPUS,

Andraemo is said by the poet Martial to be his equal in fame despite his eleven-footed verse.

Martial 10.9; *ILS* 5289.

Andres, "men", the oldest AGE-CLASS at most Greek athletic festivals. At Olympia, an *anēr* had to be (or to appear to be) at least 18.

Pausanias 6.14.2.

N. B. Crowther, "The age-category of boys at Olympia", *Phoenix* 42 (1988) 304–308.

Androclus, of Messenia, runner, eighth century. Androclus, winner of the STADION at Olympia in 768, may be the same man as the Androcles who ruled Messenia at the outbreak of the first war between Messenia and Sparta.

Pausanias 4.4.4.

Androsthenes, son of Lochaeus, Maenalian pancratiast, fifth century. Androsthenes was Olympic champion in *pankration* in both 420 and (?) 416.

Thucydides 5.49.1; Pausanias 6.6.1.

Ankylē (plural *ankylai*), Latin *amentum*, "noose", a piece of leather wrapped around the middle of the javelin (*akōn*), to form a loop through which the thrower inserted the index or first two fingers.

Philostratus, *On Athletic Exercise* 31.

Anniceris, of Cyrene, charioteer, fourth century. Seeking to impress the philosopher Plato, Anniceris drove his chariot around the grounds of the ACADEMY so carefully that his many circuits left just one track. (Plato, unmoved, criticized him – fussiness with petty concerns, he thought, was incompatible with serious achievements.) Anniceris is also said to have ransomed Plato when he was sold into slavery and bought the land which became his school. It is uncertain whether Anniceris drove in competitions; as a member of the elite – the poet CALLIMA-

CHUS was a grandson – he would only have done so on his own behalf or for a friend or relative.

Lucian, *Praise of Demosthenes* 23; Aelian, *Historical Miscellany* 2.27; Diogenes Laertius 3.20.

Anochos, or Anochas, son of Adamatas, of Tarentum, runner, sixth century. Anochos won both STADION race and DIAULOS at Olympia, likely in the same year, 520. He was the first to achieve this feat since CHIONIS over one hundred years before.

Pausanias 6.14.11.

Antaeus, mythical Libyan giant. Invigorated by contact with the earth, his mother, Antaeus wrestled visitors, inevitably defeated them, and used their skulls to roof a temple to his father Poseidon. He was finally overcome by HERACLES, who lifted him in the air and crushed him in his arms – in the process, upholding Greek ideas of hospitality and wrestling skill as well.

Pindar, *Isthmians* 4.56–61; Apollodorus 2.5.11.

Antenor, son of Xenares, Milesian pancratiast, fourth century. Unbeaten at any age and a PERIODONIKĒS as an adult, Antenor won the Olympic *pankration* in a walkover (AKONITI) in 308. He was made an honorary citizen of Athens in 306/5 and served as a *stephanēphoros*, "wreath bearer", in a ceremony of his native city in 279/8. Like Leontiscus, another *pankration* champion (? in 304), he was linked to the famous *hetaira* Mania.

Athenaeus 4.135D, 13.578F; Eusebius *Chronicon* 1.205–207 Schoene; *IG* 2^2 169; *SIG*^{3} 322.

Anthippasia, "riding opposite", a competitive equestrian display (perhaps a mock cavalry battle) which at Athens involved two squads, each made up of contingents from five of the city's civic tribes. It was part of the PANATHENAEA and Olympieia from at least the fourth century. Outside

Athens, it may be attested (as *hipeasia*) at Lebadeia in Boeotia.

Xenophon, *Hipparchicus* 1.20, 3.10–13; *IG* 2² 3079, 3130; *IG* 7 3087.

Kyle (1987) 189–190; Reed (1998) 56–59.

Antigonus, of Macedon, runner, third century. Antigonus was twice Olympic STADION champion, in 292 and 288.

Eusebius, *Chronicon* 1.207 Schoene.

Antilochus, son of Nestor, epic hero. Despite the slowness of his horses, Antilochus used tight turns and ruthless tactics – enough to bring accusations of foul play – to place second in the chariot race at the FUNERAL GAMES for Patroclus. An athlete too, he ran last in the footrace.

Homer, *Iliad* 23.290–797.

Antioch, city in Syria, founded by Seleucus (300 BCE) and later the capital of Roman Syria, a leading administrative and cultural centre of the Greek east. The site of lavish games celebrated by Antiochus IV (167 BCE, in the suburb of Daphne), the "contest of Eucrates" (running, flute playing), and festivals founded by the emperors Hadrian and Commodus, Antioch was best known for the longest-lived of the ancient Olympic festivals. This was originally endowed by Sosibius, a local senator in the time of AUGUSTUS, to be held for thirty days every fourth October, but those in charge stole much of the funds supplied. It was reorganized in honour of Olympian Zeus in 43/4 CE, but celebrated only occasionally before being suspended by Marcus Aurelius (175/6 CE) as punishment for Antioch's support for a revolt. Restored with a new schedule (forty-five days in July and August), organization (under an ALYTARCHĒS) and buildings in 181 CE, the games were moved to Issus in Cilicia in 196 before returning to Antioch (and Daphne) in 212. The games were very popular – spectators thronged ever-expanding reconstructions of the Ple-

thron, where preliminaries were staged. Despite their expense, which grew beyond the means of individuals to support by means of bequests and liturgies, the Antioch Olympics survived until 520 CE. The programme (of which little is known) seems to have included competitions for speakers and poets, and (at times) fights between men and beasts, as well as athletics and chariot racing. According to one source, well-born girls competed in wrestling (wearing shorts or trousers), running and reciting tragedies and Greek hymns; winners became priestesses and vowed to remain chaste for life.

Polybius 30.25–27; Libanius, *Oration* 10; John Malalas, *Chronicle* 12.10.288–289.

A. Schenk von Stauffenberg, *Die römische Kaisergeschichte bei Malalas* (Stuttgart 1911) 412–443; G. Downey, *A History of Antioch in Syria from Seleucus to the Arab Conquest* (Princeton 1961).

Antiochus, of Lepreon, pancratiast, fifth/ fourth century. Not only did Antiochus win the Olympic *pankration* (? 400), he also triumphed twice in pentathlon at both Nemea and Isthmia – an unusual combination. He is probably the man of the same name who represented the neighbouring Arcadians on an embassy to the king of Persia in 367, famous enough for Xenophon to refer to him as "Antiochus the pancratiast".

Xenophon, *Greek History* 7.1.33; Pausanias 6.3.9.

Antipater, of Miletus, boxer. Antipater won the boys' boxing at Olympia, perhaps in 388 BCE. He and his father refused a bribe from the tyrant Dionysius I to have him announced as a Syracusan and boasted that he was the first Ionian to dedicate a statue at Olympia.

Pausanias 6.2.6.

Antonius Lollianus, Marcus, of Ephesus, (?) athlete, second century CE. Lollianus was a PERIODONIKĒS in an unknown event and AGŌNOTHETĒS of games in honour of HADRIAN.

Moretti (1987) 88–89.

Antonius Niger, Marcus, GLADIATOR. A THRAEX, Niger fought eighteen times and was commemorated by his wife when he died at thirty-eight.

ILS 5090.

Apēnē, "wagon, cart", hauled by a pair of mules in a rare event in Greek games. The driver was seated. Depicted on early Panathenaic vases, the *apēnē* was introduced at Olympia in 500, perhaps in response to pressure from rich Greeks eager for more opportunities for victory and the prestige it brought. The first victor was THERSIAS of Thessaly. The three others we know all came from the wealthy west (where mule-cart races may have been popular). These were second-rank leaders, willing (it may be) to leave chariot- and horse racing to powerful figures such as HIERON and GELON. They were proud enough of their achievement to commission poems from Pindar and Simonides. Others, however, may have been less impressed (see ANAXILAS) – the curse on birthing mules in Elis can't have helped – and the event (like the KALPĒ) was dropped from the Olympic programme in 444 and is omitted from extant victor lists on papyrus and stone. Mule carts later raced at the Roman Consualia.

Aristotle, *Rhetoric* 3.1405b24; Pausanias 5.9.1–2.

B. Kratzmüller, "Synoris – Apene. Zweigespannrennen an den Grossen Panathenäen", *Nikephoros* 6 (1993) 75–91.

Aphesis, "sending forth", general term for the start or starting line (also *aphetērion*) of footraces and equestrian events.

See also: BALBIS, HYSPLĒX.

Sophocles, *Electra* 686; Diodorus 4.73.3

Aphetēs (plural *aphetai*), "starter", the official responsible for the oral command to begin a race – *apite*, "run off!" – and for working the starting mechanism. At SPARTA, the starting line of the race run by the suitors of Penelope – won by Odysseus – was marked by the image of Aphetaeus.

Aristophanes, *Knights* 1160; Pausanias 3.13.6.

P. Roos, "The start of the Greek foot race", *Opuscula Atheniensia* 6 (1965) 149–156.

Aphippodroma, "dismounting horse race". The rider dismounted and remounted in the course of the race – a feat all the more remarkable in that it was accomplished without the aid of stirrups. It is depicted on coins of Larisa in Thessaly.

IG 9.2 527.

K. Gallis, "The games in ancient Larisa. An example of provincial Olympic games", in Raschke (1988) 217–235 (220–221); García Romero (1992).

Aphippolampas, "mounted torch race". The term is attested only for the ELEUTHERIA (2) at Larisa in Thessaly, but such TORCH races themselves occurred as part of the festival for the Thracian goddess Bendis at Athens in the later fifth century, at the THESEIA in the second century, and elsewhere too in the Hellenistic and Roman periods.

Plato, *Republic* 1.328A; *IG*² 958, 960. *IG* 9.2 531

García Romero (1992).

Apobatēs (plural *apobatai*) "dismounter", a competitor in a race which combined athletic and equestrian elements. The *apobatēs* (also called *parabatēs*) drove or rode in a chariot but dismounted and ran for a portion of the course. Unlike other equestrian events, therefore, competitors had to appear in person. This combination was associated with Attica and Boeotia above all, but is attested elsewhere too; a Thessalian variant involved a two-horse chariot, in which both driver and runner won prizes. The *apobatēs* may have concluded equestrian programmes in Boeotia and elsewhere, as the race in armour was the final competition at Olympia.

[Demosthenes] 61.23–29; Dionysius of Halicarnassus, *Roman Antiquities* 7.73.2–3; *IG* 9.2 527.

N. B. Crowther, "The apobates reconsidered (Demosthenes lxi 23–9)", *JHS* 111 (1991) 174–176; S. Müller, " 'Herrlicher Ruhm im Sport oder Krieg' – Der *Apobates* und die Funktion des Sports in der griechischen Polis", *Nikephoros* 9 (1996) 41–69; Reed (1998) 42–55.

Apodytērion, "undressing room", a room in the PALAESTRA or GYMNASIUM where athletes disrobed. Plato describes young men playing knucklebones in a corner of an *apodytērion*. At some sites (? Epidaurus, ? Nemea), the *apodytērion* may have been a separate structure.

[Xenophon], *Constitution of the Athenians* 2.10; Plato, *Lysis* 206E.

Apollo, son of Zeus and Leto, Greek god. The image of aristocratic youth, Apollo is said to have competed at the first Olympics, defeating even HERMES (2) (swift messenger of the gods) in the footrace and warlike Ares in boxing. It was as a result of this triumph that the winner of the AULOS event in the PYTHIAN festival for Apollo played for the jump in the Olympic pentathlon. Apollo also outboxed Phorbas, who used to set upon travellers to Delphi and force them to compete against him in PANKRATION, wrestling, running and the discus. (He killed the losers, as Apollo did him.) Discus throwing with Hyacinthus was less successful: a gust of wind made the discus hit the SPARTAN boy in the head. As well as the Pythian games, Apollo was honoured at other festivals (the most famous the APOLLONIA on Delos) and at GYMNASIA such as Athens's LYCEUM.

Pausanias 5.7.10; Philostratus, *Pictures* 1.24, 2.19.

Apollonia, name of several festivals for APOLLO, the most important on the island of Delos. It featured musical competitions in particular, as well as equestrian and athletic events and a TORCH race. Athletes competed as PAIDES, AGENEIOI and ANDRES; the oldest group ran the HIPPIOS. Though some athletes were off island, most were local; this helps account for Theodorides' four victories in 269 (STADION, *hippios*, race in armour, pentathlon) and for Philarchus's as a boy wrestler in both 269 and 267. Athletic victors earned prizes valued at as much as 10 drachmas, though most were significantly less. In comparison, the annual cost of flute-players for the festival was 3,470 drachmas. The relationship between the Apollonia and another well known festival, the Delia, is unknown.

IG 11² 203, 205, 233, 274, 287.

I. R. Arnold, "Local festivals at Delos", *AJA* 37 (1933) 452–458.

Apollonius Rhantes Alexandrian boxer, the first Egyptian to run afoul of the Olympic rules (93 CE). Late for the games, Apollonius claimed to have been delayed by contrary winds. In fact – as his fellow-countryman Heraclides showed – he had been picking up prize money at games in Ionia. The Eleians disqualified Apollonius and awarded Heraclides the crown AKONITI. The infuriated Apollonius put on his boxing thongs and assaulted Heraclides, earning himself a fine.

Pausanias 5.21.12–14.

Apollonius, son of Archestratus, athlete, first century CE. Another example of how much we don't know about ancient competitors, Apollonius was PERIODONIKĒS in an unknown event in the mid-first century CE.

SEG 17.381.

Moretti (1987) 75.

Aporrhaxis, "hitting off", a children's ball game in which the winner bounced the ball with the hand most often.

Pollux 9.103, 105.

Apotomas, competitive JAVELIN.

Hesychius α 32.

Aquilo, "North Wind", Roman chariot horse, first/second century CE. Aquilo, the sire or grandsire of HIRPINUS, won 130 races for the Red CIRCUS FACTION, placing second eighty-eight times and third on thirty-seven occasions.

ILS 5295.

Aratus, of Sicyon, commander and athlete, 271–213. The leader of the Achaean Confederacy, Aratus was a successful pentathlete in his youth (he is said to have looked athletic in his STATUES) and later a chariot winner at Olympia (? in 232). Hostility to Argos prompted him to arrange for Cleonae, the original host, to hold the Nemean games in 235. The Argives responded with a celebration of their own, during which they seized Achaean competitors in defiance of the sacred TRUCE.

Plutarch, *Aratus* 3.1–2; Pausanias 6.12.6.

Arbēlas, Greek term for a type of GLA-DIATOR, perhaps the *CONTRARETIARIUS.* The *arbēlas,* who wore a spherical helmet with a smooth, semi-circular crest and a quilted tunic belted at the waist, carried a dagger in one hand. An *arbēlos,* a semi-circular blade used in leather-cutting, was attached to his other forearm.

Artemidorus 2.32.

M. Carter, "Artemidorus and the *arbēlas* gladiator", *ZPE* 134 (2001) 109–115.

Arbylē (plural *arbylai*), "shoe", a slot in the floor of a Greek racing chariot into which the driver fitted his feet.

Euripides, *Hippolytus* 1189.

H. A. Harris, "The foot-rests in Hippolytus' chariot", *CR* 18 (1968) 259–260.

Arcesilaus 1. of Megalopolis, runner, second century. STADION victor at Olympia in 188, Arcesilaus may be the man of the same name who played a leading role in the activities of the Achaean League in the early 160s.

Polybius 28.6, 29.5.6; Eusebius, *Chronicon* 1.209 Schoene.

2. king of Cyrene, winner of the Pythian (462) and Olympic (460) chariot races. Pindar's poem for the Pythian victory pays unusual attention to the charioteer, Arcesilaus's brother-in-law Carrhotus, perhaps because he alone of the forty-one entrants managed to finish.

Pindar, *Pythians* 4, 5.

C. Dougherty, *The Poetics of Colonization. From City to Text in Archaic Greece* (Oxford 1993) 103–119.

3. of Sparta, winner of the chariot race at Olympia, 448–444. His first victory – inspired perhaps by that of his Libyan namesake – started a string of seven Spartan chariot victories in eight Olympiads (one by his son, LICHAS). The Athenian oligarch Critias wished for the wealth of the Scopiads, the magnanimity of Cimon, and the victories of Arcesilaus.

Critias 88 B 8 DK; Pausanias 6.2.2.

Archelaus, son of Perdiccas, king of Macedon (413–399) and equestrian victor, about 460–399. Chariot victor at both Olympia (? 408) and Delphi, Archelaus' nine-day festival for Zeus and the nine Muses, held every fourth autumn at Dion at the foot of Mt Olympus, was the first of many to borrow the designation "Olympic".

Diodorus 17.16.3; Arrian, *Anabasis* 1.11.1; Dio Chrysostom 2.2; Solinus 9.16.

M. Mari, "Le Olimpie macedoni di Dion tra Archelao e l'età romana", *RFIC* 126 (1996) 137–169.

Archemorus *see* OPHELTES

Archery, a rare event in Greek festival competition. In the FUNERAL GAMES for Patroclus, it was won by Meriones of Crete – Cretans were famous as archers. They were no less known as runners and liars, a symptom of the Greek feeling that a man who fought from a distance might be suspect. Nevertheless, HERACLES won Iole in an archery contest, and Odysseus's skill with the bow announced his claim to his own wife Penelope in the *Odyssey*. As archery gained military importance in the Hellenistic period, archers appeared among the instructors of EPHEBES, and competitions (sometimes linked to javelin throwing) entered some Greek games. At Coressia on Ceos, winners among the ANDRES took home cash, arrows and quivers – they were of fighting age – PAIDES, pieces of meat.

Homer, *Iliad* 23.850–883; Aristotle, *Constitution of the Athenians* 42.3; SIG^3 958.

Archias, son of Eucles, of Hybla (Sicily), herald *(KĒRYX)*. Archias was the first herald from outside Elis to win the Olympic competition (perhaps in 368, 364, 356). He also won at the Pythian games.

Pollux 4.92.

Archippus, son of Calliphanes, Mytilenaean boxer, fourth/third century. Archippus was men's boxing champion at all four festivals of the PERIODOS before he was twenty-one. His Olympic victory may date to 300.

Pausanias 6.15.1.

Archon, son of Cleinus, of Pella, equestrian victor, fourth century. One of ALEXANDER III's officers and governor of Babylonia after his death (he was killed trying to hold it in 321), Archon's two-horse chariot teams won at Delphi and Isthmia sometime before 333/2.

Arrian, *Indica* 18.3; *SEG* 18.222.

Ebert (1972) 145–147.

Arena *see HARENA*

Aretē, "goodness, excellence", the quality which enabled Greek competitors (and their horses) to succeed and was demonstrated by their victory. Its components include natural ability (usually inherited), physical effort and financial expense, and luck, the favour of the gods.

Homer, *Iliad* 23.276–278, *Odyssey* 8.236–240; Pindar, *Olympians* 7.87–90; Isocrates 16.34; Lucian, *Anacharsis* 14; Plutarch, *Agesilaus* 20.1.

H. M. Lee, "Athletic arete in Pindar", *AncW* 7 (1983) 31–37.

Argos, an important Greek city-state in the northeastern Peloponnese, centre of the legendary Bronze Age kingdom of Agamemnon and long-time rival of SPARTA. The Argives often exploited festival sites and competition for political prestige. King PHEIDON is said to have controlled Olympia and presided over the games in the early seventh century, and the later democracy sponsored victorious entries in the Olympic horse race (480) and chariot race (472). After the amalgamation ("synoecism") of Argos and Corinth, the Argives were about to celebrate the Isthmian festival until forced to withdraw by the Spartan king AGESILAUS (390). Corinthian dissidents held the games as Agesilaus stood guard and the Argives put them on again after his departure. (Some won twice.) Fifty years later, the Argives took over stewardship of the Nemean games and moved them to Argos by 250. Argos also hosted its own panhellenic competitive festival, the Hecatombaea, later also called the HERAEA (1). Part of the PERIODOS of later antiquity, it generally ranked below the others, perhaps because of its unusual prize, a bronze shield; this led to the use of the term Aspis, "shield", to identify the festival. It was, however, important enough to inspire a saying, "Proud as if he'd won a shield at Argos", and to attract leaders like Demetrius Poliorcetes and

King Philip V of Macedon to preside. The full programme included the *hippios* race and (in later times at least) musical competitions. One runner, Aeschyllus, won the stadion four times and the race in armour thrice.

Pindar, *Olympians* 7.83, *Nemeans* 10.22–23; Herodotus 1.31; Xenophon, *Greek History* 4.5.1–2; *IG* 4 583.

I. R. Arnold, "The shield of Argos", *AJA* 41 (1937) 436–440; L. Moretti, "Dagli *Heraia* all'*Aspis* di Argo", *MGR* 16 (1991) 179–189.

Aristeas, or Menander, of Stratoniceia, HEAVY athlete, first century CE. Aristeas won wrestling and *pankration* on the same day at Olympia in 13 CE, the first to so match HERACLES since MARION.

Pausanias 5.21.10; Eusebius, *Chronicon* 1.213 Schoene.

Aristides, of Elis, runner, (?) second century CE. The versatile Aristides won *HIPPIOS* for *PAIDES* at Nemea, and *HOPLITĒS* at Olympia and *DIAULOS* at the Pythian games as an adult.

Pausanias 6.16.4.

Aristis, son of Pheidon, of Cleonae, pancratiast, sixth century. Aristis was one of the early stars at nearby Nemea, winning *pankration* four times in the first decades after the festival's foundation in 573.

SEG 11.290.

Ebert (1972) 36–37.

Aristodemus, son of Thrasys, Eleian wrestler, fourth century. Aristodemus won at Olympia (388) and twice at both Delphi and Nemea. The inscription on his victory statue at Olympia boasts that he won through skill rather than size. The Aristodemus of Elis who wrote on the history of the Olympics may be the same man.

Pausanias 6.3.4; Hephaestion pp. 60, 65 Cronsbruch; Eusebius, *Chronicon* 1.205 Schoene.

Ebert (1972) 113–115; C. Wacker, "The record of the Olympic victory list", *Nikephoros* 11 (1998) 39–50.

Aristomenes, of Rhodes, HEAVY athlete, second century. Aristomenes won wrestling and *pankration* on the same day at Olympia in 156, the first to do so since CAPRUS.

Pausanias 5.21.10.

Ariston, of Thurii, runner, first century. Ariston was twice Olympic STADION champion, in 40 and 32.

Eusebius, *Chronicon* 1.213 Schoene.

Aristonicus *see* CLITOMACHUS

Aristophon, son of Lysinus, Athenian pancratiast, fourth century. Winner of the *pankration* (perhaps in 312), Aristophon had his statue at Olympia dedicated by the people of Athens and he himself made a dedication to the healing god Asclepius on the Athenian Acropolis.

Pausanias 6.13.11; *IG* 2² 4397.

Arktoi, "bears", unmarried girls in the service of the goddess Artemis at Brauron and Munichion in Attica. Vases depict girls, nude or in short tunics, either running in pre-nuptial races (common throughout the Greek world) or engaged in a more unusual ritual chase.

T. F. Scanlon, "Race or chase at the Arkteia of Attica?", *Nikephoros* 3 (1990) 73–120.

Armentarius, GLADIATOR, first century BCE/CE. Armentarius, a MURMILLO, bore a strong resemblance to Cassius Severus, a likeness for which that famous orator was taunted.

Pliny, *Natural History* 7.12.55.

Armour, race in *see* HOPLITĒS

Arrichion or Arrachion, of Phigalia (Bassae), pancratiast, sixth century. Twice winner in *pankration* at Olympia (572, 568), Arrichion reached the finals again in 564. About to succumb to a choke-hold, he responded to his trainer ERYXIAS's encouragement – "What a wonderful epitaph: 'He did not yield at Olympia' " – by dislocating his opponent's ankle (or toe). It was his rival who conceded, and Arrichion, though dead, was awarded his third crown.

Pausanias 8.40.1–2; Philostratus, *On Athletic Exercise* 21, *Pictures* 2.6.

R. H. Brophy III, "Deaths in the pan-Hellenic games: Arrachion and Creugas", *AJP* 99 (1978) 363–390.

Arsilochus, of Thebes, chariot victor, fifth century. Arsilochus won the Olympic chariot race in 480 along with his fellow citizen Daetondas – the only such joint entry we know of.

Oxyrhynchus Papyri 222.

Arsinoe II, daughter of PTOLEMY I Soter and BERENICE I, chariot victor, c.316–270. Arsinoe married her full brother, the Egyptian king PTOLEMY II Philadelphus, in the 270s and, like him, valued equestrian victory. She was the first to win all three chariot races at the same Olympic festival, the two- and four-horse events for adult teams and the four-horse for colts (the race for colt pairs was introduced only after her death).

Posidippus, *P.Mil.Vogl.* 8 309.XII.26–27.

Artemidorus, of Ephesus, later second century CE, author of a work on dreams as omens of the future. Many involve sport in the Greek world of the Roman Empire. For example, it is bad for an athlete to dream that he has milk in his breasts or is nursing a child, since women's bodies are weaker.

Harris (1964) 244–261; H. Langenfeld, "Artemidors Traumbuch als sporthistorische Quelle", *Stadion* 17 (1991) 1–26.

Aryballos (plural *aryballoi*), a small round pottery vessel with a wide lip and small mouth, used for an athlete's OIL and hung by a strap from his wrist. The *aryballos*

(or *lekythos*) identifies the athlete on archaic Greek grave reliefs.

J. D. Beazley, "Aryballos", *ABSA* 29 (1927–28) 187–215; C. H. E. Haspels, "How the aryballos was suspended", *ibid.* 216–223.

Arybbas, son of Alcetas, king of Epirus and chariot victor, fourth century. Arybbas was king of the Molossi of Epirus from about 359. His niece Olympias married PHILIP of Macedon, who later drove him from the throne, and he then took refuge in Athens, where his father had been granted citizenship, dying there in 342/1. Arybbas's chariot victories, two at Olympia (perhaps in 360 and 352) and one at Delphi, must have been part of his rivalry with Philip.

IG 2² 226.

J. Heskel, "The political background of the Arybbas decree", *GRBS* 29 (1988) 185–196.

Asclepieia, the name of two important panhellenic competitive festivals in honour of the healing deity Asclepius. **1.** The Asclepieia of Epidaurus in the northeast Peloponnese, a centre of Asclepius's cult in the classical period, is known from about 520. Held every four years, nine days after the Isthmian games in early May, it was managed by an AGŌNOTHETĒS and HELLANODIKAI; it was they who fined athletes who cheated, musical contestants who did not appear and, in one instance, a workman judged responsible for the malfunctioning of the HYSPLĒX. The Asclepieia included a full athletic programme for PAIDES and ANDRES, including the HIPPIOS race and, in the mid-first century CE, a STADION race for girls (see HERMESIANAX (2)). It was held in a stadium which seated about 6,000 and was later enlarged (about 160) to hold some 14,000. There were also musical and equestrian contests. Winners (who included such famous figures as the pancratiast DORIEUS of Rhodes in the classical period) wore a laurel wreath. In the first century CE, the festival was augmented by the Caesareia, and in the third it was designated Asclepieia Olympia, but it was no longer a competition of the first rank.

Pindar, *Nemeans* 3.148, 5.97, *Isthmians* 8.147–150; *IG* 4² 1.98–100.

M. Sève, "Les concours d'Épidaure", *REG* 106 (1993) 303–328.

2. The Asclepieia of the island of Cos in the southeast Aegean was first organized as a quadrennial festival in 242, with the support and financial contributions of many Greek city-states and rulers, and soon rivalled the earlier Asclepieia in prestige. Victors came from the Greek mainland and as far east as Babylonia. It included musical, equestrian and athletic competitions. Athletes were grouped in four age-classes: PAIDES *Pythikoi*, PAIDES *Isthmikoi*, AGENEIOI, ANDRES. All took part in the STADION and the three combat events, *ageneioi* also in the pentathlon, *paides Pythikoi* also in the DOLICHOS and DIAULOS. The HIPPIOS was added to the programme for *paides Isthmikoi*, while *andres* competed in the HOPLITĒS too. Second-place finishers were awarded prizes. Coins of Cos bore a depiction of a discus-thrower.

Klee (1918) 3–19, 33–34.

Aspis *see* ARGOS

Astyanax, of Miletus, pancratiast, fourth century. Astyanax won at Olympia three times in succession (324–316) and may have been an unchallenged PERIODONIKĒS (see AKONITI). Like many HEAVY athletes, he was storied for his size – two urns could hardly hold his bones after cremation – and DIET. Invited to dinner by the Persian Ariobarzanes, he ate the food of all nine male guests and, when asked to sing for his supper, broke off a bronze lentil-shaped ornament from a couch and pulled it flat with his bare hands. Astyanax also competed as a boxer.

Menander, *Colax* 100; Athenaeus 10.413AC.

Astylus, of CROTON, runner, fifth century. Astylus won both STADION and DIAULOS at Olympia in 488, repeated this in 484, and added HOPLITĒS in 480, a triple crown not matched for 300 years. The victories in 488 (or 484) were the last in Croton's extraordinary string of athletic successes: recruited by HIERON, Astylus won his later victories as a Syracusan. In response, the Crotoniates tore down his statue and turned his home into a prison. One of those Plato mentions as abstaining from SEX during training, Astylus denied himself less in other areas, commissioning a victory song from SIMONIDES and a statue from Pythagoras of Samos.

Simonides 1, *PMG*; Plato, *Laws* 8.840A; Pausanias 6.13.1.

Young (1984) 141–144.

Atalanta, legendary female huntress, wrestler and runner. The daughter of a king – Iasus of Arcadia, Boeotian Schoeneus – Atalanta was rejected by her father, who wanted a son, and raised by hunters. She grew up to excel at this masculine pursuit; the only woman among those who fought the Calydonian boar, her arrow drew first blood. Atalanta took part in other activities otherwise restricted to men as well. She wrestled Peleus at the FUNERAL GAMES for Pelias (and is often said to have beaten him) and outran all those who sought her hand in marriage, despite giving them a head start. In the end, she was defeated by Melanion or Hippomenes, armed with the advice of Aphrodite and golden apples which he dropped whenever Atalanta was about to overtake him. Her successes were disastrous for the men who knew her. Meleager slew the boar, awarded Atalanta part of its body to signal her own contribution, killed his uncles when they objected, and was soon the victim of his mother's revenge. Her unsuccessful suitors paid with their lives and Melanion/Hippomenes, forgetful of what was owed the gods, made love with her in a sanctuary and was transformed into a lion. As for Peleus, his failure to outwrestle Atalanta was a mark of his fate, to father a son (ACHILLES) far better than himself. In her effect on men no less than her masculine strength and skill, Atalanta was an Amazon.

Plato, *Republic* 10. 620B; Apollodorus 3.9.2.

R. A. and M. L. Howell, "The Atalanta legend in art and literature", *JSH* 16 (1989) 127–139; A. Ley, "Atalante – von der Athletin zur Liebhaberin. Ein Beitrag zum Rezeptionswandel eines mythologischen Themas auf Vasen des 6.-4 Jhs. v. Chr.", *Nikephoros* 3 (1990) 31–72; J. M. Barringer, "Atalanta as model: the hunter and the hunted", *CA* 15 (1996) 48–76 (66–74).

Ateleia, freedom from taxes and other civic obligations. *Ateleia* was one of the rewards for victors in Greek crown games (see AGŌNES) under the Roman empire.

Code of Justinian 10.54.

Athanichus, of Thebes, HEAVY athlete, third or second century. Athanichus was a victorious pancratiast at Nemea and won three times, as PAIS and adult, at the BASILEIA at Lebadeia. He may also have won as a boxer before dying in battle and being commemorated by his mother or wife.

IG 7 4247.

Ebert (1972) 209–211.

Athenaeus, of Athens, athlete, first century CE. Athenaeus is called a PERIOD-ONIKĒS on an early second century CE inscription in honour of his son Athenaeus.

IG 2² 3577.

Athenion, of Stratoniceia, runner, undated. Athenion won both DIAULOS and DOLICHOS for boys at the Pythian games.

SEG 38.1104.

Athenodorus, of Aegium (Achaea), runner, first century CE. Athenodorus was Olympic STADION champion three times,

in 49, 53 and 61 CE – a long career for a sprinter.

Eusebius, *Chronicon* 1.215 Schoene.

Athenopolis, son of Pythotimus, of Priene, wrestler, second century. Athenopolis defeated three in his AGE-CLASS (likely the PAIDES) to win at the ASCLEPIEIA (1) of Epidaurus, and later won at the Pythian games as well.

Inscr. Prien. 268 II.

Ebert (1972) 218–221.

Athlētēs (plural *athlētai*), "competitor, athlete". The term becomes common for any expert, especially in war.

Homer, *Odyssey* 8.159–164; Plato, *Republic* 8.543B; Aristotle, *Politics* 6.1321a26.

Athlon (plural *athla*), the PRIZE in a competition.

C. P. Pavese, "*Athloi e athla*", *SIFC* 14 (1996) 3–9.

Athlos (plural *athloi*; epic *aethlos*), "competition, struggle, labour", a strenuous activity directed towards a goal. The plural is used for HERACLES' Labours as well as for competitive festivals.

T. F. Scanlon, "The vocabulary of competition: *agōn* and *áethlos*, Greek terms for contest", *Arete. The Journal of Sport Literature* (now *Aethlon*) 1.1 (1983) 147–162.

Athlothetēs (plural *athlothetai*), "prize giver", the organizer or supervisor of a competition; often synonymous with AGŌ-NOTHETĒS. At Athens, ten *athlothetai* were appointed for four-year terms to oversee the PANATHENAEA; they were also responsible for the HERACLEIA at Marathon.

IG 1³ 3, 370, 375; Aristotle, *Constitution of the Athenians* 60, 62.2.

B. Nagy, "The Athenian athlothetai", *GRBS* 19 (1978) 307–313; E. Vanderpool, "Regulations for the Herakleian games at Marathon", *Studies Presented to Stirling Dow on his Eightieth Birthday* (*GRBS* Monograph 10: Durham 1984) 295–296.

Attalus, son of Philetaerus, of Pergamum, chariot victor, third century. Son of the founder of the royal dynasty of Pergamum and father of Attalus I, Attalus's victory in the Olympic chariot race for colts (perhaps in 276) was celebrated in one of the most detailed of surviving epinician epigrams. Attalus was also a victor at a festival in Asia. His grandsons (including King Eumenes II) were equestrian victors at the PANATHENAEA about a century later.

Diogenes Laertius 4.30; *Inscr. Perg.* 10, 11.

Ebert (1972) 176–181.

Attinas, son of Hippocrates, of Adramyttium (Mysia), boxer, first century. In a speech delivered in 59, Cicero gives Attinas (Olympic boxing victor in 72) as an example of a well known person killed by pirates.

Cicero, *For Flaccus* 13.31; Phlegon, *FGrH* 257 F 12.

Moretti (1987) 72–73.

Auctoratus (plural *auctorati*), "hireling", a free person who chose to serve as a GLADIATOR. Driven by financial need or simply thrill-seekers, *auctorati*, especially those of equestrian or senatorial rank, shared the social stigma and legal limitations of their fellows. Some emperors outlawed or discouraged *auctorati*, but their measures did not succeed for long.

Livy, 28.21.2; Horace, *Satires* 2.7.58–59; Tacitus, *Histories* 2.62.

Mosci Sassi (1992) 70–82.

Augustus (Gaius Octavius, Octavian), first Roman emperor (27 BCE–14 CE), 63–14 CE. While not an athlete himself (he did enjoy BALL play and taught his grandsons to swim), Augustus was as innovative and influential in the area of Greek and Roman sport as in most others during his long reign, establishing practices and patterns that endured or were developed for many years to come. He celebrated his decisive naval victory over

Antony and Cleopatra at Actium (in 31 BCE) by expanding an existing competitive festival into the ACTIAN games at Nicopolis – these immediately became part of the PERIODOS of prestigious games – and later established the SEBASTAN games, almost as important, at Naples. At Rome itself, Augustus built wooden stands in the Campus Martius and sponsored athletic exhibitions which he watched (especially the boxers) with evident interest – he did not want to demonstrate the disdain shown by his assassinated adoptive father, Julius Caesar. He also instituted LUDI *pro valetudine* (or *salute*) *Caesaris*, "for Caesar's health/safety", celebrated quadrennially from 28 to at least 9 CE. A Greek-style competitive festival, this featured boys (*PAIDES*) and men from the elite as well as a Roman flavour, prisoners of war fighting in armour. As in other such competitions he attended, Augustus provided prizes for all athletes who took part. The emperor also patronized traditional Roman contests – Suetonius says he surpassed all before him in the frequency, variety and magnificence of his spectacles. He expanded the calendar of *ludi* with chariot races to include the *ludi saeculares* of 17 and the inaugural celebration of the *ludi Martiales* in 2, and put on frequent performances of the LUSUS TROIAE (until dissuaded by an injury to a senator's grandson). It is interesting in this connection that Roman elite interest in chariot competition at Olympia likely revived during Augustus's reign (see GERMANICUS, TIBERIUS).

Augustus was also involved in gladiatorial spectacles (*MUNERA*), expanding the ruler's role as he restricted the freedom of potential rivals among the elite. Within his first decade in power, he limited the number and size of shows magistrates could produce while he himself regularly exceeded those limits (boasting in the official record of his achievements that he had exhibited 10,000 fighters in all). He also systematized the procurement and presentation of GLADIATORS throughout the empire, linking them both to existing festivals at Rome (the Quinquatrus to Minerva, the Saturnalia) and to emperor cult elsewhere, set up training schools (*LUDI*) and the first permanent AMPHITHEATRE at Rome, established (or regularized) the standard programme (beast hunts, executions of common criminals, then gladiatorial combats in the afternoon), and limited the social mobility of freed slave gladiators. (These could never become citizens or make or benefit from a will.) Augustus was no less concerned to maintain and demonstrate hierarchies among spectators, requiring adult male citizens to wear the toga and relegating women (except the Vestal Virgins) to seats furthest from the action or (in the case of Greek athletics) excluding them altogether.

Cassius Dio 53.1.4–6; Augustus, *Achievements* 22–23; Suetonius, *Augustus* 43–45, 64.3.

Caldelli (1993) 21–24; R. W. Fortuin, *Der Sport im augusteischen Rom. Philologische und sporthistorische Untersuchungen* (Stuttgart 1996).

Aulos (plural *auloi*), wind instrument played to accompany the jump in the PENTATHLON. Apparently helping to set the jumper's rhythm, at Olympia, the *aulos* was played by the reigning champion in that musical competition at the Pythian games. The *aulos* was also used in other athletic contexts at times – to accompany wrestling in the Athenian games at ARGOS, boxing among the ETRUSCANS, exercise in the GYMNASIUM.

Plutarch, *Moral Essays* 1140C; Pausanias 5.7.10, 6.14.10; Philostratus, *On Athletic Exercise* 55.

W. J. Raschke, "Aulos and athlete: the function of the flute player in Greek athletics", *Arete. The Journal of Sport Literature* (now *Aethlon*) 2.2 (1985) 177–200; D. H. J. Larmour, *Stage and Stadium* (Hildesheim 1999) 67–74.

Aura, or Ouros, "Breeze", a mare owned by PHEIDOLAS of Corinth. Aura finished first in the horse race at Olympia despite losing her jockey and had her STATUE dedicated in the ALTIS. The story has a moral: the relative importance of the owner's judgement in breeding or buying horses and the rider's skill.

Pausanias 6.13.9–10.

Aurelius ....., Marcus, son of Timocles, Aphrodisian runner, third century CE. An early third-century member of a prominent family of Aphrodisias, Aurelius's victories came mainly in DOLICHOS at festivals nearby in Asia Minor, but he also ran DIAULOS and the race in armour, and won as far afield as the Pythian and Actian games.

Moretti (1953) 235–237.

Aurelius Abas, Marcus, of Adada (Pisidia), runner, second/third century CE. Abas won DOLICHOS at several important festivals of the later second or early third century CE, including the HERAEA (I) at ARGOS, the CAPITOLINE games at Rome, and the ARTEMISIA at Ephesus (where he also won DIAULOS).

IGRom. 3.370.

Moretti (1953) 222–224, (1987) 81.

Aurelius Agathopus, Marcus, of Aegina, runner, second century CE. Winner of the STADION race at Olympia in 173 and 177 CE, Agathopus may be the Marcus Aurelius Agathopus of Aegina mentioned as a winner of the race in armour at the ELEUTHERIA (I) in a Smyrnan inscription. Another (fragmentary) inscription may say he was PERIODONIKĒS four times.

Eusebius, *Chronicon* 1.217 Schoene.

Moretti (1987) 76.

Aurelius Alexander, Gaius Perelius, of Thyatira (Lydia), pancratiast, second/third century CE. A PERIODONIKĒS and later high priest of the association of athletes at Rome (XYSTOS), Alexander's city sent him to ask the emperor Elagabalus for permission to establish a new competition.

TAM 5.1017–1020.

C. P. Jones, "The pancratiasts Helix and Alexander on an Ostian mosaic", *JRA* 11 (1998) 293–298.

Aurelius Asclepiades, Marcus, of Alexandria, wrestler, second century CE. Though less famous than his fellow citizen AURELIUS Asclepiades "Hermodorus", the pancratiast, the wrestler outstripped him with two sets of victories in the PERIODOS. His Olympic crowns may have come in 193 and 197.

IG 5.1 666.

Aurelius Asclepiades, Marcus ("Hermodorus") of Alexandria, pancratiast, second century CE. The son of M. Aurelius Demetrius, "Harpocration", wrestler and PERIODONIKĒS in *pankration* who was later head priest and XYSTARCHĒS of his GUILD and Director of the Imperial Baths, Asclepiades had similar success as pancratiast and held the same positions. A member of the Councils of Naples, Elis and Athens, and an honorary citizen of other cities as well, his many triumphs in Italy, Greece and Asia Minor include those at Olympia (181 CE), Delphi, Isthmia (twice) and Nemea (twice); he boasts that he was never beaten or tied and often won AKONITI. After competing for six years, he retired in 182 CE at twenty-five "because of the dangers and jealousies which were gathering around" him; forced to return to competition (in ? 196 CE), he won at the local Olympic festival at Alexandria.

IG 14 1102–1104; *P. London* 1178.

H. A. Harris, "Notes on three athletic inscriptions", *JHS* 82 (1962) 19–24 (19–20); Poliakoff (1987) 125–127.

Aurelius Chrysippus, Marcus, of Smyrna, wrestler, second century CE. Chrysippus is cited as a PERIODONIKĒS in a papyrus of 194 CE.

P. London 1178.

Aurelius Demostratus Damas, Marcus of Sardis, HEAVY athlete, second century CE. One of the most famous athletes of his day, Damas was a good enough boxer to win at the Pythian games, but achieved most success as a pancratiast. He was PERIODONIKĒS in this event, claiming two victories at Olympia (perhaps in 173 and 177 CE), at least two at Nemea, three at Delphi and five at Isthmia among a total of at least 108. In addition to his many honorary citizenships, the emperors Septimius Severus and Caracalla appointed him to high office in the athletes' GUILDS of many communities. Damas passed on many of his honours and some of this athletic ability to his four sons, who erected a statue in his memory between 212 and 217 CE.

IG 14 1105; *Delph.* 3.1 556, 557; *ISardis* 79; *P. London* 1178.

Moretti (1953) 244–249, (1987) 78.

Aurelius Granianus Fanius Artemidorus, Publius, of Miletus, athlete, second/third century CE. Artemidorus was a PERIODONIKĒS in an unknown event at the end of the second century CE.

IDidyma 81, 182, 188, 189, 243, 244.

Moretti (1987) 79.

Aurelius Heliodorus, Marcus, son of Heliodorus, Thespian pancratiast, fourth century CE. Heliodorus won at Olympia as both PAIS and adult in the mid-fourth century CE.

J. Ebert, "Zur neuen Bronzeplatte mit Siegerinschriften aus Olympia (Inv. 1148)", *Nikephoros* 10 (1997) 217–233.

Aurelius Helix, of Phoenicia, pancratiast and wrestler, second/third century CE. The first to win both his events at the CAPITOLINE games at Rome, Helix aimed to become the eighth man (after HERACLES) to do the same at Olympia (in ? 217 CE). (He had already won the men's wrestling when just too old to compete as a PAIS, in ? 213.) Though he was successful in *pankration*, the officials cheated him of his chance by failing to announce the wrestling event in the usual way. PHILOSTRATUS regards his training regimen as a boy (clapping the hands, massage) as a model.

Cassius Dio 80.10.2; Philostratus, *On Athletic Exercise* 46; *Heroïcus* 16.23–17.5.

C. P. Jones, "The pancratiasts Helix and Alexander on an Ostian mosaic", *JRA* 11 (1998) 293–298.

Aurelius Heras, Marcus, of Chios, runner, second century CE. Heras won STADION races as a boy and an AGENEIOS, *stadion*, DIAULOS, DOLICHOS and armoured races as an adult (including both *stadion* (157 CE) and *dolichos* at Olympia).

SEG 37.712.

J. Ebert, "Neues zu den Inschriften für Aurelios Heras aus Chios", *Nikephoros* 1 (1988) 85–102.

Aurelius Hermagoras, Marcus, of Magnesia on Sipylus, wrestler, second century CE. Perhaps the son of the Olympic wrestling champion of 137 CE, Hermagoras himself was victorious in twenty-nine crown games and 127 others. At Olympia (in ? 177) he fought to a DRAW in the finals, one of nineteen such results he claims on an inscription. Hermagoras led the athletes' GUILD which organized the Actian games and the board of officials for the Olympic games at Ephesus and Smyrna.

IG 14 739.

Moretti (1953) 224–226.

Aurelius Hierocles, Marcus, of Nysa, athlete, second/third century CE. As so often, Hierocles' career, successful though it was – he was a PERIODONIKĒS – is known only through an inscription which offers no other information except that he was also an honorary citizen of Tralles.

MDAI(A) 21 (1896) 113 no. 2.

Aurelius Liber, Marcus, Roman CHARIOTEER, second/third century CE. Liber, both manager and driver for the Green CIRCUS FACTION, was given a memorial on the occasion of his 3000th victory.

ILS 5296.

Horsmann (1998) 243–246.

Aurelius Menander, Aelius, of Aphrodisias, pancratiast, second century CE. Me-

nander won as boy, *ageneios* and adult in three successive years and, in a competitive career which stretched from Italy to Arabia, earned crowns at Delphi, Isthmia, Nemea and the Capitoline games at Rome. Following a pattern common among successful athletes under the Empire, he was later XYSTARCHĒS of his athletic GUILD, citizen and councillor of several cities, and willing and able to underwrite the costs of some local games and their prizes. For his efforts, Menander's guild commended him in a letter to emperor Antoninus Pius.

CIG 2.2810b, 2811b.

Aurelius Mollicius Tatianus, Marcus Roman CHARIOTEER, second/third century CE. A native of Rome like his father AURELIUS Polynices, Tatianus shared his brother Macaris's fate, death in a chariot crash, at twenty. He had won 125 times, eighty-nine victories for the Red CIRCUS FACTION, twenty-four as a Green, five as a Blue, and seven as a White, twice earning purses of 40,000 sesterces.

ILS 5286.

Horsmann (1998) 253–255.

Aurelius Philosebastus, Marcus, of Ephesus, athlete, second century CE. An inscription found at Ephesus, dated to the end of the second century CE, declares Philosebastus victor in the PERIODOS in an unspecified event.

Année épigraphique (1938) 84.

Aurelius Phoebammon, son of Posidonius, of Egypt, pancratiast, third century CE. Phoebammon was PERIODONIKĒS in *pankration* sometime in the first quarter of the third century CE.

P. London 1243.

Aurelius Polycrates, of Cibyra (Lycia), runner and pentathlete, third century CE. Polycrates was a good enough runner to win STADION races as an AGENEIOS, but earned more fame in the pentathlon, where he sometimes swept the first three events. In later life, he enjoyed the citizenship of many communities and was XYSTARCHĒS for life of a festival at Philadelphia.

IGRom. 4.1761.

Moretti (1953) 239–241.

Aurelius Polynices Macarius, Marcus, Roman CHARIOTEER, second/third century CE. A native of Rome, Polynices died at twenty-nine after winning 739 races – 655 for the Red CIRCUS FACTION, fifty-five as a Green, twelve as a Blue, seventeen as a White – and purses totalling 1,065,000 sesterces. His victories included three with six-horse teams, eight with eight horses and nine with ten horses. Polynices left two sons, Macaris and AURELIUS Tatianus, drivers who were both apparently killed in chariot crashes.

ILS 5286.

Horsmann (1998) 269–270.

Aurelius Sarapammon, or Didymus, of Oxyrhynchus, athlete or herald (KĒRYX), third century CE. Sarapammon is called a PERIODONIKĒS in a papyrus dated to 298 CE.

Oxyrhynchus Papyri 1643, *PSI* 456.

Moretti (1987) 80.

Aurelius Zopyrus, Marcus, son of Zopyrus, Athenian boxer, fourth century CE. Zopyrus's brother M. Aurelius Eucarpides was Olympic *pankration* champion among the boys in 381 CE. Zopyrus won the boys' boxing event in 385 CE, to become our latest datable Olympic victor.

J. Ebert, "Zur neuen Bronzeplatte mit Siegerinschriften aus Olympia (Inv. 1148)", *Nikephoros* 10 (1997) 217–233.

Auriga (plural *aurigae*), or *aurigarius* (plural *aurigarii*), Roman charioteer. The term usually describes an inexperienced or less successful driver, still racing two-horse teams. Cf. AGITATOR.

Suetonius, *Nero* 5.2; *ILS* 5313, 9348.

J.-P. Thuillier, "*Auriga/agitator*: de simples synonymes?", *RPh* 61 (1987) 233–237.

Autolycus, son of Lycon, Athenian pancratiast, fifth century. Autolycus won the *pankration* for boys or AGENEIOI at the PANATHENAEA in 421, a victory which provided the occasion for a comedy by Eupolis, a satyr play by EURIPIDES (both called *Autolycus*), and Xenophon's *Symposium* (set at a celebration hosted by Autolycus's lover CALLIAS (4)). Autolycus's beauty and modesty were well known. Perhaps they helped when he had a property dispute with a Spartan, Eteonicus, and the enemy general Lysander nevertheless found in his favour. Another conflict, with another Spartan, the garrison commander Callibius, is said to have led to his death at the command of the Thirty Tyrants at the end of the fifth century. Soon afterwards, Autolycus's father Lycon was one of the prosecutors of Socrates. In the later fourth century, Autolycus came to represent the best and the brightest of Athens's glorious past, and his statues were set up in the Prytaneum at Athens and at Delphi.

Xenophon, *Symposium* 1.2, 8–9; Plutarch, *Lysander* 15.5; Pausanias 1.18.3, 9.32.6; *SEG* 34.380.

C. Vatin, "Un athlète athénien à Delphes: Autolycos", in H. Walter (ed.) *Hommages à Lucien Lerat* (Paris 1984) 841–847.

Avilius Teres, Roman CHARIOTEER, early second century CE. Perhaps a slave freed by L. Avilius Planta, Teres once held the Red CIRCUS FACTION's record for lifetime victories (1,011) and for wins in races for four chariots only in a single year. He earned at least 1,380,000 sesterces.

ILS 5287; *CIL* 6.37834.

Horsmann (1998) 294–296.

Azan, son of Arcas, legendary Arcadian king. His FUNERAL GAMES were sometimes said to have been the occasion for the first equestrian and (perhaps) athletic contests. In the chariot race, Apis was run over by Aetolus, the first attested casualty among spectators.

Pausanias 5.1.8, 8.4.5.

B

Bacchylides, of Iulis on Ceos, lyric poet, c.520–450. Like his uncle SIMONIDES, Bacchylides was commissioned to write poems in honour of the victors in the major competitive festivals. Fourteen are known from a papyrus purchased in Egypt in 1896 (by a nice coincidence, the date of Baron de Coubertin's first Olympics). Bacchylides' patrons included HIERON of Syracuse, for whom he wrote three poems (he may have stayed at his court in Syracuse), and competitors from Metapontum, Phlius and Thessaly as well as his native Ceos. Like SIMONIDES and his contemporary PINDAR, Bacchylides wrote many works in other genres: dithyrambs, hymns, paeans, maiden songs. That it is mostly his victory songs which have survived is not entirely coincidental: they were important to more Greeks than those who paid for them.

See also: EPINICIANS.

A. P. Burnett, *The Art of Bacchylides* (Cambridge MA 1985).

Balbis (plural *balbides*), "platform, start", a stone sill at either end of the Greek STADIUM used for the start and finish of footraces, the take-off board (BATĒR) of the jump, and the place from which the discus and javelin were thrown. Parallel grooves were often cut along the width of *balbides* for runners' toes.

See also: HYSPLĒX

Sophocles, *Antigone* 131; Aristophanes, *Knights* 1159; Philostratus, *Pictures* 1.24.

P. Valavanis, *Hysplex. The Starting Mechanism in Ancient Stadia. A Contribution to Ancient Greek Technology* (Berkeley and Los Angeles 1999); N. B. Crowther, "The finish in the Greek foot-race", *Nikephoros* 12 (1999) 131–142 (133–135).

Ball-play, a form of exercise and entertainment. Ball games were never part of Greek and Roman competitive festivals. In the theatre of Hellenistic SPARTA, however, five teams of fourteen *sphaireis*, "ball-players", competed in a rough-and-tumble version of EPISKYROS as the last stage of their transition to adult warrior status at twenty. Victorious teams sacrificed to HERACLES and set up commemorative monuments (with boasts of winning without a BYE); their members may have served as officials for later tournaments. Though such competitions for teams of EPHEBES were widespread in the Greek world, this was the only one to involve ball-play.

Ball-play is attested as a pastime and means of training from the time of Homer: Princess Nausicaa and her companions play ball at the beach while they wait for their laundry to dry and a pair of youths demonstrate their skill at throwing and catching to entertain Odysseus at his Phaeacian feast. (Rhythm and song mark both occasions.) Later authors refer to balls of various sizes and materials, from a small ball stuffed with hair or feathers to a larger air-filled bladder and a tightly packed two-pound monster; many were enclosed with cloth or leather patchwork, sometimes coloured, but others of terracotta or glass are known as well. The famous physician Galen recommends exercise with the small ball: it is convenient, inexpensive (Aristotle noted that even a good quality ball is cheap enough for a child's gift), suited for individuals as well as groups, for old and young alike (Spurinna was playing at seventy-seven), valuable for both strength and speed, for both the upper and lower body, and training for the eye and mind as well. (Ball-play is said to help commanders and administrators seize an enemy's goods and protect what they've won.) In addition, unlike most forms of exercise, it is safe (though a Roman lawsuit arose from a ball player breaking the leg of a slave he ran into). Prominent Greeks and Romans seem to have agreed: Sophocles included ball-play among his artistic gifts, ALEXANDER III's retinue included a ball player, Aristonicus of Carystus, who won Athenian citizenship, the younger Cato shrugged off electoral defeat by playing ball in the Campus Martius, Maecenas played after dinner and his friend AUGUSTUS was only the first Roman emperor to amuse himself in this way. It is uncertain, however, if the Greeks or Romans ever played ball games with equipment – the possibility arises from the late archaic Athenian relief showing what might be a hockey ball and sticks and from Cicero's possible reference to "club and ball' – or whether the *SPHAIRISTĒRION* of Hellenistic GYMNASIA was a space for ball-play or for boxing.

See also: APORRHAXIS, EPISKYROS, PHAININDA, TRIGŌN, URANIA.

Homer, *Odyssey* 6.99–118, 8.370–380; Aristotle, *Nicomachean Ethics* 4.1123a14; Plutarch, *Cato the Younger* 50.1; Lucian, *Anacharsis* 38;

Pollux 9.103–107; Galen, *On Exercise with the Small Ball* (5.899–910 Kühn); Athenaeus 1.14D–20F; *IG* 5 674–679; Cicero, *On Old Age* 16.58; Horace, *Satires* 1.5.49; Martial 14.45–48; Suetonius, *Augustus* 83; *Digest* 9.2.52.4.

Harris (1972) 85–111; N. M. Kennell, *The Gymnasium of Virtue. Education and Culture in Ancient Sparta* (Chapel Hill 1995) 59–63.

Balteus (plural *baltei*), a GLADIATOR's belt, broad enough to provide protection for his belly.

Juvenal, *Satires* 6.256.

Basileia, name of several Greek competitive festivals. Some at Hellenistic Alexandria and Ephesus, in Macedonia and perhaps on Euboea, celebrated living kings (*basileis*), but the most widely known, at Lebadeia in Boeotia, was established to mark Zeus Basileus's help in the Theban victory over Sparta at Leuctra in 371. Organized (in August/September, perhaps every four years) first by the Thebans and later by a pan-Boeotian college, the Basileia included a few musical and (perhaps) literary events as well as athletic and equestrian programmes. Victors included a king of Egypt (in a chariot race); they won wreaths and perhaps prizes as well. The festival was funded largely by donations from Boeotian cities and rents from the sanctuary's land. One AGŌNOTHETĒS met the entire cost himself; others were negligent enough that their successors complained or even fined them. Poverty under the Roman empire led the Boeotians to focus on the PAMBOEOTIA and let the Basileia lapse. It is possible that it had by then become identical with a festival for the local oracular hero, Trophonius.

Diodorus 15.53.4; *IG* 7 552, 2532, 3078.

A. Schachter, *Cults of Boeotia* 3 (London 1994) 111–118; L. A. Turner, "The Basileia at Lebadeia", in J. M. Fossey (ed.) *Boeotia Antiqua 6. Proceedings of the 8th International Conference on Boiotian Antiquities (Loyola University of Chicago, 24–26 May 1995)* (Amsterdam 1996) 105–126.

Batēr, "treading place, threshold", a stone sill used as the take-off board in the JUMP (and perhaps also as the starting line for footraces). The Greek proverb "He has made the *batēr* sound" corresponds to the English "He's hit the nail on the head".

Pollux 3.151.

E. N. Gardiner, "Phaÿllus and his record jump", *JHS* 24 (1904) 70–80 (74–77).

Battalia, or *battualia*, the training exercises of GLADIATORS.

Cassiodorus, Keil, *Grammatici Latini* 7 178.4.

Mosci Sassi (1992) 82.

Berenice I, queen of Egypt and equestrian victor, third century. The wife of one Olympic chariot victor (King PTOLEMY I) and the mother of two others (PTOLEMY II, ARSINOE), Berenice's own chariot triumph at Olympia is said (in an epigram by POSIDIPPUS) to have obscured the fame of CYNISCA. Along with her husband, she was commemorated by the PTOLEMAIEIA.

Posidippus, *P.Mil.Vogl.* 8 309.XII.22–27, XIII.31–XIV.1.

Berenice II, queen of Cyrene and wife of Ptolemy III Euergetes of Egypt, chariot victor, *c.*273–221. Berenice won the chariot race at Olympia (248), at Isthmia, and twice at Nemea, where she also triumphed in the pairs race and the four-horse race for colts. The resulting (fragmentary) poem by CALLIMACHUS is one of our few victory songs for a woman.

Callimachus 254–268C *Supplementum Hellenisticum*; Posidippus, *P.Mil.Vogl.* 8 309.XII.20–XIII.14.

P. J. Parsons, "Callimachus: Victoria Berenices", *ZPE* 25 (1977) 1–50.

Beryllus, GLADIATOR. A Greek ESSEDARIUS, Beryllus was freed after twenty fights. His wife erected his memorial when he died at twenty-five.

ILS 5095.

Bibasis, a dance and a training exercise for boys and girls at SPARTA. They jumped and brought their heels up to touch the buttock; one girl did 1,000 repeats.

Aristophanes, *Lysistrata* 82; Pollux 4.102.

Biga or *bigae*, Latin term for two-horse CHARIOT team.

Varro, *The Latin Language* 9.39.63.

Bigarius (plural *bigarii*), driver of a Roman two-horse chariot team (*BIGA*).

ILS 5300.

Bilistiche, of Macedon, chariot victor, third century. One of the many girlfriends of King PTOLEMY II Philadelphus of Egypt, Bilistiche won the four-horse chariot race for colts (*PŌLOI*) at Olympia in 268 and then the two-horse race at the following festival. That was its inaugural run: perhaps her royal friend had arranged for its adoption into the Olympic programme, and perhaps she wanted a triumph his late wife ARSINOE had not enjoyed.

Plutarch, *Moral Essays* 753E; Pausanias 5.8.11; Athenaeus 13.596E; Eusebius, *Chronicon* 1.207 Schoene; *Oxyrhynchus Papyri* 2082.

A. Cameron, "Two mistresses of Ptolemy Philadelphus", *GRBS* 31 (1990) 287–311 (295–304); V. Matthews, "Sex and the single racehorse: a response to Cameron on equestrian double entendres in Posidippus", *Eranos* 98 (2000) 32–38.

Biton *see* CLEOBIS

Boat races, a rare event at major competitive festivals. Despite the importance of the sea in Greek and Roman life – not least in warfare – boat races were held at only a few festivals. Among the games of the PERIODOS, only Isthmia – next to the sea – may have featured a race for rowers; a legend credited the Argonauts with the first victory. The PANATHENAEA included a race for EPHEBES representing the civic tribes. The winners won three bulls, 300 drachmas and 200 free meals – perhaps an indication that they raced triremes; the runners-up, two bulls and 200 drachmas. There was also a trireme race off Cape Sounium in Attica – a sponsor spent 1,500 drachmas, a considerable sum, to equip the winner. At sea-side Hermione, Dionysus Melanaegis was honoured every year with swimming and boat competitions; on Delos, a boat race was part of the Posideia for the sea god. Elsewhere, we hear of boat races as part of FUNERAL GAMES for Euagoras of Salamis on Cyprus and informal races organized on campaigns – ALEXANDER III's men raced triremes and quadriremes on their way back from India. AUGUSTUS's ACTIAN games later included a regatta in honour of his naval victory over Antony and Cleopatra. This inspired the funeral games of Anchises in Virgil's *Aeneid*; it replaces and often echoes the chariot race in the *Iliad*.

Lysias 21.5; Isocrates 9.1; Arrian, *Anabasis* 7.23.5; Dio Chrysostom 37.15; Pausanias 2.35.1; *IG* 2² 2311; Virgil, *Aeneid* 5.114–285.

P. Gardner, "Boat-races among the Greeks", *JHS* 2 (1881) 90–97; "Boat-races at Athens", *ibid.*, 315–317; Harris (1972) 126–132.

Boxing, Greek *pyx*, one of the core HEAVY events in Greek games. Boxers appears on objects and monuments from Bronze Age Mesopotamia, Egypt, MYCENAEAN Greece and Minoan Crete (where some bear helmets, hand coverings and footwear). Boxers in the FUNERAL GAMES for Patroclus in Homer's *Iliad* already use the distinctive Greek hand coverings, the thongs (HIMAS). Termed "painful boxing", its prize is the mule, famous for its long-suffering endurance: the Greeks thought boxing the most demanding and dangerous of events. Boxers' depictions highlight scarred faces, bloody noses, swollen ears; dreams of boxing presage deformity and loss of blood; we hear of several deaths (see AGATHOS DAIMON, CREUGAS). The traditional date of boxing's entry into the Olympic programme was 688, after wrestling and before *pankration*. The first victor, ONOMASTUS of Sicyon, is some-

times credited with the rules. (Another theory identified the SPARTANS.) These forbad clinching, scratching and (probably) kicking. There were no rounds or other scheduled breaks and efforts were made (see KLIMAX (1)) to bring boxers into contact. As a result, though bouts continued until one adversary gave in or could not go on, they were probably brief. There were no weight classes, so size and strength gave significant advantages. The ideal boxer had long hands, strong forearms, solid hips for support, and straight calves. PHILOSTRATUS even finds merit in a big belly – it keeps an opponent at a distance. But skill was valued too: Epeius, the winner of the *Iliad*'s mule, was a craftsman, the designer of the Trojan Horse, and Greek science was often contrasted with barbarian brawling (see AMYCUS). It was technique which characterized PYTHAGORAS (2) of Samos. A small man, he was refused entry into the boys' class at Olympia in 588 (despite his youthful long hair) but went on to win the men's event. Boxers' tactics included shifting ground to put the sun into a rival's eyes, blows with both hands (straight jabs, uppercuts, chops downward) to the whole body from the eyes – a target for the thumbs – to the genitals. Some Roman writers describe particularly brutal bouts among the heroes of legend, their gloves reinforced by iron and spattered with blood and brains. It is unlikely, however, that this reflects a regular form of Greek or Roman boxing, and identifications of such reinforced gloves in art are probably mistaken (see HIMAS). Boxing was very popular among the Romans, a feature of Tarquinius Priscus's first games in legends of the time of the kings, a favourite of AUGUSTUS, frequent in mosaic pavements from all over the western empire.

Homer, *Iliad* 23.612–699; Plato, *Protagoras* 342C; Demosthenes 4.40; Aeschines 3.206; Theocritus 22; Lucillius, *Greek Anthology* 11.75–81; Plutarch, *Moral Essays* 638EF; Pausanias 6.12.6; Artemidorus 1.61–62; Diogenes

Laertius 8.47–48; Philostratus, *On Athletic Exercise* 9–10, 34, 57; Livy 1.35.8; Virgil, *Aeneid* 5.362–484.

Poliakoff (1987) 68–88; N. B. Crowther, "Evidence for kicking in Greek boxing", *AJP* 111 (1990) 176–181; W. Fiedler, "Der Faustkampf in der griechischen Dichtung", *Stadion* 18 (1992) 1–67; G. Doblhofer and P. Mauritsch, *Boxen* (Vienna 1995).

Boys *see* PAIDES

Brabeus (plural *brabeis*), judge of a Greek contest.

Sophocles, *Electra* 690, 709; Plato, *Laws* 12.949A.

Brabeutēs (plural *brabeutai*), BRABEUS.

Pollux 3.145.

Bubalus, Roman chariot horse, early second century CE. An African horse, owned by the Blue CHARIOT FACTION, Bubalus was part of teams which won 134 races for Pontius EPAPHRODITUS (2).

ILS 5287.

Bull-leaping, an activity depicted on objects from Bronze Age (Minoan) Crete. They appear to show a figure (once perhaps female) who somersaults over a bull's horns or uses them to vault over its back from the side; helpers (perhaps female as well as male) hold the animal. The courtyards of Minoan palaces were spacious enough for such activities and for the spectators who are sometimes shown watching them. But even if the images (which vary) depict any activity

accurately, they are unlikely to represent a competition (unless it was organized by the bulls).

See also: TAUROTHĒRIA.

J. G. Younger, "Bronze Age representations of Aegean bull-leaping", *AJA* 80 (1976) 125–137; N. Marinatos, "The bull as an adversary: some observations on bull-hunting and bull-leaping", *Ariadne* 5 (1989) 23–32; T. F. Scanlon, "Women, bull sports, cults and initiation in Minoan Crete", *Nikephoros* 12 (1999) 33–70.

Bustuarius (plural *bustuarii*), a GLADIATOR who fought at the grave or funeral pyre (*bustum*) of a dead person. Some ancients thought gladiatorial combat (see MUNUS) originated in such graveside combats, a form of human sacrifice, but this is unlikely.

Cicero, *Against Piso* 9.19; Servius, *On Aeneid* 10.519.

Mosci Sassi (1992) 83.

Bybon, son of (?) Pholas, strong man, sixth century. A sandstone block found near Olympia bears the inscription "Bybon the son of (?) Pholas with one hand threw me over his head". The block weighs about 315lbs (143kg).

See also: EUMASTUS.

IvO 717.

N. B. Crowther, "Weightlifting in antiquity: achievement and training", *G&R* 24 (1977) 111–120 (112–113).

Bye *see* EPHEDROS

C

Caestus see HIMAS

Calippus, of Athens, pentathlete, fourth century. Calippus bribed his opponents at the Olympiad of 332. Caught, the other cheaters paid their fines. The Athenians, however, sent the famous orator Hyperides to Elis to plead for Calippus and, when he was rebuffed, boycotted the games. Finally, Apollo's oracle at Delphi refused to respond to them until they paid up. The fine paid for six statues of Zeus (ZANES).

Plutarch, *Moral Essays* 850B; Pausanias 5.21.5.

I. Weiler, "Korruption in der Olympischen Agonistik und die diplomatische Mission des Hypereides in Elis", in A. D. Rizakis (ed.) *Achaia und Elis in der Antike. Akten des 1. Internationalen Symposiums Athen, 19–21 Mai 1989* (Athens 1991) 87–93.

Calliades, equestrian victor, fourth century. After winning at Delphi and Isthmia sometime in the mid-fourth century, Calliades added an equestrian victory at Olympia.

Delph. 3.1 510.

Moretti (1953) 65–66.

Callias 1. son of Didymias, Athenian pancratiast, fifth century. Callias was victor at the Panathenaea (as a boy, 480), at Olympia (472), twice at Delphi, four times at Nemea and five at Isthmia – the first Athenian PERIODONIKĒS. His Olympic victory was accomplished in the dark, after *pankration* was delayed by chariot racing and pentathlon. (After this, the HEAVY events were held on a separate day.) Callias was ostracized from Athens (? 443/2); his sons erected a statue on the Athenian Acropolis to commemorate his career around 430.

[Andocides] 4.32; Pausanias 5.9.3, 6.6.1; *IG* 1³ 826; *IvO* 146.

Kyle (1987) 202–203.

2. son of Phaenippus, of Athens, equestrian victor, born about 590. Already an equestrian victor at Delphi, Callias took first place in the horse race and second in the chariot at Olympia in 564. This effort demonstrated his wealth – he was famous for his extravagance – and the name of his son Hipponicus ("Horse-victor") announced its success.

Herodotus 6.122.1.

3. son of Hipponicus and grandson of Callias (2), born about 520. An ancient scholar reports, probably wrongly, that a Callias was a triple Olympic chariot victor (? 500, 496, 492 or 496, 492, 484). He certainly had the resources if not the reality – he was the richest Athenian of his time.

Scholiast on Aristophanes, *Clouds* 64.

4. son of Hipponicus and grandson of

Callias (3), Athenian chariot victor, about 450–370. The scion of a rich and influential family – among other distinctions, they were hereditary priests of the Eleusinian Mysteries – Callias boasted achievements of his own. He hosted the gatherings described in Plato's *Protagoras* and Xenophon's *Symposium* (a party in honour of his boyfriend, the young pancratiast AUTOLYCUS), served as a general in the Corinthian war (391), and led a successful embassy to Sparta in 371. He also won two chariot victories at Nemea and one each in the Pythian and Isthmian games. His dedication at Delphi excuses his lack of an Olympic crown by saying his family already had one (see CALLIAS (2)).

Andocides 1.117–123; Xenophon, *Greek History* 6.3.3–6; *Delph*. 3.1 510.

J. Bousquet, "Deux épigrammes grecques (Delphes, Ambracie)", *BCH* 116 (1992) 585–606 (585–596).

5. son of Sosicrates, Athenian pancratiast, second century. Winner of the men's *pankration* at the PANATHENAEA in 182 and 178, Callias served on an embassy about the festival to Ptolemy VI Philometor in 169 – the historian Polybius identifies him as "the pancratiast" – and later, in 159/8, as magistrate in charge of the EPHEBES.

Polybius 28.19.4; *IG* 2² 1027, 2314.

Callicrates 1. of Magnesia on Maeander, runner, fourth century. Callicrates won the race in armour at Olympia twice, perhaps in 344 and 340.

Pausanias 6.17.3.

2. of Samos, commander and equestrian victor, third century. Long an admiral in the service of King PTOLEMY II of Egypt, Callicrates, like that king and his family, was an equestrian competitor, winning the Pythian chariot race for colts sometime after 270. According to a newly discovered epigram by POSIDIPPUS, the race between Callicrates and a Thessalian en-

try was so close that the AGŌNOTHETAI threw down their judges' rods and were about to decide it by drawing LOTS. However, one of Callicrates' team, a mare trace horse on the right side (DEXIOSEIRA), picked up the rod much to the delight of the crowd, which numbered in the tens of thousands. This clamoured (successfully) for Callicrates to be crowned.

Posidippus, *P.Mil.Vogl.* 8 309.XI.33–XII.7.

Callimachus, of Cyrene, scholar and poet, third century. Callimachus was the author of a prose work on competitive festivals and is said to have arranged the poems of PINDAR and BACCHYLIDES. He also wrote some of the last Greek EPINICIANS, poems celebrating the victories of Queen BERENICE II, SOSIBIUS – another important figure at the courts of the Ptolemies – and Polycles. Callimachus's epinicians incorporate many elements drawn from early examples: mythic foundation stories, abrupt transitions, echoes of language, victory catalogues. But they also ring characteristic changes, varying dialect and metre, introducing one victor, Sosibius, as a speaker in his poem.

T. Fuhrer, "Callimachus' epinician poems", in M. A. Harder, R. F. Regtuit and G. C. Wakker (eds) *Callimachus* (Groningen 1993) 79–97.

Callipateira *see* PHERENICE

Callippus Pisanus, son of M. Antonius Alexion, Eleian equestrian victor, first century CE. Winner of the horse race at Olympia (in perhaps 53 CE), Callippus belonged to a prominent Eleian family. His mother, Claudia Cleodice, erected a statue to commemorate his win as his grandfather M. Antonius Pisanus had similarly honoured his own patron, GERMANICUS.

IvO 223.

Callistratus, son of Philothales, of Sicyon, HEAVY athlete, second/first century. As a boy, Callistratus won victories at Isthmia (*pankration*), Nemea (boxing) and (among other festivals) the NAEA at Dodona and the Rhieia at Rhion (in each instance, in all three combat events). He went on to triumph in boxing as both AGENEIOS and adult at the same Isthmian festival – another rare feat – and to many other adult victories, including those at the Pythian games (boxing), at Isthmia (boxing), at Nemea (*pankration* three times, with one in boxing at the same festival), and to repeat his remarkable sweep of all three combat events at the Rhieia.

IG 4.1 128.

Moretti (1953) 103–108; P. Cabanes, "Les concours des *Naia* de Dodone", *Nikephoros* 1 (1988) 49–84 (64–67).

Calliteles, of Sparta, wrestler, sixth century. Calliteles, Olympic wrestling champion (perhaps in 508), was the father of a victor in the chariot race, Polypeithes (perhaps in 484).

Pausanias 6.16.6.

Calpurnianus, Publius Aelius Gutta, Roman CHARIOTEER, (?) late second century CE. Calpurnianus's monument, built on his behalf during his lifetime, records 1,127 victories – 583 for the Blue CIRCUS FACTION, 364 as a Green, 102 as a White, 78 as a Red (including one in an otherwise unattested race for four chariots in each faction, likely only two in this case). He won eight times with three-horse teams (*TRIGAE*), once with horses that had never run before, and once as the driver of a race (*pedibus ad quadrigam*) in which a teammate finished on foot (like the Greek APOBATĒS). This brought a large prize, 60,000 sesterces; those listed on the monument amount to 1,325,000 sesterces. Calpurnianus was at pains to mention a number of horses he'd driven to victory, but some of the figures on the

monument (including 429 victories as a Green with VICTOR) are inconsistent with its other information.

ILS 5288.

L. Friedländer, *Roman Life and Manners under the Early Empire* (trans. A. B. Gough: London 1913) 4.148–154; D. Matz, "*Pedibus ad quadrigam* in Roman chariot racing", *CW* 79 (1985) 34–36; Horsmann (1998) 228–229.

Capitolia, "Capitoline games", the first and most important regularly scheduled Greek-style competitive festival at Rome. Established as a quadrennial festival in honour of Jupiter Capitolinus by Domitian in July/August 86 CE, the Capitolia was immediately welcomed into the PERIODOS of great crown games, sometimes ranking second to or even before the Olympics in lists, and inspiring "isocapitoline" games at Aphrodisias and elsewhere. With the ACTIAN and SEBASTAN games, which were scheduled in the same year, it made up a summer tour of the west for Greek athletes. Celebrated into the fourth century CE, it included full athletic, equestrian and musical programmes as well as prose recitations in Greek and Latin and a race for unmarried girls; the chariot races featured Rome's CIRCUS FACTIONS. Winners received a wreath of oak, Jupiter's tree, often from the emperor's hand; he also customarily granted them Roman citizenship. The festival was the occasion for building Rome's first permanent stadium, on the site of the present Piazza Navona, and for renovating the CIRCUS MAXIMUS. The Capitolia should not be confused with the *ludi Capitolini*, founded (according to tradition) by Romulus (for Jupiter Feretrius) or by Camillus (for Jupiter Optimus Maximus) and held at Rome annually in October. This included boxing matches and footraces.

Suetonius, *Domitian* 4.4; Martial 4.1.6; *IG* 14 747.

Caldelli (1993); B. Rieger, "Die Capitolia des Kaisers Domitian", *Nikephoros* 12 (1999) 171–203.

Caprus, son of Pythagoras, Eleian HEAVY athlete, third century. Caprus defeated PAEONIUS in wrestling and CLITOMA-CHUS in *pankration* on the same day at Olympia in 212, the first to achieve this double distinction since the legendary HERACLES.

Pausanias 5.21.10, 6.15.4–5.

Carcer (plural *carceres*), "cell", starting-gate in the Roman CIRCUS. Twelve *car-ceres*, stone piers fronted by wooden gates, stood at the open end of the Roman circus. They were arranged in a shallow curve so that each chariot travelled more or less the same distance in its lane before reaching the break-out line beyond which they could move inside; those at the end were a little closer. Charioteers drew LOTS for the chance to choose their *carceres*. Since horses often butted or shoved the wooden gates with their hooves, occasion-ally throwing their drivers, attendants stood by to calm and restrain them. At a signal from the presiding magistrate (see MAPPA), in position above the *carceres*, the gates were opened simultaneously by a mechanical device and the teams rushed out.

Varro, *The Latin Language* 5.153; Cicero, *On Divination* 1.48.108; Ovid, *Metamorphoses* 2.153–155; *Tristia* 5.9.29–30; Pliny, *Natural History* 8.65.160; Silius Italicus, *Punica* 8.278–283; Symmachus, *Relationes* 9.6.

J. H. Humphrey, *Roman Circuses. Arenas for Chariot Racing* (London 1986) 18–24, 132–174.

Casia Mnasithea, daughter of Marcus Vetulenus Laetus, Eleian chariot victor, first century CE. A member of one of Elis's most prominent families, Casia Mnasithea won the Olympic chariot race for colts (*PŌLOI*) in 21 CE. A descendant, Lucius Vetulenus Laetus, played an important role in linking Greek athletic GUILDS with Rome.

IvO 233; *SEG* 40.391.

S. Zoumbaki, "Zu einer neuen Inschrift aus Olympia: Die Familie der Vettuleni von Elis",

ZPE 99 (1993) 227–232.

Casmylus, son of Euagoras, Rhodian boxer, fifth century. Casmylus won the Pythian boxing crown and later (perhaps in 462), the Isthmian – a victory marked by a lost poem by PINDAR.

Greek Anthology 16.23; Scholiast on Lucian, *Dialogues of the Dead* 255–256 Rabe.

Ebert (1972) 185–186.

Castor *see* POLLUX

Catervarius, one of a troop (*caterva*) of fist fighters at Roman spectacles. *Cater-varii* were participants in mass brawls rather than boxers in individuals bouts, but (like GLADIATORS) might take pride in their profession.

Suetonius, *Augustus* 45.2; *CIL* 8.7413, 7414, 10.1074.

Celadus, GLADIATOR, first century CE. A *THRAEX* who won and was crowned three times, Celadus is mentioned on Pompeian graffiti as a favourite of female fans.

ILS 5142, a, b, c, d.

Ceras, of Argos, wrestler, fourth/third century. Like PULYDAMAS, Ceras – Olym-pic wrestling champion, 300 – was said to be able to hold back a bull by the hoof.

Eusebius, *Chronicon* 1.207 Schoene.

Chaeron, of Pellene, wrestler, fourth cen-tury. Despite his extraordinary success – he won four times at Olympia (perhaps from 356 to 344 and twice (?) at Isthmia) – the people of Pellene in the Peloponnese wouldn't even say Chaeron's name. Estab-lished as tyrant by ALEXANDER III the Great, he allegedly exiled the elite and gave their wives and property to their slaves – this though (or because) he had been a pupil of Plato.

Demosthenes 17.10; Pausanias 7.27.7; Athe-naeus 11.509B.

Charinus, of Elis, runner, undated. Charinus won both *DIAULOS* and the race in armour at Olympia.

Pausanias 6.15.2.

Charioteer, driver of a chariot or (loosely) a mule-team. (Charioteers stood, mule-team drivers sat.) Homer's heroes drove their own chariots in the FUNERAL GAMES for Patroclus, and some wealthy Greek owners in historical competitions emulated them, clad in the charioteer's long, belted robe, and bearing a long rod to spur on the horses: HIERON, tyrant of Syracuse (at the Theban Iolaia, mid-470s), Herodotus of Thebes (at Isthmia, about 470), DAMONON, winner of forty-three races in and around his native Sparta in the early fourth century. Damonon makes frequent references to his hands-on self-sufficiency in the inscription which lists his victories; it may never have been common, even in local games. More often, the charioteer was a family member or connection, or (in most cases) a hired professional: driving a racing chariot required unusual strength, skill and courage. Yet we know the names of very few charioteers and drivers – one, Carrhotus, kept his chariot unscathed when forty others crashed at Delphi (see ARCESILAUS (2)) – and victory songs and statues regularly contrive to leave them out of account. Charioteers, after all, drove their flimsy rigs to glory (or ruin) in plain view when their owners might not be present at all, and they might garner a fillet or even a wreath for their brow which was very like a victory crown. The wealthy elite which commissioned poems and monuments might well wish to slight or ignore the charioteer's contribution. Unease about the charioteer's role is evident in myth, another vehicle of aristocratic ideology. PELOPS pilots his own chariot when he wins HIPPODAMEIA as his wife, while her father, King Oenomaus, is betrayed by his charioteer Myrtilus.

At Rome, charioteers were of low status, often slaves, but success could bring them freedom, privilege, wealth and fame. Often members of a family of performers (with mothers who danced in mime as well as charioteer fathers), they joined one of the CIRCUS FACTIONS young – Celsus won at thirteen – and took on the charioteer's tunic (it reached mid-thigh), close-fitting cap and short whip. Some stayed with the same faction. The more successful, however, like professional athletes today, were in demand and moved from one to another, especially in their early years. Since they kept a portion of the prizes they won, some grew very rich; Lacerta owned one hundred times a lawyer's estate, DIOCLES' purses amounted to 35,863,120 sesterces. Leading charioteers were popular heroes, the subjects of portraits and poems, adored by fans – one threw himself on the pyre of a favourite driver, FELIX of the Reds – and the intimates of emperors (Eutychus of Caligula, Hierocles of Elagabalus), who valued their association with victory as well as the charisma it produced. (NERO, however, refused to countenance their cheating and robbing at will.) They also attracted envy: curse tablets, accusations of sorcery (the explanation of their luck). In part at least as a defence against black MAGIC, many adopted a professional name in place of the one they were given at birth. This did not always protect them from the risks of their calling – risks increased by the showy Roman practice of wrapping the reins around the waist. (Charioteers carried a knife, but were not always able to disentangle themselves in a crash.) Two brothers, born slaves and sons of a charioteer, both died on the course in their twenties. In late antiquity, when the circus factions took over management of popular entertainments of all kinds, they were often headed by charioteers.

Pindar, *Olympians* 6; *Pythians* 2, 5; *Isthmians* 1, 2; Thucydides 5.50.4; *IG* 5.1 213; Pliny, *Natural History* 7.53.186; Martial 4.67, 5.25,

10.50, 53, 74; Juvenal 7.114; Suetonius, *Nero* 16; Ammianus Marcellinus 26.3.3, 28.1.27, 29.3.5; *ILS* 5278–5316.

Harris (1972) 198–210; A. Cameron, *Porphyrius the Charioteer* (Oxford 1973); Horsmann (1998).

Chariot faction *see* CIRCUS FACTION

Chariot racing, a central event at Greek competitive festivals and Roman spectacles. Depicted on Bronze age MYCENAEAN artefacts, chariot racing (with two horses, SYNŌRIS) occupies the first and longest section of the FUNERAL GAMES for Patroclus in Homer's *Iliad*. It is therefore remarkable (and unlikely) that chariot racing (in its four-horse form, TETHRIPPON, also known to Homer) is said to have entered the Olympic programme only in 680. This is probably a reflection of the debate over the relative merits of equestrian and athletic success which helped shape both that programme and HIPPIAS's account of its development. Certainly the *tethrippon* was one of the events of the Pythian games since their inception. At both festivals, the pairs race came much later, in 408 (Olympia) and 398 (Delphi); other kinds of races (involving colts (PŌLOI), war chariots drawn by cavalry horses, dismounting (APOBATĒS)) are attested there and elsewhere, but they never supplanted the four-horse race in status. Nor in expense: our only price for a four-horse team, paid by ALCIBIADES, is five or eight talents (30,000 or 48,000 drachmas) at a time when a family of six could be supplied with grain for a year or two for 500 drachmas and a workman's wage was one or one and a half drachma per day; fodder for the horses, wages or maintenance for stable hands and charioteers, and the cost of tackle would be extra. No wonder some communities (ARGOS, DYSPONTIUM, ELIS) pooled resources to enter (and win) chariot races at Olympia, a practice attested as late as the victory of Antinoe in Egypt in a pairs race for colts at Corinth in the mid-

second century CE (Alcibiades' was the state team of Argos). Nor that known competitors include the most powerful figures in the Greek world, from the tyrants of the west (GELON, HIERON, THERON) to the royal families of Sparta and Cyrene (DEMARATUS (1), CYNISCA, ARCESILAUS (2)) and the kings of Macedon (ARCHELAUS, PHILIP) and their successors (ATTALUS, BERENICE I). Even under the Roman empire, when the poverty of the Greek mainland reduced the prominence of chariot racing (and, in some games, the prizes for it), members of the imperial family (TIBERIUS, GERMANICUS, NERO) thought races worth winning. Some such winners, then and before, appeared in person, but young (or expert) friends and family members, hired CHARIOTEERS or slaves normally drove their horses and ran their risks. These were very real: flimsy chariots, crowded fields, rough tracks and long races combined to make crashes common and (apparently) crowd-pleasing – another insight into ideas about equestrian competition and its merits. At Olympia, the four-horse teams ran twelve laps of the HIPPODROME (at least six miles), the pairs and colt teams eight laps, the colt pairs, three; a trumpet signalled the start and the last lap. The Greeks thought mares made the best chariot horses. The central pair (ZYGIOI) of a four-horse team was harnessed abreast under a yoke at the end of a central pole; the outer pair (SEIRAPHOROI) was linked to the pole but drew the chariot by traces.

Chariot racing is said to have been one of the many legacies of the period of ETRUSCAN domination of early Rome. Its importance there may be judged from the capacity of the CIRCUS MAXIMUS (itself an Etruscan foundation), the scale of a typical programme (twenty-four races of seven laps each, with special cards of fifty under NERO and 100 [shorter races] under Domitian) and the interest in results. (Caecina, the leader of a CIRCUS FACTION in the first century CE, smeared swallows with the colours of the winning team and sent them as announcers to his friends in the countryside.) There is evidence that the Roman elite entered (and perhaps even drove) their own chariots in races on the Greek pattern until the fifth century or so. Afterwards, the state paid horse breeders to provide teams – this was regarded as a very profitable form of stock raising – and the elite sought credit for organizing, funding (at least in part) and presenting the spectacles (*LUDI*) at which races were held. In time (perhaps as early as the late fourth century or as late as the early first century) they contracted with the circus factions, whose monopoly and popularity gave them a powerful bargaining position. (In one negotiation, they threatened to withhold their services if their demands went unmet and a magistrate responded by arranging for scabs – racing dogs.) Like the Greeks, the Romans gave pride of place to the four-horse team (*QUADRIGA*), though races for pairs (*BIGA*) were common (usually with less experienced charioteers) and teams of three (on the Etruscan model) and six or more not unknown. The starting arrangements of the Circus Maximus allowed for no more than twelve chariots, three for each faction; this became the canonical maximum everywhere in the Roman world. The first race of the day, however, the most prestigious, may have had just four. Chariot horses began their careers late, at the age of five, and extended them for many years. (One team included a son and his sire; another was so experienced that it not only won after its driver had fallen out but stopped at the finish line.) Veterans ran as a central pair under the yoke; the team's key member was the right-hand yoke horse (unlike in Greece). Favoured breeds came from Spain, North Africa, Sicily, Hirpinum in Italy, and Cappadocia.

Homer, *Iliad* 11.698–702; 23. 262–650; Pindar, *Olympians* 3.33–34; *Pythians* 5.49–51; Sophocles, *Electra* 681–756; Isocrates 16.46; Dio Cassius 61.6.2; Ovid, *Amores* 3.2; Pliny, *Natural History* 10.34.71, 18.67.263, 21.5.7.

Harris (1972) 151–243; D. S. Potter, "Entertainers in the Roman Empire", in Potter and D. J. Mattingly (eds) *Life, Death and Entertainment in the Roman Empire* (Ann Arbor 1999) 256–325 (285–303).

Charitesia, competitive festival of Orchomenus (Boeotia). As befits a festival for the Charites ("Graces"), the Charitesia stressed musical and dramatic competitions, but there was an athletic programme too.

IG 2^2 3160; *IG* 7 3195–3197.

A. Schachter, *Cults of Boiotia* 1 (London 1981) 142–144.

Charmis, of Sparta, runner, seventh century. The likely victor in the Olympic *STADION* race of 668 – a triumph sometimes credited to his countryman CHIONIS – Charmis is said to have been the first athlete to follow a training DIET, of dried figs.

Eusebius, *Chronicon* 1.197 Schoene.

Cheating. Sharp practice was a part of Greek sport as early as the FUNERAL GAMES of Patroclus, where Antilochus forces Menelaus's chariot off the track and the god Apollo knocks the whip from Diomedes' hand. (When confronted, Antilochus offers to give up his prize; Apollo displays no such regrets.) Cheating thus entered the epic tradition: tripping mars the footrace in Virgil's *Aeneid*, hairpulling, in Statius's *Thebaid*. Other athletic fouls included false starts (footraces), testicle twisting (wrestling), gouging and biting (*pankration*); all invited a blow from the referee's rod. We hear more of fouls outside competition itself. These too have a long pedigree, from the trickery and treachery which gave PELOPS victory in Olympia's charter chariot race. Despite our earliest Olympic law (unfortunately fragmentary), which forbids deception and bribery, the Olympic oath, and PHILOSTRATUS's insistence that Olympia remained unsullied by scandal, corruption occurred even there. The athletes, their fathers, their trainers – all were bribed. Even the HELLANODIKAI fell under suspension for favouritism and worse. They were penalized for awarding the STADION crown to their fellow-citizen EUPOLEMUS in 396, excluded from competition after their fellow judge TROILUS's equestrian victories in 372. (An AGŌNOTHETĒS at the Athenian Theseia was honoured for taking special care to prevent fraud in the torch races and other events.) Other Olympic infractions included missing the thirty-day training period – to earn prizes elsewhere or to maintain a training routine. At Delphi, wine was forbidden near the stadium. Manipulation of the LOT which set pairings was a concern in HEAVY events; similarly, Roman GLADIATORS were matched only shortly before a spectacle (MUNUS) to avoid collusion. Penalties at Olympia are the best known, hefty fines which paid for the ZANES, bronze statues of Zeus with admonitory inscriptions. Those at Epidaurus were substantial as well, 1,000 staters in the third century; in contrast, the tariff for flouting the wine taboo at Delphi was small, with half paid to the informer. In one instance, authorities at Delphi helped the *Hellanodikai* collect a fine: the oracle refused to answer the Athenians until they made good CALIPPUS's debt. Plato's legislation for his ideal Cretan city includes an odd provision that anyone who keeps a rival from entering a competition be fined and, if successful, forfeit his prize to his victim. Nothing like this is attested in practice.

Homer, *Iliad* 23.382–611; Herodotus 2.160, 8.59; Aristophanes, *Clouds* 25; Plato, *Laws* 12.955AB; Pausanias 5.21, 6.1.4–5, 3.7; Philostratus, *On Athletic Exercise* 45; Athenaeus 13.582B; *IG* 2² 956, 4².1 99; *CID* 1.3; Virgil, *Aeneid* 5.335–338; Statius, *Thebaid* 6.615–617.

C. A. Forbes, "Crime and punishment in Greek athletics", *CJ* 47 (1951–2) 169–173, 202; E. Klingenberg, "Diakōlyein antagōnistēn. Eine platonische Bestimmung des griechischen Wettkampfrichts: Pl. Lg. 955A2-B4", in *Studi in onore di Arnaldo Biscardi* (Milan 1987) 435–470; P. Siewert, "The Olympic rules", in W. Coulson and H. Kyrieleis (eds) *Proceedings of an International Symposium on the Olympic Games (5–9 September 1988)* (Athens 1992) 113–117.

Chilon 1. son of Chilon, of Patrae, wrestler, fourth century. A PERIODONIKĒS, Chilon won twice at Olympia (perhaps in 332 and 328), twice at Delphi, four times at Isthmia and three at Nemea before he was killed in war and buried by the Achaeans at public expense.

Pausanias 6.4.6, 7.6.5; *Greek Anthology Appendix* 249.

Ebert (1972) 157–159; I. L. Merker, "Cheilon periodonikes", *AncW* 22 (1991) 43–48.

2. Spartan leader, mid-sixth century. One of the most famous of Sparta's early ephors (magistrates with special responsibility for the kings), and one of the "Seven Sages" of Greece, Chilon is said to have died of joy following a son's Olympic victory in boxing.

Diogenes Laertius 1.72–73; Pliny, *Natural History* 7.32.119.

N. B. Crowther, "A Spartan Olympic boxing champion", *Antiquité classique* 59 (1990) 198–202.

Chimon, of ARGOS, wrestler, fifth century. Chimon defeated TAUROSTHENES to win the Olympic crown for wrestling in 448 and was the subject of two statues which PAUSANIAS considered among Naucydes' best work. One was brought to Rome by Vespasian; a statue of his son Aristeus, winner of DOLICHOS in perhaps 420, stood by the other at Olympia.

Pausanias 6.9.3; *Oxyrhynchus Papyri* 222.

Chionis, of Sparta, runner, mid-seventh century. Chionis is credited (perhaps by a confusion with CHARMIS) with three (? 664, 660, 656) or four victories in the Olympic STADION race, and three more in *diaulos*, and others too, but he is best known for a fifty-two-foot jump. However, we know nothing of the circumstances – he is not reported to have won the pentathlon – and the Armenian and Latin versions of Eusebius's Greek text give the jump's length as 22 cubits (33 feet), so its value as evidence for the nature of the Greek JUMP is uncertain. Chionis is numbered among the founders of Cyrene. Two hundred years later, the Spartans had his STATUE (by the famous sculptor Myron) dedicated at Olympia next to that of ASTYLUS – an echo of Sparta's rivalry with Syracuse for the leadership of the Greeks against Persia.

Pausanias 3.14.3, 4.23.4, 6.13.2, 8.39.3; Eusebius, *Chronicon* 1.197 Schoene.

Chrēmatitēs *see* AGŌN.

Chrysogonus, of Nicaea (Bithynia), runner, second century. Chrysogonus was twice Olympic STADION champion, in 116 and 112.

Eusebius, *Chronicon* 1.211 Schoene.

Cimon, son of Stesagoras, Athenian chariot victor, born about 585. Cimon won the Olympic chariot race three times with the same mares (536, 532, 528). An exile from Athens at his first victory, he earned his return by allowing Athens's tyrant, PISISTRATUS, to claim credit for his second. After his third, he was murdered on the orders of Pisistratus's sons and successors, too new to power to brook such success. Cimon's half-brother MILTIADES was also an Olympic chariot victor (560, 548); his son (another Miltiades) engineered the defeat of the Persian invasion at Marathon; his grandson Cimon, another great politician and commander, developed the ACADEMY. As for his mares, they were buried near the family's tombs and depicted in bronze.

Herodotus 6.103; Plutarch, *Cato the Elder* 5.4; Aelian, *Historical Miscellany* 9.32.

Circus, "ring", site for Roman chariot racing. The circus was a large structure, with two long parallel sides and shorter ends, one semi-circular (often featuring an arch), and the other equipped with twelve starting-gates (CARCERES). Tiered seating – relatively close to the action because of the circus's shape – flanked all except the open end. The arena or track was divided lengthwise by a central barrier (EURIPUS or *spina*), with a turning post (META) at each end and monuments of various kinds on top. It was composed of sand laid over a firm mortared base and marked by lines to keep chariots in their lanes at the start, a break-out line beyond which they could leave their lanes, and a finish line halfway down the right side of the barrier. The track sloped gently towards the barrier, where ditches were dug to aid drainage, and was regularly raked to remove ruts. Circuses – especially the largest, the CIRCUS MAXIMUS at Rome – might also be used for horse races, athletic displays, boxing, wrestling, long-distance runs, wild beast hunts, gladiatorial combat and other spectacles.

J. H. Humphrey, *Roman Circuses. Arenas for Chariot Racing* (London 1986).

Circus factions, Roman chariot-racing teams. The circus factions were rather like modern motor-racing teams: they owned stables, horses, chariots and other equipment, owned or employed charioteers, veterinarians, grooms and other staff (a FAMILIA), and hired all these out to those who provided or presided over games (LUDI). In place perhaps as early as the fourth century, and originally run by independent businessmen from the Roman elite, the circus factions were eventually taken over by the emperors and managed by leading charioteers (*factionarii*). They also became responsible for shows of many different kinds, including beast hunts and theatrical displays. There were four factions, two (Green and Blue) more popular, two (White and Red) less prominent and sometimes allied with them. Many emperors shared their subjects' enthusiasm

for chariot-racing and were staunch supporters of their major factions – Caligula,
Nero and Commodus of the Greens,
Vitellius and Caracalla of the Blues.
Domitian, a Green, introduced two additional colours, Purple and Gold, but
these did not catch on.

Martial 11.33; Suetonius, *Caligula* 55.2–3;
Nero 22.1; *Domitian* 7.1; Cassius Dio 63.6,
65.5.1, 67.4, 69.14, 77.10.2, 80.14.2; *ILS*
5313.

A. Cameron, *Circus Factions. Blues and Greens
at Rome and Byzantium* (Oxford 1976).

Circus Maximus, "greatest circus", the
largest and most impressive CIRCUS in the
Roman world. Laid out in the valley
between the Palatine and Aventine hills
by the Etruscan kings in the sixth century, the Circus Maximus was redesigned
and embellished under Julius Caesar and
AUGUSTUS, rebuilt and enlarged under
Trajan. Its external dimensions measured
about 620m × 140m, its arena about
580m × 80m – roughly twelve times the
area of the COLOSSEUM's – and it seated
about 155,000 spectators, with room for
perhaps 100,000 more on the hills
nearby. The Circus Maximus included a
raised area for the images of the gods
and the emperor (PULVINAR), a box
(above the CARCERES) for the presiding
magistrate, and three tiers of seating,
with areas (of stone) marked off for
senators and *equites* and wooden stands
for others. Men (required to wear togas)
and women sat together in each section.
Upper tiers were steep, their seating shallow – knees often dug into the backs of
those below – and hard; it was customary
to bring a cushion. The façade and arena
of the Circus also incorporated a temple
of the Sun, a shrine of Murcia, and
several altars (Consus's was subterranean)
(see Figure 2).

See also: EURIPUS, META.

J. H. Humphrey, *Roman Circuses. Arenas for
Chariot Racing* (London 1986).

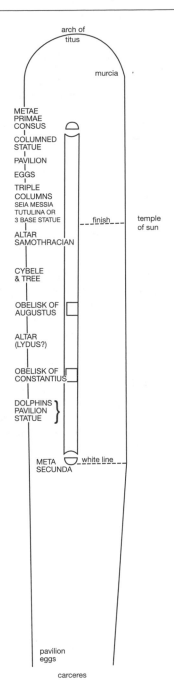

Figure 2 Relative location of the monuments on the barrier of the Circus
Maximus (not to scale)

Source: J. H. Humphrey, *Roman Circuses. Arenas for Chariot Racing* (London 1986) 290.

Cirrus, topknot worn by some athletes in the Roman world. These often have their hair shaved or cropped as well. The *cirrus* is usually thought to mark the professional athlete, but (since most who wear it are beardless) it may instead distinguish younger competitors from those in older AGE-CLASSES.

Suetonius, *Nero* 45.

J.-P. Thuillier, "Le *cirrus* et la barbe. Questions d'iconographie athlétique romaine", *MEFRA* 110 (1998) 351–380.

Claudius Artemidorus, Tiberius, of Tralles, pancratiast, first or second century CE. Unsuccessful in *pankration* for PAIDES at Olympia because of his extreme youth, Artemidorus developed so swiftly that on the same date at Smyrna he defeated those who'd competed with him earlier, the AGENEIOI, and the ANDRES. He later won the competition for *andres* at Olympia (69 CE) and became a PERIODONIKĒS.

Pausanias 6.14.2–3.

Claudius Nicanor, Tiberius, of Seleucia Pieria (Syria), first century CE. Nicanor was PERIODONIKĒS in an unknown event in the mid-first century CE.

IGL Syrie 1186.

Moretti (1987) 87.

Claudius Patrobius, Tiberius, of Antioch (Syria), wrestler, first century CE. Patrobius won many wrestling crowns, including three at Olympia (perhaps in 49, 53, 57 CE), one at Delphi, two at Nemea and two or more at Isthmia – he was a PERIODONIKĒS. He was awarded citizenship at Alexandria.

SEG 14.613.

Moretti (1953) 174–179; (1987) 75.

Claudius Rufus, Tiberius, of Smyrna, pancratiast. Early in the first century CE, Rufus fought an Olympic rival to a DRAW until darkness fell. Impressed by his endurance against a man who'd earlier drawn a BYE, Eleian notables thought him worthy of a victor's rewards and privileges. His social standing – he was the acquaintance of emperors – probably helped too. Later members of the family also won fame in the combat sports: a father (Claudius Apollonius) and a son (Claudius Rufus) were once and twice PERIODONIKAI (winning at Olympia in (?) 189 and (?) 229 and 233 CE).

IG 14 1107; *IvO* 54, 55, 233.

R. Merkelbach, "Der unentschiedene Kampf des Pankratiasten Ti. Claudius Rufus in Olympia", *ZPE* 15 (1974) 99–104; J. Ebert, "Zur neuen Bronzeplatte mit Siegerinschriften aus Olympia (Inv. 1148)", *Nikephoros* 10 (1997) 217–233.

Cleaenetus, son of Epicrates, Argive runner, fourth century. A victor in the STADION race and the race in armour sometime in the later fourth century, Cleaenetus may have been notable for his size as well as his speed. He claimed crowns at the Pythian, Isthmian (six times) and Nemean games, among others.

SEG 35.267.

P. Charneux, "Inscriptions d'Argos", *BCH* 109 (1985) 357–384 (357–375); Moretti (1987) 84.

Cleisthenes, of Sicyon, tyrant and chariot victor, sixth century. Cleisthenes won the inaugural Pythian chariot race in 582 – he may have been involved in the foundation or reorganization of the festival –, the Olympic in 576 or 572. He used the occasion of his Olympic victory to invite suitors for the hand of his daughter Agariste to Sicyon, where he built a racecourse (DROMOS) and PALAESTRA for their use. The Pythian games at Sicyon may have been his innovation.

Pindar, *Nemeans* 9.8–12 (with Scholiast); Herodotus 6.126; Pausanias 10.7.7.

M. F. McGregor, "Cleisthenes of Sicyon and the Panhellenic Games", *TAPA* 72 (1941) 266–287.

Cleitostratus, of Rhodes, wrestler, second century. Cleitostratus won the Olympic wrestling event in 192; he was famous for his stranglehold on the neck.

Eusebius, *Chronicon* 1.209 Schoene; *Suda* s. *T* 921.

Cleobis, of Argos, athlete, sixth century. A prize-winning athlete like his brother Biton (who may have competed at Nemea), Cleobis joined him in stripping, oiling and substituting for oxen to draw the cart of their mother Cydippe, a priestess of Hera, to the goddess's sanctuary some 10km (6 miles) from town. While they rested, their mother prayed to the goddess to grant them fitting thanks; they never woke up. Cleobis and Biton were further honoured by a statue from the Argives at Delphi and by Solon's judgement that they were among the most fortunate of men.

Herodotus 1.30–32; Pausanias 2.19.5; *Greek Anthology* 3.18; Cicero, *Tusculan Disputations* 1.47.113.

D. Sansone, "Cleobis and Biton in Delphi", *Nikephoros* 4 (1991) 121–132.

Cleoetas, son of Aristocles, of Athens, inventor of the starting system for the HIPPODROME at Olympia.

Pausanias 6.20.14.

Cleomachus, of Magnesia on the Maeander, boxer, fifth century. Despite being Olympic boxing champion (in perhaps 424), Cleomachus was said to imitate the sexual habits and mannerisms of effeminates.

Cratinus fragment 17 Kassel-Austin; Strabo 14.1.41.

Cleombrotus, son of Dexilaus, of Sybaris, athlete, early sixth century. After a victory at Olympia – his opponent or his victory STATUE may have been his equal in height and breadth – Cleombrotus dedicated a tithe to Athena. Our earliest surviving inscription about an Olympic victory, this difficult text raises a number of questions. In particular: if Cleombrotus's prize was the usual olive wreath, did he dedicate a tenth of a cash payment from his native city?

SEG 29.1017.

Ebert (1972) 251–255; Moretti (1987) 81–82.

Cleomedes, of Astypalaea, boxer, fifth century. When Cleomedes fouled and killed his opponent Iccus of Epidaurus (492), the HELLANODIKAI disqualified him and fined him the enormous sum of four talents. On his return home, he tore down a schoolhouse and killed the sixty boys inside. The townsfolk stoned Cleomedes and pursued him to a temple of Athena, where he hid in a chest. The Astypalaeans broke it open but found no trace of him. Upon inquiry, the Delphic oracle advised them to offer sacrifices to Cleomedes, the most recent of HEROES, as he was no longer mortal.

Plutarch, *Romulus* 28.4–5; Pausanias 6.9.6–8.

Cleopatra II, daughter of Ptolemy V Ephiphanes and Cleopatra, queen of Egypt and chariot champion, about 185–116. Wife and sisters to two kings (Ptolemy VI Philometor from 175 and Ptolemy VIII Euergetes II from 145), Cleopatra was not always successful in the dynastic struggles and civil wars which marked her long life, but she did win the chariot race at the PANATHENAEA in 162.

Hesperia 60 (1991) 188–189.

Cleosthenes, son of Pontis, of Epidamnus, chariot victor, sixth century. Cleosthenes won the Olympic chariot race at Olympia in 516 with the horses Corax, Cnacias, Phoenix and Samus, and became the first such winner to include a statue of himself in his dedication.

Pausanias 6.10.6–8.

Ebert (1972) 42–43.

Cleoxenus, of Alexandria, boxer, third century. An unwounded PERIODONIKĒS – quite a feat for a boxer –, Cleoxenus's Olympic victory dates to 240.

Eusebius, *Chronicon* 1.207 Schoene.

Clitomachus, son of Hermocrates, Theban HEAVY athlete, third century. One of the most storied athletes of his time, Clitomachus won all three combat events on the same day at ISTHMIA (the wrestling in a walkover), *pankration* three times at Delphi, and both boxing and *pankration* at Olympia in 216, the first to do this since THEOGENES. So great was his prestige that he persuaded the judges at Olympia to schedule *pankration* before boxing in 212 in an (unsuccessful) attempt to repeat as a double victor (see CAPRUS), and King Ptolemy IV of Egypt sent a picked champion, Aristonicus, to box against him. (The crowd originally cheered for the underdog Aristonicus but shifted to support Clitomachus when he claimed to be fighting for the glory of Greece rather than for King Ptolemy. Clitomachus won.) An anachronistic legend says that ALEXANDER III rebuilt Thebes in honour of his Isthmian sweep. His discipline was one element of Clitomachus's success: he was said to have left a symposium if someone so much as mentioned SEX.

Polybius 27.9.3–13; Plutarch, *Moral Essays* 710D; Pausanias 6.15.3–5; Alcaeus, *Greek Anthology* 9.588.

Fontenrose (1968) 95–97; Moretti (1987) 72.

Collega (plural *collegae*), a CHARIOTEER of a Roman CIRCUS FACTION who raced as a partner of a different faction's team; Greek SYZYGOS.

Sidonius Apollinaris 23.222.

Colosseum, or Flavian AMPHITHEATRE, main Roman site for GLADIATORIAL shows. Rome had 800 years of history before it was even begun, Caesar never saw it, AUGUSTUS, the first emperor, died over sixty years before it was finished. Yet the Colosseum is the most recognizable symbol of Rome, its name borrowed by pizzerias and sports complexes, its image displayed on the medals of the 2000 Sydney Olympics. This paradoxical fact mirrors the building's origins, a final legacy of a man who scorned much of what it stood for, and its role in the histories of two groups the Romans scorned in turn, Jews and Christians. Begun on the site of NERO's palace complex, the Golden House, by Titus Flavius Vespasianus, who became emperor after the civil wars which followed Nero's suicide, the building was dedicated by Vespasian's son and successor Titus in 80 CE and its substructure finished under Titus's brother Domitian; hence the Roman name, Amphitheatrum Flavium. The amphitheatre, Roman in design and purpose, was meant to signal Vespasian's support for traditional pastimes, in opposition to Nero's despised philhellenism; much of the labour was supplied by prisoners captured during Titus's subjection of Judaea, some of the entertainment by Christians thrown to the beasts and otherwise executed during Domitian's persecutions. It took the name by which we know it from the colossal statue of Nero which once stood nearby.

The Colosseum was an oval structure, measuring 188m × 156m along its axes and 52m high, comprising three storeys, each featuring half-columns of one of the traditional orders of Greek architecture (modified Doric, Ionic, Corinthian) and topped by a masonry attic in whose façade there alternated windows and bronze shields. A projecting rim marked off each storey from the one above it; masts on top of the attic secured ropes for an awning against the sun. Seating was arranged in five tiers, with those of higher status enjoying reserved seats of marble. Closest to the action, on the podium, were the emperor and his family at one of the amphitheatre's narrow ends, the presiding magistrate and Vestal Virgins who faced them, and the senators, priests and foreign dignitaries along the long sides. Members of the equestrian order occupied the *ima cavea*, Roman citizens clad in their official peacetime uniform, the toga, the *media cavea* above them.

(These were further subdivided. For example, boys sat apart with their slave attendants, *paedagogi*.) These privileged groups likely made up more than half the audience of about 55,000. Citizens too poor or careless to wear the toga shared the next level, the limestone *summa cavea*, with freedmen, slaves and other non-citizens, while women were furthest away, in the wooden *summum maenianum in ligneis*. Tickets led spectators to their places via marked entrances and stairways, and attendants made sure they kept to them.

Spectators looked down on an arena 77m × 46m (about the size of an American gridiron). Its sand covered the timber roof of a two-storey substructure containing animal cages, equipment and stage props, and lifts to bring them to the surface. The action, including beast hunts (*venationes*) and the execution of criminals (*noxii*) as well as gladiatorial shows, was potentially dangerous to spectators. The arena was therefore separated from them by netting, a smooth marble wall 3.6m high, and a bronze railing; and archers stood at the ready for extra security.

Martial, *Book of Spectacles*; Suetonius, *Vespasian* 9.1; *Titus* 7.3; *ILS* 5049.

P. Quennell, *The Colosseum* (New York 1971); A. Gabucci (ed.) *The Colosseum* (Los Angeles 2000).

Columbus, GLADIATOR, first century CE. When the MURMILLO Columbus was slightly hurt in winning a match, the emperor Caligula had his wound rubbed with poison – he was a fan of the THRAECES.

Suetonius, *Caligula* 55.2.

Commodus Antonius, M. Aurelius, GLADIATOR and Roman emperor (180–192 CE), 161–192 CE. The son of Marcus Aurelius, Commodus was very different from that conscientious and contemplative emperor, a fan of both the CIRCUS and the HARENA. He dressed in the garb of a professional CHARIOTEER (he favoured the Greens) and is said to have desired to drive in the circus spectacles. Though he stopped short of this step, he fought wild beasts and appeared over 1,000 times as a gladiator – an unusual combination – garbed in a purple robe with gold spangles and wearing a gold crown studded with Indian gems. Proud of his prowess (he fought left-handed against athletes or gladiators armed with only a wand), Commodus styled himself Primus PALUS of the SECUTORES. He was strangled by a slave with whom he trained in 192 CE, part of a conspiracy which involved the commander of his bodyguard and his girlfriend. It was rumoured that he intended to kill both of Rome's consuls and appear as consul from the cell he maintained in the gladiators' quarters; after his death he was reviled as murderer and gladiator. Commodus was a fan of Greek competitions as well as Roman, and was honoured by the use of the term Commodeia for at least sixteen new or existing festivals all over the Greek world; the renaming of the Commodeia Dionysia HERACLEIA at Thebes was especially appropriate in the light of Commodus's predilection for being identified with HERACLES. Most were sacred games (*hieroi* AGŌNES), but that at Athens, one of the first (founded in 176 or 180 CE), was restricted to EPHEBES, young men like Commodus himself. The Spartan was one of the very few new Greek festivals to be granted the status of an eiselastic AGŌN. Commodus's reputation was rehabilitated not long after his death, and his festivals continued at least until the mid-third century CE.

Cassius Dio 73.16–22; *Historia Augusta, Commodus* 2.9, 5.5, 8.7, 11.10–12, 15.3, 8.

E. Miranda, "Testimonianze sui *Kommodeia*", *Scienze dell'Antichità* 6–7 (1992–1993) 69–88; O. Hekster, *Commodus. An Emperor at the Crossroads* (Amsterdam 2002).

Communis, Roman CHARIOTEER, early second century CE. Communis, winner of 1,000 races (*MILIARIUS*) for the Blue CIRCUS FACTION, was one of DIOCLES' (I) rivals.

ILS 5287.

Horsmann (1998) 192–193.

Conditor (plural *conditores*), "founder, builder", member of a Roman chariot-racing *FAMILIA*, responsible for the care of horses.

ILS 5295, 5313.

G. Horsmann, "Zur Funktion des *conditor* in den *factiones* des römischen *circus*", *Nikephoros* 12 (1999) 213–219.

Contraretiarius (plural *contraretiarii*), or *contrarete* (plural *contraretes*), "anti-netman", type of GLADIATOR who fought against *RETIARII*, perhaps a synonym for *ARBELAS*, *SAMNIS*, or *SECUTOR*.

ILS 5084, 5084a.

Corax, Roman charioteer, first century CE. A CHARIOTEER of the White CIRCUS FACTION, Corax was thrown in the starting-gate at games of the emperor Claudius (47 CE). Nevertheless, his team took the lead, impeded rivals as if a skilled charioteer were at the reins, won the race and then stopped dead at the finish line.

Pliny, *Natural History* 8.65.160.

Corbeidas, of Thebes, HEAVY athlete, fourth century. Corbeidas won *pankration* and perhaps boxing for boys at the same Pythian festival in the later fourth century.

IG 7 2533.

Ebert (1972) 148–151.

Cornelius Ariston, Publius, son of Irenaeus, Ephesian pancratiast, first century CE. Ariston won the Olympic *pankration* for boys in 49 CE in three bouts without a BYE.

IvO 225.

Ebert (1972) 225–229.

Cornelius Sulla Felix, Lucius, Roman dictator, *c.*138–79. After the Athenians celebrated the Sylleia in his honour in 84, Sulla established the *ludi Victoriae Sullanae*, "Games for Sulla's Victory", at Rome in 81 to commemorate the battle which gave him control of the city. Mostly given over to dramatic performances, they also included athletic competitions. In 80, these were augmented by the presence of the leading Greek athletes; as a result, only boys' events (perhaps the *STADION* alone) were held at Olympia that year.

Appian, *Civil War* 1.99; *IG* 2² 1039.

V. J. Matthews, "Sulla and the games of the 175th Olympiad (80 BC)", *Stadion* 5 (1979) 239–243.

Coroebus, of Elis, runner, eighth century. Coroebus was the first recorded Olympic victor, in the *STADION* race, 776. A fictional cook in a work written one thousand years later calls him the son of a cook, but this lacks corroboration (or Coroeboration) elsewhere. His tomb, at the eastern edge of the territory of Elis, figured in claims to land in that area.

Strabo 8.3.30; Pausanias 5.8.5–6, 8.26.3–4; Athenaeus 9.382B.

Coryceum, room in a *PALAESTRA* where boxers and pancratiasts trained with the punching bag (*KŌRYKOS*).

Vitruvius, *On Architecture* 5.11.2.

Cotynus, Roman chariot horse, early second century CE. Paired on the inside with POMPEIANUS, Cotynus took part in 445 victories by the famous CHARIOTEER DIOCLES, including ninety-nine in one year.

ILS 5287.

Crates, of Elis, herald, fourth century. Crates won the first Olympic competition for heralds (see *KĒRYX*), in 396.

Eusebius, *Chronicon* 1.205 Schoene.

Cratinus 1. of Aegeira (Achaea), wrestler, third century. The most handsome man of his time (so says PAUSANIAS) and the most skillful wrestler, when Cratinus won the wrestling competition for boys at Olympia (perhaps in 272) he set up a statue of his TRAINER as well as his own.

Pausanias 6.3.6.

2. of Megara, runner, seventh century. Cratinus won the STADION race at Olympia in 652 and his brother Comaeus the boxing event – the first pair of brothers to become Olympic champions.

Eusebius, *Chronicon* 1.197 Schoene.

Crauxidas, or Crauxilas, of Crannon, race horse victor, seventh century. Crauxidas won the first running of the horse race at Olympia, in 648. This was also the first Thessalian victory – the region was famous for its rich plains and the horses they nourished.

Pausanias 5.8.8.

Crescens 1. GLADIATOR, first century CE. The RETIARIUS Crescens and his appeal to women are featured on Pompeian graffiti.

ILS 5142 d, e.

2. Roman CHARIOTEER, second century CE. A native of Mauretania in North Africa, Crescens won in his twenty-fourth race, in 115 CE, and triumphed for the Blue CIRCUS FACTION forty-seven times in all (in 686 starts) in a nine-year career which ended with his death at twenty-two. Nineteen of his victories came in races for a single team from each faction, twenty-three against seven other entries, five in races for three teams per faction. His winnings amounted to 1,558,346 sesterces.

ILS 5285.

Horsmann (1998) 193–194.

Creugas, of Epidamnus, boxer. When night fell as Creugas and a Syracusan boxer, Damoxenus, were fighting at Ne-mea, the two men agreed to trade one blow each to decide the match. Creugas first hit Damoxenus in the face. In return, Damoxenus asked him to raise his arm and then struck him in the rib cage with rigid fingers. He is said to have penetrated Creugas's abdomen, seized his entrails, and so killed him. The Argive judges disqualified Damoxenus – his fingers had struck one blow each – declared Creugas victor and set up his statue at Argos.

Pausanias 2.20.1, 8.40.3–5.

R. H. Brophy III, "Deaths in the pan-Hellenic games: Arrachion and Creugas", *AJP* 99 (1978) 363–390.

Crison, of Himera, runner, fifth century. A three-time winner of the Olympic STADION race (448, 444, 440), Crison figures in Plato as an exemplar of speed and self-control (like some other famous athletes, he abstained from SEX during training). Plutarch tells an anachronistic tale (inspired perhaps by Plato's account) in which Crison lets ALEXANDER III outrun him, to the famous conqueror's annoyance.

Plato, *Protagoras* 335E-336A; *Laws* 8.840A; Plutarch, *Moral Essays* 58F, 471E; Eusebius, *Chronicon* 1.203 Schoene; *Oxyrhynchus Papyri* 222.

Crispina Meroe, Roman woman, first century CE. About 68 CE, Crispina set up a memorial for a twenty-five-year-old charioteer of the Blue CIRCUS FACTION whose name is lost. He won forty-seven times with four-horse teams and nine times with two, placing in the top three 354 times.

ILS 5284.

Crixus, GLADIATOR and rebel, first century. Crixus, a Gaul, was an early and important leader in the slave rebellion headed by SPARTACUS.

Livy, *Summaries* 95–96.

Crocinas, of Larisa, runner, fifth/fourth century. Crocinas won the STADION race at Olympia in 404, the DIAULOS in 396.

Xenophon, *Greek History* 2.3.1; *Oxyrhynchus Papyri* 2381.

Croton, Greek city in south Italy, home of Pythagoras the philosopher, the famous doctors Alcmaeon and Democedes, and many top-flight athletes (ASTYLUS, MILON, PHAŸLLUS). The Greek cities of Sicily and south Italy produced many victors at the Olympic and other crown festivals in the sixth and early fifth centuries, but none dominated like Croton. Of seventy-one known athletic victors from 588 to 488, twenty were Crotoniates; the next largest group, of SPARTANS, totals four. Eleven of the twenty-six identified STADION champions were from Croton, as against two each from Corcyra and Elis. Crotoniate sprinters once made up the first seven finishers; "the last of the Crotoniates was the first of all other Greeks". Explanations for Croton's extraordinary record include wealth and the willingness to use it to recruit first-class athletes from other cities, its stable oligarchy and, conversely, a democratic spirit which encouraged competitors from every social class and put them into contact with the best medical advice. Whatever its causes, Croton's supremacy came to an end: we know of no Crotoniate victories at any major competition after 480.

Strabo 6.1.12.

Young (1984) 134–147; Stephen G. Miller, "Naked democracy", in P. Flensted-Jensen, T. H. Nielsen and L. Rubinstein (eds) *Polis and Politics. Studies in Ancient Greek History Presented to Mogens Herman Hansen on his Sixtieth Birthday, August 20, 2000* (Copenhagen 2000) 277–296 (284–287).

Crupellarius (plural *crupellarii*), a type of GLADIATOR, heavily clad in armour like Gallic defenders.

Tacitus, *Annals* 3.43.

Cryptarius (plural *cryptarii*), "vaultman", the manager of the enclosed area (*crypta*) in which GLADIATORS waited for their turn in the HARENA.

ILS 5084, 5084a.

Mosci Sassi (1992) 93.

Cursor (plural *cursores*), "runner". **1.** A competitor in footraces at Roman LUDI.

2. A kind of DESULTOR.

3. A slave member of a gladiatorial FAMILIA.

Suetonius, *Augustus* 43.4; *ILS* 5127, 5278.

J.-P. Thuillier, "Les *cursores* du cirque étaient-ils toujours des coureurs à pied?", *Latomus* 47 (1988) 376–383.

Cylon, Athenian runner, seventh century. A member of a wealthy and powerful family, Cylon won the Olympic DIAULOS (640) and married the daughter of Theagenes, tyrant of Megara. Advised by the oracle of Delphi to act at the time of Zeus's greatest festival, he took some of Theagenes' troops and his own friends and seized the Athenian Acropolis during the Olympiad of 632. The oracle seems to have had another festival in mind, however – the Diasia (?) – and the Athenian people, far from flocking to Cylon's support, besieged the Acropolis. Cylon escaped, but his friends were put to death. Some had surrendered on guarantees of safety, others were murdered at the altars of the gods, and the magistrate Megacles and his family, the Alcmaeonids, came under a curse. The curse did not prevent later Alcmaeonids (MEGACLES, ALCIBIADES) from winning wreaths of their own.

Herodotus 5.71; Thucydides 1.126; Plutarch, *Solon* 12; Pausanias 1.28.1.

Cynisca, daughter of King Archidamus of Sparta, chariot victor, fourth century. The daughter and sister of Spartan kings, Cynisca boasted that she was the first Greek woman to keep (or perhaps breed) horses and win a chariot race at Olympia (four-horse race, 396, 392). Her achievements earned her a heroine's shrine at Sparta, close to where the young girls ran, and the emulation of later victors like BERENICE I. According to a hostile tradition, however, Cynisca's entries were prompted by her brother AGESILAUS, who wished to demonstrate that chariot victories were the result of wealth more than merit.

Xenophon, *Agesilaus* 9.6; Posidippus, *P.Mil. Vogl.* 8 309.XIII.31–34; Plutarch, *Agesilaus* 20.1; *Moral Essays* 212B; Pausanias 3.8.1, 15.1, 5.12.5, 6.1.6; *IvO* 160 (= *Greek Anthology* 13.16); *SEG* 36.394.

Cynosarges, Athenian GYMNASIUM. Located in a sanctuary for HERACLES, perhaps in Athens's southeastern suburbs, Cynosarges was likely less well equipped than Athens's two older gymnasia, the ACADEMY and the LYCEUM, and more often associated with marginal groups and ideas. ("Go to Cynosarges!" was an expression of abuse.) Though used as a base of operations by the democratic leader Themistocles in the early fifth century and provided with ample grounds for riding, it seems to have played little role in classical Athenian intellectual and military life. It was later linked with Antisthenes the Cynic and other unorthodox thinkers.

Andocides 1.61; Demosthenes 24.114; [Plato], *Axiochus* 364A; Plutarch, *Themistocles* 1.3; Diogenes Laertius 6.13.

J. Bremmer, "*Es Kynosarges*", *Mnemosyne* 30 (1977) 369–374; Kyle (1987) 84–92; M.-F. Billot, "Le Cynosarges, Antiochos et les tanneurs. Questions de topographie", *BCH* 116 (1992) 119–156.

D

D ... **gonus**, boxer, second century. An inscription declares that this man (whose name is only partly legible) was twice boxing champion at all four games of the PERIODOS. His Olympic wins may date to 160 and 156.

IvO 185.

Daetondas *see* ARSILOCHUS

Daicles, of Messenia, runner, eighth century. Daicles, winner of the STADION race at Olympia in 752, is said to have been the first to be awarded the olive wreath.

Phlegon *FGrH* 257 F 1.10–11.

Daippus, of Croton, boxer, seventh century. Winner of the boxing wreath in 672, Daippus was the first Olympic champion among western Greeks.

Phlegon *FGrH* 257 F 6.

Damagetus *see* DIAGORAS

Damarchus, or Demaenetus, son of Dinytas, Parrhasian boxer, (?) fifth century. Damarchus is said to have tasted the flesh of a boy roasted during a sacrifice to Zeus Lycaeus ("the wolf") in Arcadia and to have been changed into a wolf for ten years as a result. (It's a story Pausanias can't swallow.) When he regained human form, he trained (by abstaining from meat) and became Olympic boxing champion, perhaps in 400.

Pausanias 6.8.2; Pliny, *Natural History* 8.34.82; Augustine, *City of God* 18.17.

Damaretus, or Demaretus, of Heraea, runner, sixth century. The most renowned (according to Pausanias) of Arcadian athletes, Damaretus won the first race in armour (HOPLITĒS) at Olympia in 520 and repeated four years later. His son and grandson, both named THEOPOMPUS, were Olympic champions after him, the first family to triumph in three generations.

Pausanias 5.8.10, 8.26.2; *IG* 2² 2326.

Damatrius, son of Aristippus, Tegean runner, third/second century. Winner of the Olympic STADION race for boys (perhaps in 208), Damatrius was a PERIODONIKĒS in the long race (DOLICHOS) as an adult, champion at Olympia (? in 200), at Delphi twice, two or three times at Isthmia, four at Nemea.

IG 5.2 143.

Damiscus, of Messene, runner, fourth century. Winner of the STADION race for boys in 388, Damiscus is the youngest Olympic champion we know. He later won the pentathlon at both Isthmia and Nemea.

Pausanias 6.2.10–11.

Damon, of Thurii, runner, fourth century. Damon won the STADION race at Olympia twice, in 376 and 372.

Pausanias 4.27.9, 6.3.5, 5.3, 8.27.8.

Damonon, Spartan athlete and equestrian, fifth/fourth century. Damonon's competitive career, detailed on a marble stele dedicated in the sanctuary of Athena of the Bronze House on the Spartan Acropolis, includes both athletic and equestrian triumphs, eleven as a boy in STADION and DIAULOS, forty-three in four-horse chariots and eighteen in horse races (the stele is topped with a relief of a chariot). Damonon stresses that he bred and drove his own chariot teams and notes that his son sometimes won races on the same day as his horses. That son, Enymacratidas, improved on his father's record as an athlete, adding victories in DOLICHOS; on one occasion, he won *stadion, diaulos* and *dolichos* on one day and added the race on horseback – a taste, no doubt, of things to come when he (like his father) grew too old for athletics. Their success suggests how crowded the competitive calendar could be in some Greek communities and how eagerly victory – especially distinctive victory – might be sought, whatever the quality of the opposition. Neither father nor son can claim a crown at a major festival – a result, perhaps, of Sparta's exclusion from Olympia from 420 to about 400 and of the disruptions of the Peloponnesian war.

IG 5.1 213.

S. Hodkinson, *Property and Wealth in Classical Sparta* (London 2000) 303–307.

Dandis, of Argos, runner, fifth century. Dandis, a PERIODONIKĒS, won twice at Olympia (DIAULOS, 476, STADION, 472), three times at Delphi, twice at Isthmia – and fifteen times at Nemea, the crown festival nearest his home. His Nemean victories must include those as a PAIS and AGENEIOS.

Greek Anthology 13.14; *Oxyrhynchus Papyri*

222.

Ebert (1972) 66–69.

Decemiugis (plural *decemiuges*), Latin term for ten-horse chariot team and race. Suetonius, *Nero* 24.2; *ILS* 5286.

Decoratus, GLADIATOR. Decoratus, both RETIARIUS and (unusually) SECUTOR, killed his opponent in his ninth fight but died himself, leaving a wife to mourn him. Their owner erected a tomb and inscription for both fighters on account of the success of his show.

ILS 5123.

Deinolochus, son of Pyrrhus, Eleian runner, fourth century. Deinolochus's mother dreamed that her baby son was crowned. He was therefore trained and grew up to win the STADION race for boys at Olympia (perhaps in 380).

Pausanias 6.2.4–5.

Deinosthenes, son of Deinosthenes, Spartan runner, fourth century. The winner of the STADION race in 316, Deinosthenes set up a monument indicating the distance from the ALTIS to his native Sparta (something over 100km = 60 miles) – perhaps an indication that he was a courier (*hēmerodromos*) who had run the distance to report his victory.

Diodorus 19.17.1; Pausanias 6.16.8; *IvO* 171.

Moretti (1953) 79–82.

Demades, son of Demeas, Athenian politician and equestrian victor, c.380–319. Despite his origins outside the traditional elite, Demades' gifts as a speaker brought him prominence and power in an Athens dominated by Macedon until he was put to death by Cassander in 319. His equestrian victory, dating perhaps to 328, may reveal a desire to identify with the pursuits of Athenian aristocrats – or of Macedonian kings.

Suda δ 415

Demaenetus, son of Demeas, Athenian equestrian victor, fourth century. Like his sons Demeas and Demosthenes, Demaenetus led an Athenian tribe in an *ANTHIP-PASIA* competition in which it was part of the winning team.

IG 2² 3130.

Moretti (1953) 66–68.

Demaratus 1. king of Sparta (*c*.515–491) and chariot victor. Though highly esteemed by his people for his chariot victory at Olympia (perhaps in 504), Demaratus was later deposed and accompanied the Persian king Xerxes on his invasion of Greece in 480.

Herodotus 6.70.3.

2. of Ephesus, runner, first century BCE/ CE. Demaratus was twice Olympic champion in the *STADION* race, in 4 BCE and 1 CE.

Eusebius, *Chronicon* 1.213 Schoene.

Demetrius, of Salamis (Cyprus), runner and pentathlete, third century CE. Demetrius won the *STADION* race at Olympia at three festivals in a row (perhaps 229, 233, 237) twice adding the pentathlon crown as well. He also won at the Pythian and Isthmian games and once defeated eighty-six rivals at the SEBASTAN games in Naples. Demetrius's victories in games which were *TALANTIAIOI* or *hēmitalan-tiaioi* totalled forty-seven. The cities which held them awarded him citizenship, and two emperors appointed him XYS-TARCHĒS of the athletes' GUILD for life.

Moretti (1953) 253–257; H. A. Harris, "Notes on three athletic inscriptions", *JHS* 82 (1962) 19–24 (21–24); Moretti (1987) 79–80.

Democrates 1. Son of Democrates, of Magnesia on Maeander, HEAVY athlete, first century CE. A *PERIODONIKĒS* in boxing, Democrates won three times at Olympia (perhaps in 25, 29 and 33), twice at both Nemea and Isthmia, at Delphi, as well as three times at the ACTIAN games and twice at the HERAEA (1) of ARGOS. His many other victories include all three HEAVY events at the festival of the Lycian federation.

IvO 211, 212; *IMagn.* 149.

Moretti (1953) 162–164.

2. Son of Hegetor, Tenedan wrestler, third century. Arriving at Olympia with a foot illness (perhaps in 204), Democrates stood in the stadium, drew a circle around himself, and dared his rivals to drag him outside it. When they failed, he stepped over the line and was crowned wrestling champion. Like his father before him, Democrates received citizenship and other honours from the Eleians; his brother Polycrates was Panathenaic wrestling winner *c*.190.

Pausanias 6.17.1; Aelian, *Historical Miscellany* 4.15; *IvO* 39; *IG* 2² 2313.

3. Son of Lysis, Athenian equestrian competitor, born *c*.470–460. Democrates, his father and other members of this wealthy family won chariot and horse races at Delphi, Isthmia and Nemea, using hired charioteers. Their achievements figure in the flattery his wooers aim at Democrates' son, another Lysis, in the Platonic dialogue which bears his name.

Plato, *Lysis* 205C, 208A.

Demostheneia, a quadrennial competitive festival endowed at his native Oenoanda (Lycia) by C. Iulius Demosthenes in 125 CE. The inscription recording Demosthenes' foundation (discovered in 1967) is our richest source of information on the arrangements such a festival required. It is all the more unfortunate for our purposes that athletics is very much de-emphasized in comparison to musical, rhetorical and dramatic competitions: it takes up only the twenty-second and last day of the programme, is open to local citizens only, and offers fees for participants rather than prizes.

SEG 38. 1462.

M. Wörrle, *Stadt und Fest in kaiserzeitlichen Kleinasien. Studien zu einer agonistischen Stiftung aus Oenoanda* (Munich 1988); S. Mitchell, "Festivals, games and civic life in Roman Asia Minor", *JRS* 80 (1990) 183–193.

Demosthenes, of Miletus, athlete, (?) first century. The most likely interpretation of a Greek epigram is that it refers to Demosthenes' three victories in the same Olympic festival. If this is correct, it suggests how spotty our evidence is: we hear nothing else about Demosthenes' athletic career.

Crinagoras, *Greek Anthology* 6.350.

Moretti (1987) 73–74.

Desultor (plural *desultores*), Roman equestrian competitor. There were two kinds of *desultor*: one (see CURSOR (2)) dismounted and ran alongside his horse to the finish line, the other jumped back and forth between two horses under his control. Despite demands and dangers, races for *desultores* were less frequent than chariot races and drew smaller prizes.

Ovid, *Amores* 1.3.5; Seneca, *Suasoriae* 1.7.

J.-P. Thuillier, "Les *desultores* de l'Italie antique", *CRAI* (1989) 33–51.

Dexioseiros (plural *dexioseiroi*), "right-hand trace horse", the horse in a Greek four-horse team who had the furthest to run and so became proverbial for energy and assistance in a time of trouble.

Sophocles, *Antigone* 140.

Diagoras, son of Damagetus, Rhodian boxer and patriarch, fifth century. Diagoras's Olympic victory in boxing (464) was celebrated in a poem of PINDAR which was later inscribed in golden letters on the walls of the temple of Athena at Lindus. He also won at Delphi, four times each at Isthmia and Nemea, as well as at the HERAEA (1) at Argos and elsewhere. Diagoras's son Damagetus was twice Olympic champion in *pankration* (452, 448); on the second occasion, he was

joined by another son, Acusilaus, in boxing. The brothers carried their father through the admiring crowd, which pelted him with flowers. A third son, Dorieus, was a PERIODONIKĒS like his father, but still more successful, a triple winner in the Olympic *pankration* (432, 428, 424), perhaps four times at Delphi (once AKONITI), eight at Isthmia, seven at Nemea, and often elsewhere. During the Peloponnesian war, he fought against Athens and was captured, but was released in recognition of his athletic feats. He was less lucky later, when he fell into Spartan hands – his native Rhodes was then an Athenian ally – and put to death. Two sons of Diagoras's daughters were also Olympic champions, Eucles and Peisidorus (see PHERENICE). A statue group of the family stood in the ALTIS at Olympia.

Pindar, *Olympians* 7; Thucydides 3.8.1; Xenophon, *Greek History* 1.5.19; Andronion, *FGrH* 324 F 46; Pausanias 6.7.1–5; *IvO* 159.

Poliakoff (1987) 119–120.

Diaulos, "double pipe' (see AULOS), one of the regular events at Greek competitive festivals. The *diaulos* was a footrace two lengths of the STADIUM (400 Greek feet) – up in lanes marked out by lime or gypsum, counter-clockwise around a post (KAMPTĒR), and back in a parallel lane. According to tradition, it joined the Olympic programme second, in 724; the first winner was HYPENUS of Pisa. Only men ran *diaulos* at Olympia, Isthmia and Nemea. At the Pythian games, however, it was on the original programme for both *paides* and men. *Diaulos* runners needed to be stronger than sprinters but lighter than HOPLITE racers (who ran the same distance, in armour); however (according to Galen), even a champion would be slower at this distance than a gazelle. Unchallenged by gazelles, some *diaulos* runners enjoyed success over many years: an Argive won at Olympia four times running (208–196), a feat matched and surpassed by LEONIDAS of

Rhodes (164–152, adding victories in STADION and race in armour as well). Double victories in *stadion* and *diaulos* were not uncommon. The term is also used for a horse race of two lengths of the Greek HIPPODROME.

Pausanias 5.8.6; Galen, *Exhortation* 13.36; Philostratus, *On Athletic Exercise* 33.

Stephen G. Miller, "Turns and lanes in the ancient stadium", *AJA* 84 (1980) 159–166.

Diazōma see PERIZŌMA.

Dicon, son of Callimbrotus, of Caulonia, runner, fourth century. When he won the boys' STADION race at Olympia (perhaps in 392), Dicon was proclaimed as a Caulonian. He won twice more at Olympia as an adult, in the *stadion* and another footrace in 384, now as a Syracusan: Dionysus I of Syracuse had incorporated his city's people. Dicon also won five Pythian victories, three at Isthmia and four at Nemea.

Diodorus 15.14.1; Pausanias 6.3.11; *Greek Anthology* 13.15.

Didas, of the Arsinoite nome in Egypt, boxer, second century CE. Didas won the Olympic boxing event in 125 CE but was fined along with his opponent and fellow-citizen Sarapammon, apparently because they had made a side bet on the bout.

Pausanias 5.21.15.

Diet. According to tradition, athletes once ate grain, soft cheese and dried figs, a simple diet much like that of other Greeks. Then, about 500 BCE, they began the heavy eating, especially of meat, which marked them throughout antiquity. One story ascribes the innovation to the famous philosopher Pythagoras, whose advice led to the victory of EURYMENES of Samos in a HEAVY event at Olympia about 532. Pythagoras was better known for promoting vegetarianism, however, and an alternative version credits DROMEUS (1) of Stymphalus, twice victor in

dolichos at Olympia around 480. (His statue was sculpted by a different Pythagoras, hence perhaps the confusion.) The wrestler MILON is said to have consumed extraordinary amounts of bread, wine and meat, including a whole bull in a single day; it is heavy athletes (ASTYANAX, THEOGENES) whose bulk was an advantage in events with no weight classes, who generally figure in critiques of athletic gluttony and praise of unusual abstinence. PHILOSTRATUS mocks the doctors and trainers of his own time for their subtle refinements: bread sprinkled with poppy seeds, pork from pigs fed on berries and acorns only. (Pigs pastured near water were to be avoided.) Modern athletes (like the baseball player featured in L. H. Addington's limerick) sometimes come in for similar criticism: "The Dodgers have Del Bissonette/No meal has he ever missed yet/The question that rises/Is one that surprises:/ Who paid for all Del Bissonette?" Roman GLADIATORS were also encouraged to bulk up, but through a much cheaper means, the coarse mash called SAGINA. Much like death-row convicts today – or like the elite banqueters they also resembled – they enjoyed a special meal before a match.

Euripides fragment 282 N²; Xenophon, *Memories of Socrates* 3.14.3; Athenaeus 10.412DF; Pausanias 6.7.10; Philostratus, *On Athletic Exercise* 43–44; Diogenes Laertius 8.12; Porphyry, *Life of Pythagoras* 15.

Harris (1964) 171–173; J. M. Renfrew, "Food for athletes and gods", in Raschke (1988) 174–181.

Diludium (plural *diludia*), pause in a GLADIATORIAL combat or an interval between spectacles.

Horace, *Epistles* 1.19.47–48.

Mosci Sassi (1992) 97–98.

Dimachaerus (plural *dimachaeri*), type of GLADIATOR, armed with two daggers.

Artemidorus 2.32; *ILS* 5097.

Mosci Sassi (1992) 98.

Diocles, Gaius Appuleius, Roman charioteer, early second century CE. Diocles'
career, detailed on an honorific plaque, is
one of our most important sources of
evidence on Roman chariot racing. Born
in Lusitania in 104 CE, Diocles joined the
White CIRCUS FACTION at eighteen, won
his first victory two years later, moved to
the Greens in 128, to the Reds in 131,
and competed in their colours for fifteen
years, retiring at forty-two in 146 CE. He
raced four-horse chariots 4,257 times,
placing 2,900 times – first 1,462, second
861, third 576, fourth (in a race with an
unusually large purse) once. Of his victories, 1,064 came in the races with the
best drivers, those in which each faction
entered one team, 347 in races with two
entries for each faction, fifty-one in full
fields (three entries each). In addition, he
occasionally raced two-horse chariots and
once a seven-horse team without a yoke –
the first time such a race was held. One
hundred and ten times Diocles won the
programme's first and most prestigious
race. His purses, as much as 60,000
sesterces, totalled 35,863,120 sesterces.

Diocles' inscription is remarkable for
the attention it gives to the ways he won –
leading from the outset (815 times),
snatching victory at the end (502), coming
from behind (67) – and notes that he
came in first even when he was not his
faction's lead driver (36 times). It is also
ingenious in identifying distinctions and
making Diocles' claim to outshine other
named charioteers. Thus Diocles was the
best driver of African horses, won 134
races in one year, made eight horses
winners one hundred times and one, two
hundred. His record of victories might be
surpassed but Diocles was unmatched in
high-stakes races.

ILS 5287; *CIL* 14.2884.

L. Friedländer, *Roman Life and Manners under
the Early Empire* (trans. A. B. Gough: London
1913) 4.154–164; Horsmann (1998) 194–198.

Diocles, of Corinth, runner, eighth century. Winner of the Olympic STADION

race in 728, Diocles and his lover Philolaus (a member of the ruling Bacchiad
clan) left Corinth for Thebes, where
Philolaus became a famous lawgiver.
When they died there, Diocles made
certain that Corinth was not within eye-
sight of his tomb – he had been disgusted
by his mother's sexuality.

Aristotle, *Politics* 2.1274a34.

Diogenes, son of Dionysius, Ephesian
trumpeter, first century CE. A five-time
winner at Olympia (beginning perhaps in
69 CE), Diogenes also won twice at the
Pythian games, three times at both the
Isthmian and the Nemean, and over
eighty times at other games.

IvO 232.

Diognetus, of Crete, boxer, (?) fifth century. The Eleians refused to award Diognetus the Olympic crown (perhaps in 488)
after he killed his opponent in a boxing
match, perhaps on the grounds that the
dead man shared the name of the hero
HERACLES. He went into exile but was
worshipped by his fellow citizens as a
HERO himself.

Photius, *Library* 151a.

Dionysia *see* HERMESIANAX (2)

Dionysius Sameumys, of Alexandria, runner, second century CE. Dionysius was
twice Olympic champion in the STADION
race, in 125 and 129.

Eusebius, *Chronicon* 1.217 Schoene.

Dionysodorus, of Thebes, Olympic victor,
fourth century. Along with other Greek
ambassadors to the Persian king, Dionysodorus fell into ALEXANDER III's hands
after the Battle of Issus (333) but was
freed, perhaps in part due to his Olympic
victory in an event now unknown.

Arrian, *History of Alexander* 2.15.2.

Diophanes, son of Empedion, of Athens, pancratiast, fourth century. Diophanes won *pankration* for AGENEIOI at Isthmia in the earlier fourth century, apparently duplicating the feat of a grandfather of the same name or of a brother, Progonus or Stephanus.

IG 2² 3125; *SEG* 46.255.

Ebert (1972) 133–134; J. S. Traill, "The case of the mal-aligned *bouleutai*", in *Studies Presented to Sterling Dow on his Eightieth Birthday* (*GRBS* Monograph 10: Durham 1984) 283–294 (289 n8).

Diophon, son of Philon, pentathlete, fifth century. An epigram attributed to SIMONIDES says Diophon won pentathlon at the Pythian and Isthmian games and lists the events: the jump, swiftness of foot, discus, javelin, wrestling.

Greek Anthology 16.3.

Ebert (1972) 181–182.

Dioxippus, of Athens, pancratiast, fourth century. Victor in the Olympic *pankration* in a walkover (AKONITI) in 336, and supposedly one of the strongest men in Greece – strong enough to scare any man off from insulting his sister – Dioxippus was on campaign with ALEXANDER III (in 325) when he overcame a Macedonian soldier who had challenged him to a single combat. (Dioxippus's physical presence joined with the club he carried brought HERACLES to mind.) This demonstration of an athlete's strength and skill did not sit well with some of Alexander's entourage; Dioxippus was accused of theft and committed suicide (to the disgust of some who tell his story).

Hyperides 1a.6; Diodorus 17.100–101; Aelian, *Historical Miscellany* 10.22, 12.58; Curtius 9.7.12–25.

T. S. Brown, "Alexander and Greek athletics, in fact and fiction", in K. Kinzl (ed.) *Greece and the Eastern Mediterranean in Ancient History and Prehistory. Studies Presented to Fritz Schachermeyr* (Berlin 1977) 76–88.

Diskos, "discus", one of the distinctive events of the PENTATHLON. The *diskos* was a disc-shaped object of stone or (later) bronze, sloping from the centre to the edges, which was thrown for distance. It does not figure among the events of the FUNERAL GAMES for Patroclus – the heroes throw a metal ingot (*solos*), and one may attract derision because his technique is better suited to the *diskos* – but both Achilles' companions and the suitors of Penelope throw *diskoi* as a pastime, and Odysseus awes his Phaeacian hosts by a mighty throw. Here and elsewhere the *diskos* was a stand-alone event, but it was usually part of the pentathlon. (Each competitor threw five times in a (?) first-century games on Rhodes.) Homer uses the length of a *diskos* throw as a measure of distance familiar to his audience. Unfortunately, it is less clear to us. The famous pentathlete PHAŸLLUS is said to have thrown 95 feet (likely measured from the front of the BALBIS to the spot where the *diskos* landed) but it is difficult to evaluate his achievement. Most known *diskoi* range in weight from 1.8 to 2.8kg (4–6 lbs). A modern athlete would do much better with a *diskos* of similar size. Phaÿllus's, however, may have been larger – Philostratus classifies *diskos* as a HEAVY event, Galen notes that it may injure practitioners, and wayward *diskoi* kill spectators in myth. Furthermore, the ancient style may not have involved the full rotation of the body which contributes so much to distance today. (The ancient *diskos* throw seems to have relied on the pendulum movement of the right arm back and forth with the left leg striding forward; long fingers helped to impart a spin to increase stability and distance.) It is likely that *diskoi* varied from place to place (as did the length of the STADION race); in addition, PAIDES threw a smaller *diskos*. At Olympia, three *diskoi* for the pentathlon were stored in the Treasury of the Sicyonians. Another, IPHITUS's, kept in the Temple of Hera, bore the terms of the Olympic TRUCE inscribed around its edges, as well as the name of Lycurgus. Marble *diskoi* were sometimes used as prizes in athletic competitions.

Homer, *Iliad* 2.774–775, 23.431–432, 523–524, 826–849; *Odyssey* 4.625–626, 8.186–198, 17.167–168; Lucian, *Philopseudes* 18; Pausanias 1.35.5, 5.20.1, 6.19.4; Galen, *On Exercise with the Small Ball* 5 (910 Kühn); Plutarch, *Lycurgus* 1.1; Philostratus, *On Athletic Exercise* 3, 31; *Heroicus* 2.3; *Pictures* 1.24; *Greek Anthology Appendix* 3.297; Statius, *Thebaïd* 6.646–730.

L. Moretti, "Un regolamento per la gara del pentatlo", *RFIC* 84 (1956) 55–60; M. K. Langdon, "Throwing the discus in antiquity: the literary evidence", *Nikephoros* 3 (1990) 177–182; M. Lavrencic, G. Doblhofer and P. Mauritsch, *Diskos* (Vienna 1991).

Diversium, type of Roman chariot race, in which the victor in a previous race drove the team of a defeated opponent. Wins in such races demonstrated the driver's skills and were much prized.

Sidonius Apollinaris 23.307–427; *Greek Anthology* 15.47, 16.337, 340, 374.

A. Cameron, *Circus Factions. Blues and Greens at Rome and Byzantium* (Oxford 1976) 50–53.

Doctor (plural *doctores*), "teacher", gladiatorial instructor. Such trainers were normally specialists, like GLADIATORS themselves; so we hear of a doctor of MURMILLONES, of THRAECES, and so on. In smaller troupes, the LANISTA might double as *doctor*.

Quintilian, *Declamations* 302.3; *ILS* 5091, 5099, 5103, 5116, 9342.

Mosci Sassi (1992) 98–99.

Dolichos, "long race", one of the regular events of Greek competitive festivals. The *dolichos* varied in length from seven to twenty-four lengths of the STADIUM – from 1,400 to 4,800 Greek feet. The race at Olympia was apparently one of the longest; only men ran here – the first winner, in 720, was ACANTHUS of Sparta. However, *dolichos* was on the original programme for *paides* as well as men at the Pythian games and is attested at

Nemea too. The *dolichos* for younger competitors may have been shorter (like all the footraces for boys and AGENEIOI Plato planned for his Cretan city). A horse (says Galen) would run *dolichos* better than a man. Among men, the ideal was a strong neck and shoulders – to hold up the hands during most of the race – and light, slender legs for a finishing sprint. A Bithynian nicknamed GRAUS won the Olympic *dolichos* three times in a row (? 213–221 CE) and FLAVIUS Metrobius claims 140 victories in the late first century CE. The achievement of POLITES of Caria, who won STADION, DIAULOS and *dolichos* on the same day at Olympia (69 CE), was as remarkable.

Plato, *Laws* 8.833C; Pausanias 5.8.6, 6.13.3–4; Galen, *Exhortation* 13.36; Philostratus, *On Athletic Exercise* 32; *Greek Anthology* 9.319; *CIG* 2682.

J. Nollé, "Grabepigramme und Reliefdarstellungen aus Kleinasien", *ZPE* 60 (1985) 117–135 (133–135); Y. Kempen, *Krieger, Boten und Athleten: Untersuchungen zum Langlauf in der griechischen Antike* (Sankt Augustin 1992).

Domitius Prometheus, Titus, of Athens, chariot victor, third century CE. Prometheus won chariot races at all four festivals of the original PERIODOS, repeating at Delphi. An EPHĒBOS – and so aged seventeen or eighteen – perhaps between 220 and 225 CE, his chariot victories, like his service as a magistrate with responsibilities for GYMNASIA, probably came before 244/5 CE.

IG 2² 2243, 3769.

Ebert (1972) 247–250.

Dorieus *see* DIAGORAS

Dracontomenes, son of Hierocles, Halicarnassian runner, first century. The winner of numerous crowns as a boy (including in both DOLICHOS and HIPPIOS at the Panathenaea and in DIAULOS at the ASCLEPIEIA (I) at Epidaurus), Dracontomenes specialized successfully in *hippios* as an adult. He won at Isthmia, the

HERAEA (1) at Argos, and the Coan ASCLEPIEIA (2) among other important festivals, but not at Olympia or Delphi, where this race was not on the programme. An ancestor, another Dracontomenes, son of Hierocles, won *diaulos* at the Coan Asclepieia about 180.

SIG³ 1064.

Moretti (1953) 144–146.

Draw. Draws were a feature of Greek athletics – reruns and rematches are very rare (see ALEXANDER I). Most occurred in the HEAVY events, but they are attested in the footraces (including the longer distances) as well; no dead heats are known in horse or chariot racing, though the possibility is raised in a recently discovered epigram by POSIDIPPUS (see CALLICRATES (2)). Some draws arose because of the inability of judges to determine a winner, some because of time constraints (as when night fell before a boxing match was decided), some by the agreement of the competitors. (An alternative, at least in boxing, was a punch-off like the one which killed and crowned CREUGAS.) In chrematitic AGŌNES, the prize might simply be divided. This can rarely have been as awkward as in the FUNERAL GAMES of Patroclus, where Ajax and Odysseus, who draw in wrestling, are to divide a tripod valued at twelve oxen and a woman valued at four. In crown games, the practice of dedicating the winner's wreath to the god of the festival is as early as the fourth century. In the Imperial period, it became more common for multiple wreaths (no more than two) to be awarded, though not at Olympia or the other leading festivals. This allowed each competitor to earn rewards on offer at the festival (such as the right to erect a STATUE) or at home. Successful athletes sometimes boast of never having shared a victory in this way.

Homer, *Iliad* 23.700–705, 736–737; Polybius 1.58.5, 29.8.9; Plutarch, *Moral Essays* 1045D; Aulus Gellius 18.2.5; *IG* 14 1102; *IvO* 56;

SEG 11.61.

N. B. Crowther, "Resolving an impasse: draws, dead heats and similar decisions in Greek athletics", *Nikephoros* 13 (2000) 125–140; P. Bernardini and L. Bravi, "Note di lettura al nuovo Posidippo", *QUCC* 70 (2002) 147–163 (156–158).

Dromeus 1. of Stymphalus, runner, fifth century. Dromeus – the name means "runner" – was PERIODONIKĒS in DOLICHOS, winning twice at Olympia (? 484 and 480) and Delphi, three times at Isthmia and five at Nemea. He is one of several given credit for originating the meat DIET of athletes. Dromeus's victories in the Pythian games brought him privileges which were claimed by his descendants several centuries later.

Pausanias 6.7.10, SIG³ 516.

2. of Mantinea, pancratiast, fifth century. The withdrawal of THEOGENES, exhausted from his boxing match with EUTHYMUS, allowed Dromeus to win the Olympic *pankration* unopposed (AKONITI) in 480 – the first such victory in that event.

Pausanias 6.11.4.

Dromos, "run", a word with many meanings in athletic and equestrian contexts: race, racecourse, pace, lane, straightaway or half-lap, circuit.

See also: STADION.

N. B. Crowther, "More on 'dromos' as a technical term in Greek sport", *Nikephoros* 6 (1993) 33–37.

Drymus, son of Theodorus, of Argos, runner, fourth century. Drymus won at Olympia in about 320 (likely in DOLICHOS) and announced his victory that same day at Epidaurus, 225km (140 miles) away.

IG 4²1 618; *SEG* 38.300.

Dust, (Greek *konis*), sprinkled on the Greek athlete after the application of OLIVE oil before exercise and scraped off with a STRIGIL after (see GLOIOS, PATOS). Dust was so much a part of Greek athletics that an unopposed victory was said to be won AKONITI, "dustlessly", and the model gymnasium had a dusting room, a *konistērion*. Dust helped prevent oiled wrestlers from slipping from each other's grasp but it had more general uses, each best fulfilled by a particular kind: thus (says PHILOSTRATUS) clay dust disinfects and cuts down perspiration – encouraged by terracotta dust – asphalt dust heats the body, yellow dust softens it and makes it more appealing. The best quality dust came from around the Nile – ALEXANDER III's generals and NERO's favourite Patrobius had it imported. Whatever its kind, dust should be sprinkled with a fluid motion of the wrist and the fingers spread so as to settle like a soft down.

Lucian, *Anacharsis* 2, 6; Philostratus, *On Athletic Exercise* 18, 42, 56; Pliny, *Natural History* 35.47.167–168; Vitruvius, *On Architecture* 5.11.2.

Dyspontium, in Elis, Greek city. In 672, the Eleians of Dyspontium became the first Greeks to win an Olympic victory as a collective when their team won the chariot race, a precedent for the people of ARGOS.

Phlegon *FGrH* 257 F 6.

E

Eirene, daughter of Ptolemaeus, of Alexandria, chariot victor, second century. Eirene's team won the four-colts chariot race at the PANATHENAEA of 170/69. Her father served the Ptolemies as governor of Cyprus and ambassador to Rome, she herself as first priestess of the cult of Queen Arsinoe Philopator from 199 to 171/0.

Hesperia 60 (1991) 188–189.

Eiselasis (plural *eiselaseis*), Latin *iselasis*, "driving in", a victor's triumphant entry into his city, generally in a chariot. Perhaps due to the example of NERO, it became the practice to make a breach in the wall for the victor's homecoming: a city with such champions was in no need of other defences. Designation as eiselastic (*eiselastikos* AGŌN) saluted a festival's status, but what was given (by the emperor under Roman rule) could also be taken away. Winners in eiselastic games often earned other rewards as well, such as *ATELEIA* or *OPSŌNIA*.

Diodorus 13.82.7; Plutarch, *Moral Essays* 639E; Cassius Dio 62.20; Vitruvius, *On Architecture* 9 *Preface* 1; Pliny, *Letters* 10.118, 119; Suetonius, *Nero* 25.1; *SEG* 41.1003 II.

Eiselastikos *see* AGŌN

Ekecheiria *see* TRUCE

Elagabalus, Roman emperor (218–222 CE), born ? 203 CE. Elagabalus brought a number of CHARIOTEERS (Protogenes, Cordius) into his entourage and appointed one, Hierocles, to high office.

Cassius Dio 79 (78).15; *Historia Augusta, Elagabalus* 6.

Eleutheria, name of two important panhellenic quadrennial festivals in honour of Zeus Eleutherios, "the liberator". 1. The Eleutheria at Plataea in Boeotia was established in memory of those who died fighting the Persians in 479 and the decisive victory they won there. Its race in armour, run on the battle's anniversary (in August/September), was famous as the longest (15 *stadia*, from the trophy which honoured the victory to the altar of Zeus) and most arduous, since runners wore heavier armour. The winner was styled "best of the Greeks". Repeaters were discouraged by a regulation which allegedly punished them with death if they lost a subsequent run. A Milesian of the first century CE boasts that he was the first to win twice (he was good enough to win STADION and DIAULOS too) and an Egyptian runner matched him, encouraged by the faith shown by a TRAINER who pledged his life if he lost. The festival was held into the third century CE at least.

Diodorus 11.29.1; Strabo 9.2.31; Plutarch, *Aristides* 21.1; Pausanias 9.2.6; Philostratus, *On Athletic Exercise* 8, 24.

Moretti (1953) 151–156; L. Robert, "*Aristos Hellēnōn*", *REA* 31 (1929) 13–20, 225–226; A. Schachter, *Cults of Boiotia* 3 (London 1994) 138–141.

2. The Eleutheria at Larisa in Thessaly dated from 196, the year after the Romans defeated Philip V of Macedon at Cynoscephalae and freed Thessaly from his control. Its AGŌNOTHETĒS was the *stratēgos*, the political and military leader of the Thessalian League. Events included PANKRATION, PENTATHLON, STADION and DOLICHOS for PAIDES, AGENEIOI and AN-DRES; a race in armour for *andres*; horse and chariot races (among them the unusual mounted torch race, APHIPPOLAMPAS, and dismounting race, APHIPPODROMIA); bull-wrestling, TAUROTHĒRIA; trumpeters and heralds; musical contests. Most victors came from Larisa or elsewhere in Thessaly, but some from as far away as Syracuse and Asia Minor. Two local women figure among the chariot champions.

IG 9.2 525–534, 614.

K. Gallis, "The games in ancient Larisa. An example of provincial Olympic games", in Raschke (1988) 217–235 (218–226).

Elis, main city of the region of Elis in the northwest Peloponnese. For all its agricultural riches and reputation for horse-breeding, Elis owned its prominence within the Greek world and its privileges under the Roman Empire to one thing: control of the sanctuary and festival of Zeus Olympios at Olympia, 60km (about 37 miles) away, where it supplanted PISA by the mid-sixth century. The steady stream of visitors and their need for food, lodging and sacrificial animals fed Elis's prosperity as well as its prestige. Eleian authority was made manifest by the training period athletes were required to spend at Elis before the games and by the procession which wended its way to Olympia over two days at the end of that period. HELLANODIKAI, ALYTARCHAI and other officials were drawn from the Eleian elite, as was the shadowy Olympic Council which heard appeals from their decisions. And the city of Elis deposited copies of treaties and laws in the sanctuary of Zeus. Eleians, as keen for competitive distinction as any Greeks, enjoyed more Olympic success than others. They make up 125 (12 per cent) of the 940 known Olympic victors, the largest number from any one city. They were most successful in the fourth, third and first centuries, and as pentathletes, equestrians and boys. There are, however, few known STADION (five of 254) or *pankration* (one of 68) champions from Elis, and they were less successful with four-horse chariots than in other, less prestigious equestrian events. Eleians clearly had a home-field advantage, since travel and the training period might be more difficult and expensive for outsiders; this would count most against boys (who needed accompaniment) and horses (and may have discouraged outlay and risk for any but the greatest reward). Their roles as officials also came into play. Elis was willing to play politics with its control of the Olympic festival – for example, excluding Spartan competitors as a consequence of a dispute over Eleian claims to Lepreon (see LICHAS) – and the HELLANODIKAI may have admitted some events to the programme as a favour to strong local contenders (Eleians won the inaugural competition in five events) and followed their bias in judging others (see EUPOLE-MUS, TROILUS). But nothing could make an Eleian a PERIODONIKĒS: they were excluded from the games at Isthmia.

Pausanias 5.2.2–5, 6.3.9, 16.2; Philostratus, *Life of Apollonius* 5.43.

N. B. Crowther, "Elis and the games", *AC* 57 (1988) 301–310; J. Roy, "Les cités d'Élide", in J. Renard (ed.) *Le Péloponnèse. Archéologie et histoire* (Rennes 1999) 151–176.

Empedocles, son of Exaenetus, of Agrigentum, equestrian victor, fifth century. Empedocles' horse won at Olympia in 496, the same festival at which his son Exaenetus was wrestling champion. He celebrated by feasting all those who attended; since he was a vegetarian, he divided an ox made up of spices among them. Empedocles was the grandfather of the famous philosopher.

Diogenes Laertius 8.51–53; Athenaeus 1.3E.

Enkrisis, examination to determine eligibility for a competitive festival or one of its AGE-CLASSES. The judges (*enkritai*) might use examination rooms (*enkritērioi oikoi*), and apparently voted to include (*enkrinein*) or exclude (*ekkritein*) competitors by secret ballot.

Xenophon, *Greek History* 4.1.40; Lucian, *For Images* 11; Artemidorus 1.59; IG 4 203.

D. R. Jordan, "Inscribed lead tables from the games in the sanctuary of Poseidon", *Hesperia* 63 (1994) 111–126 (111–115).

Enymacratidas *see* DAMONON

Epaenetus, of Argos, runner, first century. Epaenetus won the boys' *STADION* race at Olympia in 80 – the only event at that festival (see CORNELIUS Sulla).

Appian, *Civil War* 1.99.

Epaphroditus, Roman CHARIOTEER, late first century CE. Epaphroditus won 178 races for the Red CIRCUS FACTION as a slave and then, after being freed, eight more for the short-lived Purple faction established by the emperor Domitian.

ILS 5282.

Horsmann (1998) 202–203.

Epaphroditus, Pontius, Roman CHARIO-TEER, second century CE. Epaphroditus, a driver for the Blue CIRCUS FACTION in the time of the emperor Antoninus Pius (138–161 CE), is one of the famous predecessors and rivals mentioned on the memorial of DIOCLES (146 CE). He won 1,457 times, 909 in a field of four, 467 at the finish line, 134 with the African horse BUBALUS.

ILS 5287.

Horsmann (1998) 203–204.

Eperastus, son of Theogonus, Eleian runner, third century. The winner of the Olympic race in armour (perhaps in 292), Eperastus was a seer from the famous family of the Clytidae.

Pausanias 6.17.5.

Epharmostus, of Opus, wrestler, fifth century. Epharmostus was a PERIODO-NIKĒS in wrestling, winning at Olympia (468), at Delphi (466), three times at Isthmia and twice at Nemea.

Pindar, *Olympians* 9; *Oxyrhynchus Papyri* 222.

Ephebes (Greek *ephēboi*), "youths", young men just come of age who received military instruction in some Greek cities. At Athens, young men of eighteen and nineteen spent two years training (under the supervision of PAIDOTRIBAI) and doing garrison duty at the city's harbours and frontier fortifications. Teams of ephebes (and, at the THESEIA, ex-ephebes) represented their tribes in TORCH RACES at competitive festivals.

Xenophon, *Ways and Means* 4.51–52; Aristotle, *Constitution of the Athenians* 42.

Ephedros, a competitor who drew a bye in a combat event. Competitors were paired by lot. Whenever there were unequal numbers, one became *ephedros*. To win without the benefit of a bye (*anephedros*) was something to be proud of.

See also: LOT.

Lucian, *Hermotimus* 40; *IvO* 225.

N. B. Crowther, "Rounds and byes in Greek athletics", *Stadion* 18 (1992) 68–74.

Ephippios see HIPPIOS.

Ephotion, or Ephoudion, of Maenalus, pancratiast, fifth century. A PERIODO-NIKĒS in *pankration* (his Olympic victory came in 464), Ephotion was remembered (at least in comedy) for a match he fought against Acondas. Though older and white-haired, he cut a fine figure with his strong hands, good body and firm flanks.

Aristophanes, *Wasps* 1190–1194, 1382–1385.

Epichares, of Athens, runner, fourth century. The nephew of the well known Athenian politician Aristocrates (one of the generals condemned to death after the Battle of Arginusae, 406), Epichares won the Olympic STADION race for boys, perhaps in 396. His grandson, another Epichares, recalls the victory with pride in a speech meant to impress a jury, some fifty years later.

Xenophon, *Greek History* 1.7.2; Demosthenes 58.66.

Epinician, victory song (Greek *epinikion*, from *nikē*, "victory"). Epinicians were commissioned by a winner at a Greek competitive festival (or by his friends or family) from a leading poet (SIMONIDES, IBYCUS, PINDAR, BACCHYLIDES); almost all surviving examples celebrate athletic or equestrian winners at the games of the PERIODOS, those of greatest interest to the scholars who collected and preserved them.

Epinicians were typically sung by a choir of young men at or shortly after the victor's homecoming – the effect (and expense) rivalled a modern operatic chorus; shorter versions may also have been presented at the festival itself. Useful as they may sometimes be for details of particular competitions and their rules, epinicians are most valuable for the picture they provide of the elements of victory: natural ability (and the equestrian owner's sagacity in identifying it), hard work and expense, luck (the contribution of the gods). The very existence of the genre testifies to victory's value. Public presentations of epinicians were never encouraged at SPARTA; they went out of fashion elsewhere after the mid-fifth century, but were revived by exceptional champions (ALCIBIADES) and poets (CAL-

LIMACHUS, POSIDIPPUS) as late as the Hellenistic period.

M. R. Lefkowitz, *The Victory Ode: An Introduction* (Park Ridge NJ 1976); Golden (1998) 76–88.

Episkyros, "stone chip", a BALL game in which teams try to force each other over an end line by throwing a ball over their opponents' heads. It was played by youths at SPARTA as part of their transition to the status of adult warriors. The game is named for the stone chips (*skyroi*) which separated the teams; it is also called *ephēbikē*, "EPHEBE ball", and *epikoinos*, "team ball".

Pollux 9.104.

N. M. Kennell, *The Gymnasium of Virtue. Education and Culture in Ancient Sparta* (Chapel Hill 1995) 59–63.

Epistatēs (plural *epistatai*), "overseer", Greek term for TRAINER or gladiatorial instructor (Latin DOCTOR).

M. Carter, "A *doctor secutorum* and the *retiarius* Draukos from Corinth", ZPE 126 (1999) 262–268 (262–265).

Epitherses, son of Metrodorus, Erythraean boxer, second century. Panathenaic boxing champion among the AGENEIOI about 190, Epitherses became a PERIODONIKĒS as an adult. His two Olympic victories may date to 184 and 180; he may have won twice at the other games of the PERIODOS.

Pausanias 6.15.6; *IvO* 186; *IG* 2² 2313.

Eques (plural *equites*), "horseman, knight", type of mounted GLADIATOR, clad in scale armour or a tunic and carrying a round shield. *Equites* usually began their fights on horseback with lances and finished on foot with swords. They wore no greaves.

Cicero, *For Sestius* 59.126; Isidore, *Etymologies* 18.53.

Mosci Sassi (1992) 99–101.

Ergoteles, son of Philanor, of Himera, runner, fifth century. Driven from his home at Cnossus on Crete by civil strife as a young man, Ergoteles came to Himera on Sicily, where he was given citizenship and many other honours. It was understandable, then, that he chose to be proclaimed as a native of Himera when he twice became PERIODONIKĒS in DOLICHOS (first winning at Olympia in 476).

Pindar, *Olympians* 12; Pausanias 6.4.11; *SEG* 11.1223a; *Oxyrhynchus Papyri* 222.

Moretti (1987) 68.

Eryxias, trainer, sixth century. When ARRICHION was on the point of giving in during his attempt at a third successive *pankration* championship at Olympia (in 564), Eryxias inspired him to continue until victory and death. He is the earliest datable trainer we hear of.

Philostratus, *On Athletic Exercise* 21.

Essedarius (plural *essedarii*), type of GLADIATOR who fought in the guise of a Celtic war-charioteer.

Cicero, *Letters to Friends* 7.10.2; Suetonius, *Claudius* 21.6.

Mosci Sassi (1992) 101–102.

Etruscans, people who dominated central Italy (including Rome) for half a millennium from about 1000. They influenced many aspects of Roman life (the toga was Etruscan dress) and also served as a conduit for Greek culture (the Latin alphabet is derived from an Etruscan modification of the Greek). Etruscan tombs contain a rich panorama of paintings and grave goods related to competitive activity, perhaps linked to FUNERAL GAMES for men and women of the elite. Among athletes, boxers abound, though there are regional differences. Some (such as wrestlers at Chiusi) are nude, others INFIBULATED; on some Greek vases meant for the major Etruscan market athletes have had loincloths (PERIZŌMATA) painted on after firing. Boxers fought to the accompaniment of the AULOS, a means to impart rhythm or encourage ardour. There is evidence as well for the distinctive events of the pentathlon, discus, javelin, jump (with the aid of the ANKYLĒ and HALTĒRES, as in Greece), perhaps for a pole vault too. Equestrian events are particularly popular, though a mix of riding and running (like ANABATĒS or KALPĒ?) is more common than horse-racing and two- and three-horse chariots than four. Jockeys sometimes wear coloured tunics and pointed caps – precursors of the CIRCUS FACTIONS?–, charioteers wrap and knot the reins around their midriffs and carry a knife, all in the manner of Roman drivers. Both Etruscan favourites feature in the tradition that L. Tarquinius Priscus, the Etruscan ruler of Rome in the late seventh and early sixth centuries, inaugurated the CIRCUS MAXIMUS with horses and boxers from Etruria. Tomb paintings show men and women watching from covered stands; the competitors themselves were likely slaves, dependants of great families or others of low status. This is Roman, not Greek; but the panEtruscan festival for Tinia (a Zeus/Jupiter analogue), at Fanum Volturnae near Orvieto recalls Olympia, though we know nothing of its programme. However, the game (if that's what it is) of Phersu has no classical parallel: a masked figure (Phersu) puts a dog on a man who defends himself blindly with a club, his head hidden in a sack.

Herodotus 1.167.1–2; Livy 1.35.8.

J.-P. Thuillier, *Les jeux athlétiques dans la civilisation étrusque* (Rome 1985); Thuillier (ed.) *Spectacles sportifs et scéniques dans le monde étrusco-italique* (Paris 1993); H. A. Shapiro, "Modest athletes and liberated women: Etruscans on Attic black-figure vases", in B. Cohen (ed.) *Not the Classical Ideal* (Leiden 2000) 313–337.

Eu ... , equestrian victor, third century. Only the first syllable of the name of this three-time winner of the Olympic chariot race is legible on the newly discovered papyrus of POSIDIPPUS's epigrams.

Posidippus, *P.Mil.Vogl.* 8 309.XII.16–19.

Euagoras 1. of Elis, chariot champion, fifth century. Euagoras won the two-horse chariot race (*synōris, biga*) at its first running at the Olympic festival in 408.

Xenophon, *Greek History* 1.2.1; Pausanias 5.8.10; *IG* 2² 2326.

2. of Sparta, chariot victor, (?) sixth century. Like CIMON of Athens, Euagoras won three successive Olympic chariot races with the same mares, perhaps in the mid-sixth century (? 548–540). He gave his horses an elaborate burial and omitted any human representation in the statue he dedicated at Olympia.

Herodotus 6.103.4; Pausanias 6.10.8; Aelian, *Characteristics of Animals* 12.40.

Euancritus, son of Triax, Theban pancratiast, third century. Euancritus was a *pankration* champion in three AGE-CLASSES in the early third century; as a boy and an AGENEIOS at Isthmia, as an adult at Nemea.

IG 7 2470.

Ebert (1972) 169–172.

Euandria, "manliness", team competition at Athenian festivals. Athens's ten civic tribes competed in *euandria* at the PA-NATHENAEA and THESEIA. Prizes at the Panathenaea were an ox and 100 drachmas (to be shared among the victors' tribe) and shields (for the actual competitors). Just what was involved is unclear: suggestions include a tug-of-war, a dance and mock combat with two shields, and a chorus in which the front rank was chosen for good looks.

Aristotle, *Constitution of the Athenians* 60.3; *IG* 2² 956, 957, 2311.

A. L. Boegehold, "Group and single competitions at the Panathenaia", in J. Neils (ed.) *Worshipping Athena. Panathenaia and Parthe-*

non (Madison 1996) 95–105 (97–103); Reed (1998) 31–37.

Euanoridas, of Elis, wrestler and HELLA-NODIKAS, third century. Euanoridas won wrestling for boys at both Olympia (? 240) and Nemea and later served as an Olympic HELLANODIKAS, carrying on PARABALLON's plan of listing victors. He may have been the man of the same name who was among the high-ranking Eleians captured in the war against the Achaean Confederacy (218).

Polybius 5.94.6; Pausanias 6.8.1; *IvO* 299.

Euanthes, of Cyzicus, boxer, undated. Olympic champion as an adult, Euanthes had earlier outboxed the boys at both Nemea and Isthmia.

Pausanias 6.4.10.

Eubatas 1. of Cyrene, runner and chariot champion, fifth/fourth century. Told by an oracle that he would win at Olympia, Eubatas had his STATUE made beforehand and so dedicated it the same day he became STADION champion in 408. He returned to Cyrene with a painting of the famous *hetaira* Lais: he'd promised to marry her but wished neither to break training before the event nor fulfill his agreement afterwards, and brought the painting home instead. Another statue now entered the picture, one his wife made as testimony to his self-restraint. Forty years on, Eubatas won again at Olympia, in the chariot race.

Xenophon, *Greek History* 1.2.1; Pausanias 6.8.3; Aelian, *Historical Miscellany* 10.2.

2. of (?) Messenia, equestrian victor, third century. Eubatas's Aethon, "Blazing", won four horse races at the Nemean and two at the Pythian games.

Posidippus, *P.Mil.Vogl.* 8 309.XIII.27–30.

Euexia, "good health, vigour", a Greek gymnasium competition, often associated with EUTAXIA and PHILOPONIA. Winners (who might include adult men as well as boys and youths) were chosen for their fit and healthy appearance. At Beroea, the judges were three local residents chosen by lot; the prize (as at Sestos too) was a shield.

*SIG*³ 1060–1062; *SEG* 46.730.

N. B. Crowther, "Male 'beauty' contests in Greece: the *euandria* and *euexia*", *AC 54* (1985) 285–291.

Eumastus, son of Critobolus, strong man, sixth century. A black volcanic rock found on the island of Thera bears the inscription "Eumastus son of Critobolus lifted me from the ground". The rock is about 2m (6 feet) in circumference and weighs about 480kg (1,050lbs).

See also: BYBON.

IG 12.3 449.

N. B. Crowther, "Weightlifting in antiquity: achievement and training", *G&R* 24 (1977) 111–120 (111–112).

Eupolemus, or Eupolis, of Elis, athlete, fourth century. Twice victor in pentathlon at Delphi and once at Nemea, Eupolemus finished first in the STADION at Olympia in 396 – or so two of the Eleian HELLA-NODIKAI saw it. The other declared Leon of Ambracia winner. Leon appealed to the Olympic Council, which fined Eupole-mus's supporters, but it was Eupolemus whose victory statue Pausanias found in the ALTIS.

Diodorus 14.54.1; Pausanias 6.3.7, 8.45.4; *Oxyrhynchus Papyri* 2381.

N. B. Crowther, " '*Sed quis custodiet ipsos custodes?*' The impartiality of the Olympic judges and the case of Leon of Ambracia", *Nikephoros* 10 (1997) 149–160.

Eupolus, of Thessaly, boxer, fourth century. Eupolus was caught bribing his rivals in the boxing event at Olympia in 388 (including the reigning champion, PHORMION). This was the first such scandal, and the earliest monitory statues of

Zeus, ZANES, were set up with the fines they paid.

Pausanias 5.21.2–3; *IvO* 637.

Euprepes, Roman CHARIOTEER, second/third century CE. Having won more races than any other driver (? 3,782), Euprepes was put to death by the emperor Cara-calla (in ? 211CE) in his old age because he favoured a different CIRCUS FACTION.

Cassius Dio 78 (77).1.2.

Horsmann (1998) 208–209.

Euripides, son of Mnesarchides, Athenian tragic playwright, about 484–406. A pro-phecy foretold that Euripides would win crowns, so his father trained him as an athlete and tried, unsuccessfully, to enter him for the boys' wrestling at Olympia (he was too old). It is said that he did win at the Eleusinia and THESEIA before turn-ing to drama, and more reliably, that he was the author of a poem in praise of ALCIBIADES' Olympic chariot triumph (416).

Euripides 755, 756, *PMG*; Aulus Gellius 15.20.2–3.

M. F. Lefkowitz, *The Lives of the Greek Poets* (Baltimore and London 1981) 163–169; A. Iannucci, "Euripide (satiresco) e gli 'sportivi': note di lettura a Eur. fr. 282 N.²", *Quaderni del Dipartimento di filologia, linguistica e tradi-zione classica* (Turin) 11 (1998) 31–48.

Euripus, "strait, moat", the barrier divid-ing the track of the Roman CIRCUS. The *euripus* was laid out at a slight angle to the long sides of the circus in order to allow more room for chariots as they passed on the right of the near META at the start of a race. At the CIRCUS MAX-IMUS, the *euripus* was 335m long and bore a number of structures. These in-cluded a series of basins (hence the barrier's name), lap-counting devices (se-ven dolphins on the end closest to the CARCERES, turned whenever the lead char-iot rounded the near meta, seven eggs at the far end, which were lowered one by one), an Egyptian obelisk, 28m high, moved and erected by Augustus, at the mid-point (Constantius set up a second obelisk at the centre of the circus as a whole in 357 CE), a statue of the goddess Cybele mounted on a lion (and flanked by a tree), and several altars, statues and pavilions.

Cassius Dio 49.43.2; Varro, *On Agriculture* 1.2.11; Livy 41.27.6; Tertullian, *On Spectacles* 8; Isidore, *Etymologies* 18.31; *CIL* 6.710.

J. H. Humphrey, *Roman Circuses. Arenas for Chariot Racing* (London 1986) 174–294.

Eurybatus, of Sparta or Lousoi (Arcadia), wrestler, eighth century. The first Olympic wrestling winner (in 708), Eurybatus was likely one of the Spartans so prominent in our records of early victors at Olympia.

Pausanias 5.8.7; Philostratus, *On Athletic Exercise* 12.

Eurybiades (or Sybariades) of Sparta, chariot victor, fourth century. Eurybiades was the winner of the first chariot race for colts (*PŌLOI*) at Olympia, in 384.

Pausanias 5.8.10; *IG* 2² 2326.

Euryleonis, of Sparta, chariot victor, fourth century. Euryleonis followed in the footsteps of her compatriot CYNISCA (and her horses), winning the two-horse chariot race at Olympia (perhaps in 368). Her statue stood at Sparta.

Pausanias 3.17.6.

Eurymenes, of Samos, combat athlete, sixth century. A victor in one of the HEAVY events, perhaps in 532, Eurymenes is said to have been the first athlete to follow a meat DIET in training, under the care of the famous philosopher Pythagoras. Others attribute the innovation to DROMEUS (1) of Stymphalus.

Porphyry, *Life of Pythagoras* 15.

Eusebeia, Greek-style competitive festival. Established (perhaps in 142 CE) by the emperor Antoninus Pius in honour of

HADRIAN, his adopted father, the Eusebeia was held every four years at Puteoli. Including at least athletic, literary and musical competitions – horse and chariot races are not attested – it joined the Actia, Sebasta and Capitolia as the most important Greek-style competitive festivals founded by the Romans.

Artemidorus 1.26; *Historia Augusta, Hadrian* 27.3; *IG* 14 737.

Caldelli (1993) 43–45.

Eutaxia, or *eutaktia*, "good order, discipline", a Greek gymnasium competition, often associated with EUEXIA and PHILOPONIA. A gymnasium's best behaved boy or young man was awarded a prize (a shield at Beroea and Sestos) by the gymnasiarch. At Athens, the prize may have been provided for and by members of each of the ten civic tribes.

IG 2² 417, *SIG*³ 1061, *SEG* 46.730.

N. B. Crowther, "*Euexia, eutaxia, philoponia*: three contests of the Greek gymnasium", *ZPE* 85 (1991) 301–304.

Eutelidas, of Sparta, athlete, seventh century. Eutelidas won both the wrestling competition and the first and only pentathlon for boys at Olympia in 628. He was one of the few successful pentathletes who was not primarily a runner.

Pausanias 5.9.1, 6.15.8; *IG* 2² 2326.

Euthycles, of Locri (Italy), pentathlete, fifth century. A victor in the Olympic pentathlon (perhaps in 488), Euthycles later served as an ambassador and returned home with mules, gifts from a foreign friend. The Locrians, thinking them a bribe, threw him into prison, where he died, and mutilated his statue in the AGORA. An ensuing famine ended only when the Locrians honoured the statue like Zeus's image and made an altar for Euthycles' worship as a HERO.

Callimachus fragments 84–85 Pfeiffer; Eusebius, *Preparation for the Gospel* 5.34.

Moretti (1987) 68.

Euthymenes, of Maenalus, wrestler, fifth/ fourth century. Euthymenes was twice wrestling champion at Olympia, as a boy (? 400) and as an adult (? 392).

Pausanias 6.8.5.

Euthymus, son of Astycles, of Locri (Italy), boxer, fifth century. A rival of the great THEOGENES, and three-time champion at Olympia in his own right (484, 476, 472), Euthymus is one of several HEAVY athletes to receive worship as a HERO. Like others too, his career attracted tall tales. On his way home to Locri, Euthymus called in at Temesa to find the citizens at the mercy of an angry ghost. One of Odysseus's sailors, it had raped a local girl and been stoned to death; ever since, it had exacted vengeance from the Temesans and now claimed the most beautiful girl in town as its due each year. Euthymus donned armour, drove the ghost into the sea, and married the girl. When lightning struck his statues at Olympia and Locri on the same day, the oracle at Delphi advised he be worshipped. Some said he was the son of a god, the river Caecinus.

Strabo 6.1.5; Pausanias 6.6.4–11; Aelian, *Historical Miscellany* 8.18; *IvO* 144; Pliny, *Natural History* 7.47.152.

F. Costabile, *I ninfei di Locri Epizefiri* (Soveria 1991) 195–215; B. Currie, "Euthymos of Locri: a case study of heroization in the classical period", *JHS* 122 (2002) 24–44.

Exaenetus, of Agrigentum, runner, fifth century. After winning the Olympic STADION race in 416, Exaenetus celebrated his repeat victory at the following festival by entering the city in a procession which included 300 chariots, each drawn by two white horses – evidence of Agrigentum's great wealth.

Diodorus 12.82.1, 13.34.1, 82.7.

F

Factiones see CIRCUS FACTIONS

Familia (plural *familiae*), "household", term used to describe the group of GLA-DIATORS owned by a *LANISTA* and the drivers and horses of stables attached to a Roman CIRCUS FACTION.

Petronius, *Satyricon* 45; ILS 5083, 5084a, 5163, 5313.

Felix, Roman charioteer, first century. At Felix's funeral, a distraught devotee of his Red CIRCUS FACTION threw himself on his pyre in grief – an act attributed by fans of other factions to the effects of scents, incense and anything but sense.

Pliny, *Natural History* 7.54.186.

Horsmann (1998) 218.

Ferula (plural *ferulae*), "rod, cane", used to symbolize the agreement of a free man (*AUCTORATUS*) who chose to serve as a GLADIATOR to submit to the same terms and treatment as his fellow fighters.

Seneca, *Apocolocyntosis* 9.3.

Mosci Sassi (1992) 104–105.

Flamma, GLADIATOR. A *SECUTOR*, Flamma was a Syrian who fought thirty-four times – winning twenty-one fights, drawing nine, and receiving MISSIO on four occasions. After his death at thirty, a fellow gladiator, Delicatus, erected his tombstone.

ILS 5113.

Flavian Amphitheatre *see* COLOSSEUM

Flavius Archibius, Titus, of Alexandria, HEAVY athlete, first/second century CE. A *pankration* champion among the boys at Nemea and the AGENEIOI at the Pythian and CAPITOLINE games (in 94 CE), Archibius went on to a successful adult career which included two *pankration* crowns at both Olympia (101, 105) and Delphi and three at both Nemea and the Capitolia. He was also victorious as a wrestler and once won all three HEAVY events at the BALBILLEIA at Ephesus before serving as a high priest of the GUILD of athletes.

IG 14 747.

Moretti (1953) 186–191.

Flavius Artemidorus, Titus, son of Artemidorus, of Adana, HEAVY athlete, first century CE. A *PERIODONIKĒS* mentioned by the poet Martial as a model of strength, Artemidorus won *pankration* twice at Olympia (perhaps in 85 and 89), twice at both the Pythian and Nemean games, and once (as an *AGENEIOS*) at the Isthmian, as well as at the first celebration of the CAPITOLIA in 86. His numerous other victories include one as a wrestler.

Martial 6.77.3; IG 14 746.

Moretti (1953) 183–186.

Flavius Hermogenes, Titus, of Xanthus, runner, first century CE. Hermogenes, nicknamed Hippos, "the horse", won eight Olympic running events, including the STADION race in 81 and 89. He also won five times at the Pythian games, nine times at both the Isthmian and the Nemean, and likely at the first celebration of the CAPITOLIA at Rome in 86, a feat for which he may have been awarded Roman citizenship. Hermogenes also enjoyed the honour of being XYSTARCHĒS for life of all the games in his native Lycia.

Pausanias 6.13.3; Eusebius, *Chronicon* 1.215 Schoene.

Moretti (1987) 76.

Flavius Metrobius, Titus, son of Demetrius, of Iasus, runner, first century CE. A PERIODONIKĒS in DOLICHOS, Metrobius claimed some 120 victories, including one at the first celebration of the CAPITOLIA in 86, one at Olympia in 89, and others in all five cities which held the KOINA ASIAS.

Ilasos 107–109.

Moretti (1953) 181–183; (1987) 76; C. Habicht, "Titus Flavius Metrobios, Periodonike aus Iasos", in P. Kneissl and V. Losemann (eds) *Imperium Romanum: Festschrift für Karl Christ zum 75. Geburtstag* (Stuttgart 1998) 311–316.

Flavius Theodotus, Titus, son of Numenius, of (?) Nicopolis, athlete, first century CE. Theodotus was twice PERIODONIKĒS in an unknown event in the mid-first century.

Moretti (1987) 88.

Florus, Roman CHARIOTEER, uncertain date. Florus, a boy apprentice who fell from a two-horse chariot (BIGA) in practice and was killed, was commemorated by his teacher Januarius.

ILS 5300.

Horsmann (1998) 221.

Fortunatus, Roman CHARIOTEER, early second century CE. Driving for the Green CIRCUS FACTION, Fortunatus won 386 times with the famous horse Tusco and earned a prize of 50,000 sesterces nine times.

ILS 5287.

Horsmann (1998) 221–222.

Fulvius Nobilior, Marcus, Roman politician and commander, third/second century. Consul (189) and patron of the poet Ennius, Fulvius celebrated a successful campaign in Aetolia by ten days of games (186). These included hunts of lions and panthers and the first Roman appearance of Greek athletes in a traditional festival format, naked and competing in characteristic events such as pentathlon.

Livy 39.22.2.

J.-P. Thuillier, "Le programme 'athlétique' des *ludi circenses* dans la Rome républicaine", *REL* 60 (1982) 105–122; N. B. Crowther "Greek games in Republican Rome", *AC* 52 (1983) 268–273.

Funeral games, competitions accompanying the burial or cremation of a prominent figure in literature or life. Depicted (it may be) in the Bronze Age art of the MYCENAEANS, funeral games were celebrated for a number of HEROES of Greek myth (among others, ACHILLES, Oedipus, Paris, Pelias). The most famous are those for Patroclus in Homer's *Iliad*, in which his great friend Achilles acts as AGŌNOTHETĒS and the Greeks move from murderous battle with their Trojan enemies to bloodless competition among themselves; the games end with a reconciliation between Achilles and King Agamemnon which presages the end of Achilles' wrath against the Trojans too at the poem's close. This became a model for later epics (the games for Anchises in Virgil's *Aeneid*, in which a long boat race substitutes for Homer's chariots, for OPHELTES in the *Thebaid* of Statius, for Scipio's father in Silius Italicus's *Punica*), as well as for those ALEXANDER III provided his beloved Hephaestion. (All four games of the original PERIODOS are sometimes said to have originated in funeral games, the Olympics for PELOPS, the Pythian games for Python, the Isthmian for MELICERTES/Palaemon, the Nemean for OPHELTES.) Patroclus's games also displayed traits of historical Greek funeral games, such as the valuable prizes to attract the best competitors (in the *Iliad*, these include Odysseus and Ajax) and so to honour the dead all the more. Some such games were celebrated by private citizens until at least the fifth century. Others were public memorials for leaders and benefactors, often long repeated as part of the community's regular festival schedule. So the citizens of the Thracian Chersonese honoured their founder Miltiades, the Amphipolitans their defender, the Spartan Brasidas, Timoleon of Corinth earned funeral games at Syracuse, and the Achaean commander PHILOPOEMEN at Messene. At Athens, the public honours accorded those who died in battle each year included competitions (*epitaphios agōn*, Epitaphia). Instituted perhaps after the Battle of Plataea (479), these featured a torch race and a race in armour which began at the public monument for those killed in war. Winners received a prize attested for other funeral games: bronze vessels.

Homer, *Iliad* 23.257–897; Hesiod, *Works and Days* 654–659; Herodotus 6.38.1; Thucydides 5.11.2; Aristotle, *Constitution of the Athenians* 58.1; IG 1³ 523–525; IG 2² 1006, 1011, 2997–2999; SIG³ 624; Virgil, *Aeneid* 5.104–603; Statius, *Thebaid* 6.296–946; Silius Italicus, *Punica* 16.275–591.

L. Malten, "Leichenspiel und Totenkult", *MDAI(R)* 38–39 (1923–1924) 300–340; L. Roller, "Funeral games for historical persons", *Stadion* 7 (1981) 1–18; "Funeral games in Greek art", *AJA* 85 (1981) 107–119.

Fuscina (plural *fuscinae*), the trident used as a weapon by the RETIARIUS.

Juvenal 2.143; Suetonius, *Caligula* 30.3.

Mosci Sassi (1992) 105.

Fuscus, Roman charioteer, first century CE. First of all drivers (so says his memorial, erected in 35 CE) to win on his first day, Fuscus went on to place first in fifty-three races at Rome before dying at twenty-four. He drove for the Green CIRCUS FACTION.

ILS 5278.

Horsmann (1998) 222–223.

G

ILS 5117.

Gaius *see* HYPSICLES

Galata, Roman chariot horse, early second century CE. Galata was one of the horses who won 445 times for DIOCLES.

ILS 5287.

Galerus (plural *galeri*), leather or metal shoulder-piece worn in place of a shield by RETIARII.

Juvenal 8.207–208.

Mosci Sassi (1992) 105–106.

Gallus see MURMILLO

Gelon, son of Deinomenes, Sicilian tyrant and chariot victor, died 478/7. Tyrant of Gela from about 491, Gelon allied with THERON of Acragas (whose daughter he married), seized control of Syracuse, and soon commanded the most powerful military force in Greece. Like THERON and his brother HIERON, Gelon demonstrated his wealth and good fortune to mainland Greeks by equestrian success, winning the chariot race at Olympia in 488. It may have been Gelon who convinced ASTYLUS to run as a citizen of Syracuse rather than his native Croton.

Pausanias 6.9.4–5; *IvO* 143.

Generosus, GLADIATOR. Generosus, an Alexandrian, is described as undefeated as a RETIARIUS in twenty-seven fights.

Gerenus, of Naucratis, wrestler, ? third century CE. Successful at Olympia (? in 209), Gerenus partied for two days in celebration. Though he was short of sleep and out of sorts, his TRAINER insisted he carry on as usual. Gerenus died in the middle of his workout – an example (says PHILOSTRATUS) of the dangers of the tetrad training system.

Philostratus, *On Athletic Exercise* 54.

Germanicus Caesar, adopted son of TIBERIUS and father of the emperor Caligula (Gaius), of Rome, chariot victor, first century CE. Born in 16 or 15 BCE, Germanicus in 17 CE became an Olympic chariot champion like Tiberius before him.

Eusebius, *Chronicon* 1.213 Schoene; *IvO* 221.

Gigas, Roman CHARIOTEER, first century CE. Gigas drove two-horse teams (BIGAE) of the Green CIRCUS FACTION to victory twenty-six times.

ILS 5280.

Horsmann (1998) 223–224.

Gladiator (plural *gladiatores*), "swordsman", fighter in a Roman gladiatorial show (MUNUS). Most gladiators were slaves, condemned (by masters or magistrates) *ad* LUDOS for serious crimes, or prisoners captured in war. Some, however, were free men, even citizens from the elite, motivated by the need for money or the desire for adventure. Emperors too might choose to fight in the AMPHITHEATRE – Caligula (as a THRAEX), Macrinus, COMMODUS (said to have been assassinated because he wished to be invested as consul in gladiatorial garb).

Some women (including those of high status) served as gladiators. Givers of games (MUNERARII) sought to please spectators with other unusual fighters such as black Africans and dwarves as well. All had to swear the gladiator's oath – to be burnt (branded like a slave), chained, killed by an iron weapon – and share his social and civil disgrace (infamia). Gladiators entered service as novices (NOVICII), were identified as rookies (TIRONES) before their first bout, then fought as VETERANI. Most specialized in one kind of combat, being trained as RETIARII, SAMNITES, THRAECES, MURMILLONES or other less common types of gladiator, and regularly claimed that identity on their tombstones. However, a few, like the versatile HERMES (1), mastered more than one discipline. Gladiators were ranked, and their services valued by their owners, according to their success as well as their experience (see PALUS).

Some gladiators (most famously SPARTACUS) revolted. Terrible as their fate was, however, it bore comparison to those of other slaves, criminals or captives in a world in which living conditions were often grim and survival tenuous. Gladiators might win their bouts or be spared in defeat. (One fought thirty-seven times.) Victory brought rewards, from the symbolic palm leaf or crown to fame and riches. Simple survival might be enhanced by personal ties – gladiators' memorials mention wives, children, fellow-fighters. After three years, they could hope for retirement from combat; after five, for freedom. Some chose to re-enlist – they were slaves, but valuable slaves, reasonably well fed (at least before shows), able to consult physicians attached to their

gladiatorial FAMILIA. Others stayed on as trainers. Still others used their experience to work as bodyguards but maintained a link with their former lives and those who had shared it through associations (collegia) of retirees, much like the athletes to whom Greek gladiators liked to assimilate themselves.

Cicero, *For Sestius* 4.9; Petronius, *Satyricon* 117; Quintilian, *Declamations* 9.21, 302; Tacitus, *Annals* 15.32; Suetonius, *Vitellius* 12; Pliny, *Letters* 10.31.2; *Digest* 48.19.8.11.

L. Friedländer, *Roman Life and Manners under the Early Empire* (trans. A. B. Gough: London 1913) 4.171–181; T. Wiedemann, *Emperors and Gladiators* (London and New York 1992) 102–127; M. Junkelmann, *Das Spiel mit dem Tod: so Kämpften Roms Gladiatoren* (Mainz 2000).

Glaucon, son of Eteocles, Athenian politician and chariot victor, third century. A democratic leader and then (after the defeat of Athens in the Chremonidean War, 262/1) a high-ranking official in the court of the Ptolemies in Egypt, Glaucon won the Olympic chariot race, perhaps in 272. He also served as AGŌNOTHETĒS of the PANATHENAEA.

Pausanias 6.16.9; *IvO* 178, 296; *IG* 2² 3079.

Glaucus 1. GLADIATOR. A RETIARIUS from Modena in Northern Italy, Glaucus died at twenty-three in his eighth fight, "deceived by Nemesis", the goddess of fate whose shrine had a place in many AMPHITHEATRES. His memorial was erected by his wife Aurelia.

ILS 5121.

2. son of Dimylus, of Carystus, boxer, date uncertain. When Glaucus's father saw him hammer a ploughshare back into place with his bare fist, he realized his son had promise as a boxer and took him to Olympia. (The date may be 680 or, as usually thought, 520.) There he found more experienced boys as his opponents; he was about to give in to one when his father (or his TRAINER Tisias) shouted, "The ploughshare one!" Victorious,

Glaucus went on to win twice at Delphi and eight times each at Isthmia and Nemea, earning in the process a reputation for skill as well as strength. GELON later made him governor of Camarina on Sicily, where he was killed in a revolt.

Demosthenes 18.319; Pausanias 6.10.1–3; Lucian, *For Images* 19; Philostratus, *On Athletic Exercise* 20; Bekker, *Anecdota Graeca* 1.232; Scholiast on Aeschines 3.190; Quintilian 11.2.11–16.

Fontenrose (1968) 99–103.

Gloios, "gum", mixture of sweat and olive oil scraped off the bodies of those exercising or competing in gymnasia and baths, and collected and often sold for its medicinal properties.

Teles 41 Hense; Galen 12.283 Kühn; *SEG* 46.730; Pliny, *Natural History* 28.13.50–51.

N. M. Kennell, " 'Most necessary for the bodies of men': Olive oil and its by-products in the later Greek gymnasium", in M. Joyal (ed.) *In Altum. Seventy-five Years of Classical Studies in Newfoundland* (St John's 2001) 119–133 (128–133).

Glycon, Philippus, son of Asclepiades, Pergamene HEAVY athlete, first century. Styled "undefeated" by his contemporary Horace, "the glory of Asia, the thunderbolt of the *pankration*" by his funerary epigram, Glycon was apparently a triple threat in the heavy events. He was a champion in *pankration* at Isthmia, in wrestling (at the HERAEA (I) in ARGOS twice), perhaps in both as well as boxing at Olympia (? in 24), Delphi and the ACTIAN games.

Horace, *Epistles* 1.1.30–31; *Greek Anthology* 7.692; *Inscr.Perg.* 535.

Moretti (1953) 149–151; (1987) 73.

Gnathon, of Dipea (Arcadia), boxer, fifth century. The inscription on the base of his statue (seen by PAUSANIAS) stressed Gnathon's youth when he won the boxing for boys at Olympia (? in 440).

Pausanias 6.7.9.

Gorgus 1. of Elis, runner, (?) third century. Gorgus, the only man to win four Olympic pentathlons in a row, also won in *diaulos* and the race in armour.

Pausanias 6.15.9.

2. son of Eucletus, Messenian statesman and pentathlete, third century. Privileged by birth, wealth and personal beauty, Gorgus won the pentathlon event at Olympia (? in 232) and enough other crowns to become, according to the historian Polybius (his contemporary), the most famous athlete of his time. He was no less distinguished in public life – not a boor like so many athletes.

Polybius 5.5.4, 7.10.2–5; Pausanias 6.14.11.

Grammē (plural *grammai*), "line", the start or finish of a Greek foot- or horse race.

Pindar, *Pythians* 9.118–119; Euripides, *Electra* 955–956; Aristotle, *Nicomachean Ethics* 10.1174a34; Pollux 3.147.

N. B. Crowther, "The finish in the Greek footrace", *Nikephoros* 12 (1999) 131–142 (135–136).

Granianus *see* AELIUS GRANIANUS

Graus, of Bithynia, runner, third century CE. Graus (a NICKNAME) won the Olympic DOLICHOS three times in a row, perhaps in 213, 217 and 221.

Ancient Greek Inscriptions in the British Museum 609.

Gregarius (plural *gregarii*), "common man", criminal condemned to fight in the HARENA. The *gregarius* lacked the training and status of a GLADIATOR.

ILS 5163.

Guild (Greek *synodos*, plural *synodoi*), association of athletes. Attested from the mid-first century (first at Erythrae in Lydia), athletic guilds were likely modelled on associations of theatrical performers (and sometimes acted in concert or even shared an organization with them). An Ephesian association of winners in sacred crown games already carried enough weight to gain favours from the triumvir Marc Antony in 41 or 33/2, and local associations were soon widespread throughout the Greek east; there may have been an umbrella organization at Ephesus. Rome had an athletes' association from the mid-first century CE; perhaps first fostered by NERO, it grew in importance with the upsurge of Greek-style festival activity which inspired and followed the foundation of the CAPITO-LINE games in 86, and was granted a site (*curia athletarum*) with space for its cult and archives at that time or, as a result of the lobbying of M. ULPIUS Domesticus, by the emperor HADRIAN in 134; his promise was made good only after his death (in 143). This became the headquarters for a federation of local guilds, "the sacred xystic international association of those connected to Heracles". (The relationship between this term and the entire portico, *hē sympas* XYSTOS, is uncertain.) The federation was headed by imperial appointees, who generally served for life (and might hold more than one post): a high priest, a XYSTARCHĒS, a superintendent of the imperial baths. It remained active until the late fourth century CE. Athletic associations sought recognition and privileges for their members: relief from military service, billeting troops and other civic duties, the right to wear purple at festivals, the patronage of the powerful. In return, they founded and organized games in the emperor's honour. Athletes paid a fee to join and received certificates of membership.

IG 14 747, 1054, 1055, 1102; *P. London* 137, 1178.

H. W. Pleket, "Some aspects of the history of the ancient athletic guilds", *ZPE* 10 (1973) 197–227; W. C. West, "M. Oulpios Domestikos and the athletic synod at Ephesus", *AHB* 4 (1990) 84–89; M. L. Caldelli, "Curia athletarum, iera xystike synodos e organizzazione delle terme a Roma", *ZPE* 93 (1992) 75–87; U. Sinn, "Olympia und die *Curia athletarum* in Rom", *Stadion* 24 (1998) 129–135.

Gymnasiarch (Greek *gymnasiarchos*, plural *gymnasiarchoi*), official in charge of a GYMNASIUM. Since Greek cities boasted gymnasia wherever they were, the appointment and role of gymnasiarchs differed widely; in Athens, they were appointed by the ten civic tribes to oversee TORCH-RACE teams; on Sicily, some cities had dual gymnasiarchs who exercised political power. In general, however, a gymnasiarch had responsibility for the programme, upkeep and order of one or more of a community's gymnasia. Some were appointed and served as a form of taxation; others volunteered; gymnasiarchies might also be bought or inherited. They might serve for a festival, a few months, a year or more. In any case, gymnasiarchs came from the elite, and often supplemented the public funds available for the main expenses – olive OIL for athletes, fuel for baths – from their own resources; public-spirited and ambitious office-holders might take on improvements – extra oil, statues, new rooms. The gymnasiarch supposedly supervised the work of the gymnasium's staff (trainers, guards, barbers, clerks), sometimes with the aid of a subordinate *hypogymnasiarchos*. That the role was primarily financial is shown by the appointment of women and minors as gymnasiarchs; that it was an honour as well as a burden by numerous laudatory decrees and Marc Antony's appearance in the guise of a gymnasiarch (he carried a referee's rods and wore white shoes) at Athens. But failure to fulfill it or insistence on imposing strict discipline might incur hostility and legal liability.

Andocides 1.132; Plutarch, *Antony* 33.4; *Moral Essays* 754D, 755A; *IG* 5.2 46–48, 50; *SEG* 46.730.

P. J. Sijpesteijn, *Nouvelle liste des gymnasiarques des métropoles de l'Égypte romaine* (Zutphen 1986); P. Gauthier and M. B. Hatzopoulos, *La loi gynasiarchique de Beroia*

(Athens 1993); G. Cordiano, *La ginnasiarchia nelle "poleis" dell'occidente mediterraneo antico* (Pisa 1997).

Gymnasium (Greek *gymnasion*, plural *gymnasia*), Greek athletic complex. The earliest gymnasia – Athens's ACADEMY and LYCEUM – date from the early sixth century, developing at the same time as the circuit (PERIODOS) of panhellenic competitive festivals and in the wake of the ascendancy of heavy infantry (hoplite) warfare and the fellow-feeling and physical fitness it required. A "place for naked exercise" (from *gymnos*, "naked"), the gymnasium was essentially an enclosed courtyard with rooms attached (a PALAESTRA) and running tracks (a covered XYSTOS, an open PARADROMIS). Set as it often was in an ample park-like precinct dedicated to a god or HERO, and handy to shade and water, the gymnasium was also suitable for cavalry musters and manoeuvres (such as the ANTHIPPASIA). Though a public institution, the gymnasium was generally the preserve of a leisured elite, and many cities formally forbade access to outgroups; at Beroea in Hellenistic Macedonia, these included slaves, freed slaves and their sons, those involved in trade or convicted of prostitution, drunks and madmen. A community official, the GYMNASIARCH, was responsible for these and other rules. As in other areas of Greek life, gymnasiarchs and other members of the elite supplemented public funds and the money raised from the sale or lease of the gymnasium's property or from loans by initiating or supporting improvements – a tradition as old as the fifth-century Athenian political leader Cimon. From the fourth century, gymnasia became the site of still more activities, cultural and educational as well as athletic, and the entrepreneurial efforts of teachers such as Plato (at the Academy) and Aristotle (at the Lyceum), who used them as meeting places and sources of students, became institutionalized: gymnasia came to include lecture theatres and libraries. The gymnasium became a hallmark of Hellenic culture – the first use of the Greek word for "Hellenism" refers to a Jerusalem gymnasium. One of the grounds for PAUSANIAS's disdain for the claims of Panopeus in Phocis to the status of a *polis* was its lack of a gymnasium, and the Greek elite of Egypt was identified as *hoi apo tou gymnasiou*, "the gymnasial class". Many cities much smaller than Athens had several – Iasus in Caria no fewer than four – often catering to different age groups.

Antiphon 3.2.3; Xenophon, *Symposium* 2.4; Demosthenes 24.114; Pausanias 10.4.1; 2 *Maccabees* 4; Vitruvius, *On Architecture* 5.11.3–4; Isidore, *Etymologies* 8.6.17; *IG* 1^3 369, 383; *SEG* 46.730.

J. Delorme, *Gymnasion* (Paris 1960); S. L. Glass, "The Greek gymnasium: some problems", in Raschke (1988) 155–173; P. Gauthier and M. B. Hatzopoulos, *La loi gymnasiarchique de Beroia* (Athens 1993); J.-C. Moretti, "Le gymnase de Délos", *BCH* 120 (1996) 617–638.

Gymnastēs (plural *gymnastai*), athletic TRAINER. Aristotle and some later writers distinguish the *gymnastēs*, concerned with bodily workings and well-being, from the PAIDOTRIBĒS, an expert in athletic skills and techniques; Galen inveighs against the false claims of the *gymnastēs* in a manner echoed in modern turf wars between physicians and athletic therapists. It is doubtful how clear-cut this distinction really was: it is *gymnastai* who (says PAUSANIAS) were required to swear not to break the rules at Olympia and to attend nude after PHERENICE snuck into the festival disguised as her son's trainer.

Plato, *Laws* 4.720E; Aristotle, *Nicomachean Ethics* 10.1180b14; *Politics* 8.1338b9; Galen, *Exhortation* 12; Philostratus, *On Athletic Exercise* 14, 45.

Jüthner (1909) 3–8; Kyle (1987) 141–145.

Gymnastikos (plural *gymnastikoi*), athletic trainer, GYMNASTĒS.

Plato, *Gorgias* 464A; *Phaedrus* 248D; *Protagoras* 313D; *Statesman* 295C; Aristotle, *Politics* 4.1288b17.

H

Hadrian (Publius Aelius Hadrianus), Roman philhellene and emperor (117–138 CE), first/second century CE. Nicknamed "little Greek" as a youth, Hadrian fostered and founded competitive festivals when he became emperor. Most were in Asia Minor, but he showed special favour towards Athens: Hadrian founded three eiselastic crown games (Hadrianeia, Olympieia, Panhellenia) and promoted the PANATHENAEA to this status, giving Athens more than any other city. In all, some twenty-one cities added the designation "Hadrianic" to new or existing games; several others hosted festivals in honour of the emperor's boyfriend, Antinous. Hadrian supported the Greek athletic tradition in other ways, both large – funding the gymnasium at Smyrna, allowing the athletic GUILDS to establish headquarters at Rome – and small (he restored the boys' *hippios* at the Nemean games). His successor Antoninus Pius founded a new Greek-style competitive festival in his honour, the EUSEBEIA at Puteoli, only the third in Italy.

IG 2² 1102; *Historia Augusta, Hadrian* 19.2.

M. T. Boatwright, *Hadrian and the Cities of the Roman Empire* (Princeton 2000) 94–104.

Hagesistratus, son of Polycreon, of Lindus (Rhodes), wrestler, second century. Hagesistratus became the first Lindian to win the boys' wrestling at Olympia when he defeated three opponents without suffering a single fall (? in 172). His father Polycreon was wrestling champion among the AGENEIOI at Nemea.

IG 12.1 841; *ILindos* 699.

Ebert (1972) 214–217.

Hagias, son of Acnonius, of Pharsalus, pancratiast, fifth century. Hagias won in *pankration* once at Olympia (? 484) – the first Thessalian to do so –, three times at Delphi, five at Nemea, five at Isthmia. His son Daochus ruled Thessaly for twenty-seven years in the late fifth century. One brother, Telemachus, took crowns in wrestling on the same days as Hagias's – once killing his opponent; another, Agelaus, won STADION for boys at Delphi. All are commemorated in a group of statues dedicated by Hagias's great-grandson Daochus at Delphi (336–332).

*SIG*³ 274.

Ebert (1972) 137–145; W. Geominy, "Zum Daochos-Weihgeschenk", *Klio* 80 (1998) 369–402; A. Jacquemin and D. Laroche, "Le monument de Daochos ou le trésor des Thessaliens", *BCH* 125 (2001) 305–332.

Halieia, Rhodian competitive festival. Attested from the mid-fifth century, the Halieia (in honour of Helius, the sun god) was celebrated with special elaboration every four years after the amalgamation of Rhodes's cities in 408/7, and thereafter grew into the most prestigious of the island's several sets of contests. It attracted such successful competitors as the Alexandrian pancratiast M. AURELIUS Asclepiades. The full programme included musical, equestrian and athletic events, among them a TORCH race for men. The prizes, once bronze water jugs, became oil amphoras in the fourth century.

Pindar, *Olympians* 7.80 (with Scholiast); *IG* 12.1 75b, 935b, 1039; *SIG*^{3} 1067, *SEG* 40.669.

I. R. Arnold, "Festivals of Rhodes", *AJA* 40 (1936) 432–436; P. Angeli Bernardini, "Le Halieia di Rodi e lo scolio a Pind. O. 7,146ab (p. 229 Dr.)", *Stadion* 3 (1977) 1–3.

Halma see JUMP

Haltēr (plural *haltēres*), "jumping weight". The *haltēr* was a small stone or metal object (usually about 2kg [4½lbs]) shaped like a clothes iron, dumbbell or portable phone. Competitors in the JUMP carried one in each hand for balance, perhaps in the belief that they increased distance and improved landings. (It has also been suggested that they increased the event's difficulty and so the value of success, but this seems unlikely given the jump's rarity as an independent event.) *Haltēres* regularly identify athletes in Greek art – they are shown in the statue of AGŌN at Olympia – and were dedicated by victorious pentathletes. They were also used to exercise the shoulders, hands and fingers.

Aristotle, *On the Progression of Animals* 705a16; *Problems* 5.8.881b5; Pausanias 5.26.3; Philostratus, *On Athletic Exercise* 55; *IG* 1^3 988.

D. Knoepfler, "Haltère de bronze dédié à Apollon *Hékabolos* dans la collection G. Ortiz (Genève)", *CRAI* (1994) 337–379.

Harena (Latin "sand"), the sandy floor of the AMPHITHEATRE, the site of GLADIATORIAL and other shows.

Tacitus, *Annals* 14.14; Suetonius, *Nero* 53.

Mosci Sassi (1992) 111–112.

Heats, preliminary footraces. Fields in Greek competitive festivals could be large – eighty-seven competed in the pentathlon or a footrace at the SEBASTAN games at Naples in the third century CE – and tracks could accommodate only limited numbers of runners. (The HYSPLĒX at Olympia had room for twenty, but those at Corinth (seventeen), Isthmia (sixteen) and Priene (eight) smaller fields, and the *DIAULOS* may have used alternate lanes only.) Consequently, runners often had to run preliminary heats, a fact that made feats such as POLITES' victories in the *STADION* race, *DIAULOS* and *DOLICHOS* on the same day at Olympia all the more remarkable.

Pausanias 5.17.6, 6.13.3–4.

N. B. Crowther, "The number of contestants in Greek athletic contests", *Nikephoros* 6 (1993) 39–52.

Heavy events (Greek *barea*), term used for Greek sports (PANKRATION, WRESTLING, BOXING), either because they were difficult and dangerous or because they had no weight classes, so heavier competitors had an advantage. It is perhaps for this last reason that PHILOSTRATUS groups DISKOS with wrestling as the heavy events in the PENTATHLON. Successful heavy athletes such as MILON and THEOGENES were the most famous of ancient competitors and the most likely to attract worship as HEROES. But some members of the elite (at least in later antiquity) may have avoided heavy events because of the risk of disfigurement.

Plato, *Laws* 8.833D; Aeschines 3.179; Diodorus 4.14.2; Galen 6.487 Kühn; Philostratus, *On Athletic Exercise* 3.

M. W. Dickie, "*Palaistritēs/'palaestrita'*: callisthenics in the Greek and Roman gymnasium", *Nikephoros* 6 (1993) 105–151 (148–151).

Hecatomnus, of Miletus, runner, first century. Hecatomnus won *stadion*, *diaulos* and the race in armour at Olympia, 72.

Phlegon, *FGrH* 257 F12; Eusebius, *Chronicon* 1.211 Schoene.

Hedea *see* HERMESIANAX (2)

Heliodorus 1. or Trosidamas, of Alexandria, runner, third century CE. Heliodorus won two STADION races at Olympia, in 213 and 217 CE. The second is the last listed by AFRICANUS.

Eusebius, *Chronicon* 1.219 Schoene.

2. of Cos, wrestler, first century. An inscription discovered only in 1987 accompanied a statue the people of Cos set up for Heliodorus, who outwrestled four other boys at Olympia in the late first century.

SEG 43.555.

C. Habicht, "Neue Inschriften aus Kos", *ZPE* 112 (1996) 83–94 (93–94).

Hellanodikas (plural *Hellanodikai*), "judge of the Greeks", major official at panhellenic competitive festivals (ASCLEPIEIA (1) at Epidaurus, Nemea, Olympia). At Olympia, there was originally one AGŌNOTHETĒS in charge of the festival. Then, in 580, the Eleians selected two by LOT and later (likely after the amalgamation of ELIS in 471/0) nine *Hellanodikai*, three to supervise equestrian events, three for pentathlon and three for the others. The number was increased to ten shortly after and to twelve in 384, reduced to eight in 364, and restored to ten in 348 and subsequently. Each set of *Hellanodikai*, members of the Eleian elite, was responsible for one Olympic festival; they lived for ten months in the *Hellanodikaion*, a building in the AGORA at Elis. Distinctively dressed in purple robes and allowed the privilege of elevated seating (while others sat on the ground or stood), the *Hellanodikai* admitted or excluded competitors, assigned them to AGE-CLASSES, oversaw the training period, led the procession from Elis to Olympia (during which they addressed competitors and purified themselves), supervised pairings by lot, crowned winners and punished rule-breakers, and presided over the final feast. Their decisions could be appealed to the Olympic council; two were fined after awarding victory in STADION to their fellow Eleian, EUPOLEMUS (396). *Hellanodikai* were themselves eligible to compete until the chariot triumphs by TROILUS (372). In later antiquity, many (at least) of their duties were performed by ALYTARCHAI. At Nemea, the ten *Hellanodikai* wore black robes as a sign of mourning for OPHELTES.

Pindar, *Olympians* 3.9–16; Pausanias 5.9.5–6, 16.8, 24.10, 6.1.5–6, 3.7, 23.2–24.3; Lucian, *Hermotimus* 40; Philostratus, *On Athletic Exercise* 18, 54; *Life of Apollonius* 3.30; *IG* 4².1 98; *IvO* 2.

S. S. Slowikowski, "The symbolic *Hellanodikai*", *Aethlon* 7.1 (1989) 133–141.

Hēmitalantiaios *see* AGŌN

Hēniochos ekbibazōn, "charioteer dismounting", equestrian event in which a charioteer dismounted and re-entered his chariot.

IG 2² 2316.

Heracleia, name of a number of Greek competitive festivals in honour of HERACLES. That of Marathon outside Athens dates from the early fifth century. But perhaps the oldest and most famous was held at the hero's home town, Thebes, and mentioned in victory songs by the Theban poet PINDAR. In his time, it took place over two days, the first devoted to the pentathlon and equestrian competitions, the second to other athletic events. Under the empire, literary, musical and theatrical competitions were added, and the festival was known as the *Dionysia Heracleia*, *Dionysia Heracleia Antonineia*, *Commodeia Dionysia Heracleia* and *Heracleia Olympia*; its relationship to the Iolaeia for Heracles' sidekick Iolaus is unclear. Winners at the Heracleia (who included famous stars such as DIAGORAS of Rhodes) received a bronze tripod.

Pindar, *Olympians* 7.83–85; *IG* 1³ 3; *SEG* 11.338.

P. Roesch, "Les Hérakleia de Thèbes", *ZPE* 17 (1975) 1–7.

Heracles (Latin Hercules), Greek HERO and model athlete. The son of Zeus and a mortal woman, Alcmene, Heracles showed his strength at an early age by strangling two snakes Hera sent against him in his cradle – despite the proverb "Not even Heracles can take on two" – and later deployed it in his labours (ATHLOI), subduing beasts and monsters at the behest of King Eurystheus of Mycenae. These earned him the title athlete on behalf of human life and entry as a god into Olympus. The first pancratiast, Heracles was worshipped with the epithet Palaemon, "wrestler" – many of his labours involved hand-to-hand combat – and inspired later strongmen. Those who won both events on the same day at Olympia were "successors of Heracles" (*hoi aph'/meth' Hērakleous*), MILON sported his lion-skin and club in leading CROTON into battle, PULYDAMAS killed a lion in emulation of his first labour. This was sometimes thought to have led to the founding of the NEMEAN games, as Heracles' cleansing of the stables of King Augeas of Elis did the Olympics (his labours were the theme of sculptures on the Temple of Zeus). Competitive festivals (such as the HERACLEIA at Marathon and his hometown, Thebes) were held in his honour in turn and his statues frequently found in GYMNASIA and PALAESTRAE; GYMNASIARCHS at Beroea in Macedonia swore an oath in his name. At Rome, games for Hercules are attested for the first century. They may have been instituted by the dictator CORNELIUS Sulla and downgraded in importance after his death.

Hesiod, *Shield of Heracles* 301–313; Pindar, *Olympians* 3.9–38, 10.24–30; Bacchylides 13.46–57; Isocrates 10.23; Diodorus 12.9.5–6; Pausanias 6.5.5; Cassius Dio 80.10; Apollodorus 2.4.8–7.8; *SEG* 46.730.

P. Angeli Bernardini, "Mythe et agon: Héraclès fondateur des jeux olympiques", in R. Renson, M. Lämmer, J. Riordan and D. Chassiotis (eds) *The Olympic Games through the Ages: Greek Antiquity and its Impact on Modern Sport. Proceedings of the 13th International HISPA Congress, Olympia/Greece, May 22–28, 1989* (Athens 1991) 13–22; Golden (1998) 146–157; T. P. Wiseman, "The games of Hercules", in E. Bispham and C. Smith (eds) *Religion in Archaic and Republican Rome and Italy. Evidence and Experience* (Edinburgh 2000) 108–114.

Heraclides *see* APOLLONIUS RHANTES

Heraea 1. festival at ARGOS.

2. festival at Olympia, said to have been founded by Hippodameia to thank Hera for her marriage to PELOPS.

Held, like the Olympics, every four years, and in the Olympic stadium, the Heraea involved footraces for three age-groups of girls, who ran 500 Greek feet (five-sixth of the male STADION). Runners let their hair loose, and wore a short tunic which reached to just above the knee and left the right shoulder bare as far as the breast. Winners received an olive wreath, a portion of the cow sacrificed to Hera, and the right to dedicate their portraits. Chloris, sole surviving daughter of the Theban heroine Niobe, is supposed to have been the first, but the competitions likely date to the 580s. A group of sixteen married women, two for each of ELIS's eight tribes, administered the festival. They also wove a robe for Hera in their building in the AGORA at Elis and managed two choral dances, for Hippodameia and for Physcoa, an early devotee of Dionysus.

Pausanias 5.16.2–8, 6.24.10.

N. Serwint, "Female athletic costume at the Heraia and prenuptial initiation rites", *AJA* 97 (1993) 403–422; J. Scheid and J. Svenbro, *The Craft of Zeus* (trans. C. Volk: Cambridge MA 1996) 10–15; Scanlon (2002) 98–120.

Herald *see* KĒRYX

Heras, of Laodicea, pancratiast, first century CE. "Bull-bellied, like a second

Atlas", Heras was *pankration* champion at Olympia (perhaps in 33) and gained other victories at Delphi, Corinth (in the Isthmian games), ARGOS (either the HERAEA (1) or the Nemean games), Actium, Smyrna and Pergamum.

Philip of Thessalonica, *Greek Anthology* 16.52.

Hercules *see* HERACLES

Hermas, son of Ision, of Antiochia (Syria), pancratiast, first century CE. A *PERIODONIKĒS*, Hermas won twice at both Olympia (perhaps in 25 and 29 CE) and Nemea. He may be the Ti. Claudius Hermas who went along on an embassy to the emperor Claudius in 46 CE.

IvO 231.

Hermes 1. GLADIATOR, about 100 CE. The poet Martial praises Hermes as preeminent among the gladiators of his time, able to fight as a VELES, a SAMNIS or a *RETIARIUS*.

Martial 5.24.

2. Latin Mercurius ("Mercury"), son of Zeus and Maea, Greek god. Hermes' statues – like that of HERACLES – long graced GYMNASIA and PALAESTRAE, and his epithets identify him as a god of competition (*enagōnios*) and of wrestling (*palaistritēs*). Later authors credit him with the invention of wrestling – the god of thieves, he defeated Eros by stealing his legs from under him – and with a daughter Palaestra.

Simonides 50.1 West; Pindar, *Pythians* 2.10; *Isthmians* 1.60; Lucian, *Dialogues of the Gods* 7.3; Pausanias 4.32.1; Philostratus, *Pictures* 2.32.1; Athenaeus 13.561D; *Greek Anthology* 12.143, 16.188; *IG* 12.5 911.

Scanlon (2002) 250–255.

Hermesianax 1. son of Agoneus, Colophonian wrestler, fourth century. Hermesianax was boys' wrestling champion at Olympia (? 320), a feat matched by his son Lycinus's son Eicasius, perhaps in 256.

Pausanias 6.17.4.

2. son of Dionysius, of Tralles, proud father, first century CE. In 47 CE, Hermesianax set up a statue in honour of his three daughters, each a successful festival competitor. An honorary citizen of Athens and Delphi (where the statue stood), Hermesianax likely had no sons. Of his girls, Tryphosa is listed as first of the maidens (*parthenoi*) in the STADION race at the Pythian (twice) and Isthmian games. The versatile Hedea won the *stadion* race at Nemea and Sicyon, the chariot race in armor at Isthmia, and the contest for PAIDES in singing to the *kithara* at the Athenian Sebasteia. Dionysia won the *stadion* race at the ASCLEPIEIA (1) at Epidaurus and elsewhere. The equestrian and musical victories likely came in fields which included boys and men. This is much less likely for their triumphs on the track.

See also: WOMEN.

*SIG*³ 802.

H. M. Lee, "*SIG*³ 802: did women compete against men in Greek athletic festivals?", *Nikephoros* 1 (1988) 103–117.

Hero (Greek *hērōs*, plural *hērōes*), a man or women, legendary or real, worshipped after death, often at a shrine at or near a tomb and with rites like those for the dead. Heroes were linked with the founding of some important Greek competitive festivals (MELICERTES with Isthmia, OPHELTES with Nemea), and an important part of the ritual at others (as PELOPS was at Olympia). The connection continued into historical times: the people of Amphipolis regarded the Spartan general Brasidas as their city's founder and worshipped him as its saviour, with competitions in his honour after his death in battle. Some competitors were also treated as heroes after their death, including the SPARTAN equestrian princess CYNISCA and an otherwise unknown Macedonian athlete from the first century BCE or CE.

Most famous are the athletes (EUTHYCLES, EUTHYMUS, HIPPOSTHENES, OEBOTAS, PHILIPPUS (2), THEOGENES) who figure in a series of stories, often involving STATUES with special powers, which came into circulation in the early fifth century, perhaps as an elite response to internal or external threats; these tales influenced accounts of later heroized athletes (CLITOMACHUS, PULYDAMAS) as well. It is noteworthy that most of these were HEAVY athletes, bigger and stronger than most – as legendary heroes (such as Orestes) were usually thought to be.

Herodotus 1.68.3; Thucydides 5.11.1; *SEG* 40.1611.

Fontenrose (1968); F. Bohringer, "Cultes d'athlètes en Grèce classique: propos politiques, discours mythiques", *REA* 81 (1979) 5–18; L. Kurke, "The economy of kudos", in C. Dougherty and Kurke (eds) *Cultural Poetics in Archaic Greece. Cult, Performance, Politics* (Cambridge 1993) 131–163 (149–155).

Herod the Great, king of Judaea, Olympic benefactor, born *c.*73–4. On his way to Rome (probably in 12), Herod heard that the Olympic festival was in need of funds. He provided money for sacrifices and other ceremonies and established a fund for such costs in the future. In gratitude, the Eleians named him *AGŌNOTHETĒS* – not normally an Olympic designation – not just for that festival but forever. Herod also established quadrennial games in honour of AUGUSTUS to mark his rebuilding of Caesarea.

Josephus, *Jewish Antiquities* 16.136–140, 149; *Jewish War* 1.426–427.

H. W. Pleket, "Olympic benefactors", *ZPE* 20 (1976) 1–18.

Herodes Atticus (Tiberius Claudius Atticus Herodes), Athenian intellectual and philanthropist, *c.*101–177 CE. The richest Greek of his day, Herodes Atticus donated buildings all over the Greek world, including stadiums of white marble at Athens and Delphi. At Olympia, notoriously hot, dry, dusty and thronged, he saw to the provision of the first adequate supply of water, channels leading from a tributary of the Alpheius river to a monumental colonnade ("the Nymphaeum", "the exedra of Herodes Atticus") crowned by statues of Herodes himself, his wife (a priestess of Demeter at Olympia) and three Roman emperors: HADRIAN, Antoninus Pius, and his student, Marcus Aurelius. (Not everyone was pleased: Peregrinus, a rival intellectual, complained that the water would turn Greeks into women.) Herodes also celebrated FUNERAL GAMES in honour of Polydeucion, a family member who received worship as a HERO.

Lucian, *Demonax* 24; *Peregrinus* 19–20; Pausanias 1.19.6, 6.21.2, 10.32.1; *IG* 2² 3968.

L. Robert, "Deux inscriptions de l'époque impériale en Attique", *AJP* 100 (1979) 153–165 (160–165).

Herodorus, of Megara, trumpeter, fourth/third century. Herodorus won the trumpet competition (*SALPINKTĒS*) at Olympia from (perhaps) 328 through 292 – indeed, he was PERIODONIKĒS ten times. Though not particularly large, he had very strong ribs and could eat and drink a great deal (like famous athletes such as MILON), as well as play two trumpets at once. The sound of his blasts inspired Demetrius's soldiers at the siege of Argos.

Athenaeus 10.414F–415A; Pollux 4.89.

Herogeiton, of Magnesia on Maeander, runner, fourth/third century. As a boy, Herogeiton had a successful career around 300 – he won the STADION race at Delphi and Ephesus, HIPPIOS at Isthmia and the Panathenaea – but we hear nothing of later victories.

SEG 14.459.

Ebert (1972) 163–165.

Hetoemocles, of Sparta, wrestler, sixth century. Hetoemocles, like his father HIPPOSTHENES, was a repeat champion in wrestling at Olympia, winning five times from (?) 592 through 576, the first time probably as a boy.

Pausanias 3.13.9.

Hierocles, Roman CHARIOTEER, second/third century CE. Said to be a Carian slave by origin, Hierocles learned to be a charioteer from a lover, Cordius, and later became an intimate and influential adviser of the emperor Elagabalus (218–222 CE) at Rome (Cordius too was one of ELAGABALUS's circle.) He was killed after the emperor's murder.

Cassius Dio 79.15; *Historia Augusta, Elagabalus* 6.3–5, 15.2–4.

Hieromēnia see TRUCE

Hieron, son of Deinomenes, of Syracuse, equestrian victor, died 466. Ruler of Gela for his brother GELON (485–478), Hieron succeeded him as tyrant of Syracuse (478–466) and the leading power in Sicily. He was still more successful in equestrian competition, winning chariot races at Olympia (468, when he drove for himself) and Delphi (470) and Olympic (476, 472) and Pythian (482, 478) horse races, the middle two (at least) with PHERENICUS, as well as a mule-cart race (APĒNĒ) at an unidentified festival. Hieron patronized SIMONIDES and commissioned victory songs from PINDAR and BACCHYLIDES. Both *Olympians* 1 – Pindar's most beautiful – and Bacchylides 5 celebrate Hieron's first Olympic triumph; his achievements there were also marked by a bronze charioteer, flanked on either side by mounted race horses, the work of Onatas of Aegina and of Calamis and the gift of Hieron's son, Deinomenes.

Pindar, *Olympians* 1; *Pythians* 1, 2, 3; Bacchylides 3, 4, 5; Aristophanes, *Birds* 938–943 (with Scholiast); Pausanias 6.12.1, 8.42.9.

Ebert (1972) 71–73.

Himas (plural *himantes*, Latin *caestus*), "thongs", hand coverings used by Greek boxers in competition. (For practice coverings, see SPHAIRAI.) The earliest *himantes*, the soft thongs (*himantes meilichai*), were light strips of leather, about three to four metres (ten to twelve feet) in length, wrapped around the wrists and/or hands. They supported a boxer's wrists and/or protected his hands; they did not soften the force of his blows. In the fourth century, Greek boxers took to wearing heavier and more damaging coverings, the sharp thongs (*himantes oxeis*). These were gloves (again wrapped in leather bands) with holes cut to leave the fingertips and thumb free. A piece of hard leather with sharp edges covered the knuckles and the bands, which extended up the forearm, were sometimes topped with sheepskin. Both kinds of thongs were nicknamed *myrmēx*, "ant" – a biting insect – for their capacity to draw blood. From the first century CE we find depictions of long-sleeved leather gloves topped at the upper arm by fleece and including what may have been a padded half-cylinder of leather to protect the arm.

Homer, *Iliad* 23.683–685; Apollonius of Rhodes 2.51–53; Lucillius, *Greek Anthology* 11.78; Pausanias 8.40.3; Philostratus, *On Athletic Exercise* 10.

T. F. Scanlon, "Greek boxing gloves: terminology and evolution", *Stadion* 8/9 (1982–1983) 31–45; Poliakoff (1986) 54–63; H. M. Lee, "The later Greek boxing glove and the Roman caestus: a centennial reevaluation of Jüthner's 'Über Antike Turngeräthe' ", *Nikephoros* 10 (1997)161–178; F. Rausa, "*Myrmēx* = *himas oxys*: una proposta sull'origine del nome", *Nikephoros* 13 (2000) 153–161.

Hippaphesis (plural *hippapheseis*), starting-line of a HIPPODROME.

Polybius fragment 52; *IG* 7 3078.

Hippias, of Elis, polymath and polemicist, fifth century. One of the many Greek intellectuals and entrepreneurs who came to Athens to lecture and teach – he features in two dialogues of Plato – Hippias was the first to compile a list of Olympic victors, perhaps about 400. This became the basis of most later outlines of the early history of the games. Even in antiquity, however, it had critics as well as rivals, and modern archaeological research has suggested that it is unreliable at least in respect to the traditional foundation date of the games (776) and the names and origins of early victors. The precedence of footraces over equestrian events in the programme may reflect an ongoing debate over the relative importance of these kinds of contests (perhaps given new currency by the admission of the two-horse chariot race into the programme in 408); the prominence of Eleians, Hippias's local patriotism.

B. Peiser, "The crime of Hippias of Elis. Zur Kontroverse um die Olympionikenliste", *Stadion* 16 (1990) 37–65; C. Wacker, "The record of the Olympic victory list", *Nikephoros* 11 (1998) 39–50; Golden (1998) 63–65; R. Bilik, "Die Zuverlässigkeit der frühen Olympionikenliste. Die Geschichte eines Forschungsproblems im chronologischen Überblick", *Nikephoros* 13 (2000) 47–62.

Hippios (*ephippios, hippios diaulos*), "horse race", a footrace at some Greek competitive festivals. Though not run at the Olympic or Pythian festivals, *hippios* was an event at Isthmia (for men), at Nemea (for boys and men), at the (Hellenistic) Panathenaea, and elsewhere, and Plato recommended it (as *ephippios*) for males (in armour) and females of his ideal Cretan city. *Hippios* was four lengths of the stadium, 2,400 Greek feet. The name may refer to the length of the Greek HIPPODROME or to the difficulty of the race, suitable for a runner as strong as a horse. Aristides of Elis won *hippios* at Nemea as a boy, the men's *diaulos* at Delphi and the race in armour over the same distance at Olympia, an unnamed Athenian both *stadion* and *hippios* at Isthmia.

Bacchylides 10.21–28; Euripides, *Electra* 824–826; Plato, *Laws* 8.833AD; Plutarch, *Solon* 23.5; Pausanias 6.16.4.

Hippocleas, son of PHRICIAS, of Pelinna (Thessaly), runner, fifth century. Hippo-

cleas won DIAULOS for boys at the Pythian games in 498 and later two footraces (probably HOPLITĒS or *diaulos*) at Olympia (in 492 and 488) as well as another (possible) Pythian race as an adult.

Pindar, *Pythians* 10.8–9.

Hippocrates, son of Thessalus (or, of Thessaly), equestrian victor, third century. Hippocrates may have won the Olympic race for colts (PŌLOI) at its first running in 256, but this distinction is also awarded to TLEPOLEMUS of Lycia.

Eusebius, *Chronicon* 1.207 Schoene.

Hippodrome (Greek *hippodromos*, plural *hippodromoi*), an equestrian race course (cf. DROMOS). Though the word was used to refer to the Roman CIRCUS, the *hippodromos* was generally much less elaborate; at least one, on Delos, was used as farmland between festivals. As a result, few *hippodromoi* have left archaeological remains – the main exception is otherwise unusual, located high on Mt Lycaeum in Arcadia. Most were simply open areas, flanked by a natural or man-made elevation for spectators, with turning posts (KAMPTĒRES) at either end. These might be two or three STADIA distant, as at Olympia, or as many as eight (Athens, where the length of the hippodrome permitted races without a turn, AKAMPION). This openness allowed for large fields, likely from forty to sixty at both Olympia and Delphi. Some care was taken to assure fairness; the use of the LOT for starting positions is only one example. At Olympia, a mechanism (invented by CLEOETAS) ensured a staggered start. A cord running in front of each stall (see HYSPLĒX) dropped sequentially so that entrants on the ends broke for the turning post before those inside them, who were closer to it. Most hippodromes made do with a cord attached to a post to mark the starting line. The Olympic was also unusually elaborate in the decoration of its far turn post, bronze plaques showing hippodameia tying the victory ribbon (TAINIA) around PELOPS's head. In addition, bronze figures, an eagle (for Zeus), and a dolphin (for Poseidon, god of horses as well as of the sea), rose and fell to signal the start for spectators. Many hippodromes featured a _TARAXIPPOS_, a spot where chariot crashes – a thrill for spectators much as in modern motor sport – were especially frequent.

Homer, _Iliad_ 23.330; Pindar, _Pythians_ 5.49–51; Pausanias 6.20.10–19; _Etymologicum Magnum_ s. _en Echelidōn_; IG 2² 1638.

Harris (1972) 161–172; J. Ebert, "Neues zum Hippodrom und zu den hippischen Konkurrenzen in Olympia", _Nikephoros_ 2 (1989) 89–107.

Hippomachus, athletic trainer, (?) fourth century. A much storied instructor of HEAVY athletes, Hippomachus is said to have disciplined a wrestler who played to the crowd, derided the qualifications of an extra-tall boxer – wreaths were not hung up to be won by reaching – and been able to pick out his pupils even when they were bringing home meat from the market. He charged 100 drachmas as a retainer, a sum scoffed at by the high-end courtesan Gnathaena.

See also: THEOTIMUS.

Plutarch, _Dion_ 1.2; _Moral Essays_ 523CD; Aelian, _Historical Miscellany_ 2.6; Athenaeus 13.584C.

Hipposthenes, of Sparta, wrestler, seventh century. The winner of the first Olympic wrestling competition for boys in 632, Hipposthenes later won five more crowns as an adult (624–608) and may have received worship like Poseidon at Sparta as a result (see HERO). His son HETOEMOCLES was also a champion wrestler; they make up the earliest of many such father-son pairs.

Pausanias 3.13.9, 15.7, 5.8.9.

Hippostratus 1. of Thessaly, equestrian victor, third century. Hippostratus, known only through a newly-discovered epigram by Posidippus, twice won the Pythian horse race with Aethon, "Blazing".

Posidippus, _P.Mil.Vogl._ 8 309.XI.21–24.

2. of Croton, runner, sixth century. Hippostratus was twice winner in the _STADION_ race at Olympia (564, 560).

Eusebius, _Chronicon_ 1.201 Schoene.

Hirpinus, "Samnite", Roman chariot horse, first/second century CE. All the fashionable young men knew Hirpinus's pedigree, but his offspring were soon sold off as losers: breeding, the poets imply, is crucial but not conclusive. A Hirpinus identified as (?) grandson of Aquilo won 114 races for the Red CIRCUS FACTION – perhaps the same horse. It also placed second fifty-six times and third, thirty-six.

Martial 3.63.12; Juvenal 8.62–63; _ILS_ 5295.

Hockey _see_ BALL-PLAY

Hoplitēs, "shield race, race in armour", regular event in Greek athletic festivals. The common events in Greek competitions were usually much the same from place to place, but not the race in armour. Two lengths of the stadium (like the _DIAULOS_) at Olympia, it was four lengths (like the _HIPPIOS_) at Nemea and fifteen stadia at the Plataean ELEUTHERIA (1). The equipment also varied; it was heaviest at Plataea and generally became less burdensome over time, as runners, once decked out as heavy infantrymen (_hoplitai_) shed greaves and helmet and kept only the shield. The race's reputation is also difficult to fix. Oldest perhaps at Nemea, it entered the programme at Olympia only in 520, at Delphi in 498, in each case the last athletic event for men. (Boys did not run the race in armour, though it made up part of the military training of EPHEBES in Hellenistic Athens and elsewhere.) The prize for the race at Aphrodisias early in our era was equal to that for pentathlon, but smaller than all others. On the other hand, the *hoplitēs* was a favourite of vase painters – it was certainly picturesque –, one Eudoxus thought it worthwhile to donate ten shields for the Pythian event in 271, and for Plato, only races run in armour deserved a prize. The winner of the demanding (and potentially deadly) race at Plataea garnered the title "best of the Greeks". According to PHILOSTRATUS, an armoured runner (*hoplitodromos*) required a long waist, well developed shoulders, knees with an upward tilt – the better to support the shield; he should be heavier than other sprinters (though true specialists in this event were rare). Of course, not all runners measured up: one (the subject of a satirical epigram) is said to have been so slow that attendants took him for a statue and closed the stadium while he was still on the track. The placement of the *hoplitēs* on the Olympic programme, as the final event, may reflect its late addition or (as Philostratus thought) the imminent expiry of the truce and the return of armour to its accustomed use in the Greek world.

Aristophanes, *Birds* 291–292; Plato, *Laws* 8.833AB; Plutarch, *Moral Essays* 639E; Pausanias 2.11.8, 5.12.8, 6.10.4, 9.2.6; Philostratus, *On Athletic Exercise* 7–8, 24, 32–33; *Greek Anthology* 11.85; *SIG*[3] 419.

L. Robert, "*Aristos Hellēnōn*", *REA* 31 (1929) 13–20, 225–226.

Hoplomachus (plural *hoplomachi*), or *oplomachus*, "armed fighter", type of GLADIATOR, much like the SAMNIS. Armed with a long shield and high greave on the left leg, the *hoplomachus* customarily used his spear and dagger in combat with a MURMILLO or THRAEX.

Seneca, *Controversies* 3 preface 10; Suetonius, *Caligula* 35.2; *ILS* 5099.

Mosci Sassi (1992) 120–121.

Hordearius (plural *hordearii*), "barley men", a term once applied to GLADIATORS because of the important role grain played in their diet.

Pliny, *Natural History* 18.14.72.

Mosci Sassi (1992) 121–122.

Horse race (Greek *kelēs*), regular event at Greek competitive festivals. Uncommon among the ETRUSCANS and Romans – they preferred CHARIOT racing – and absent from Homer's FUNERAL GAMES for Patroclus, the horse race entered the Olympic programme only in 648, some thirty-two years after the chariots. (The first winner was CRAUXIDAS of Crannon in horse-rich Thessaly.) However, it was among the original events at the PYTHIAN games in 586 – whereas the chariot race had to wait until 582 – and grew in popularity over time until horse races outnumbered chariot at the Hellenistic PANATHENAEA and THESEIA. The inclusion of a horse race in Quintus Smyrnaeus's account of what Homer didn't tell reflects this popularity. (It was cheaper to run one horse than two or four, so the expansion of the programme made much prized equestrian success more available to these outside the super-rich.) Most horse races were of one length (AKAMPION) or lap (DIAULOS) of the HIPPODROME but the Hellenistic Panathenaea also listed a long-distance race (*hippos polydromos*). This (like many of the events at the Panathenaea and Theseia) was for war horses; race horses were lighter and more costly. (In Aristophanes' comedy *Clouds*, Pheidippides has a nightmare about 1,200 drachmas he's borrowed to buy a race horse – at a period when a daily wage was one or one and a half drachmas per day.) As in the HEAVY events for athletes, Greek horse races knew no weight categories, but came to include events for colts (PŌLOI) as well as for adult (*teleioi*) stallions and mares, from 338 at Delphi, from 256 at Olympia (in both places, some time after chariot races for colts). Dismounting races (ANABATĒS, KALPĒ) also appear at some festivals. As in all equestrian events, the winner was the owner; jockeys were boys – because of their size – likely SLAVES. Horse races were dangerous. Jockeys had whips but no saddles or stirrups and track conditions must often have been treacherous, especially where the chariots churned up the hippodrome before the horses ran. Nevertheless, though we can identify some race horses (AURA, PHERENICUS), jockeys remain anonymous. Not that the horses themselves always profited from their fame: a series of Hellenistic epigrams is put into the mouths of race horses who once swept the circuit (PERIODOS) and now grind grain in a mill.

Aristophanes, *Clouds* 22–23; Pausanias 5.8.7, 6.12.1, 13.9; Quintus Smyrnaeus, *Posthomerica* 4.545–591; *Greek Anthology* 9.19–21; *IG* 2^2 2316.

D. Bell, "The horse race (*kelēs*) in ancient Greece from the pre-classical period to the first century B.C.", *Stadion* 15 (1989) 167–190.

Hortator (plural *hortatores*), "encourager", member of a chariot racing FAMILIA who rode a horse behind or in front of a charioteer, offering encouragement or advice.

ILS 5313.

Hypenus, of Pisa, runner, eighth century. Hypenus won the DIAULOS at its introduction into the Olympic programme in 724.

Pausanias 5.8.6.

Hyposkelizein, "trip up", to bring a wrestling opponent down.

Plato, *Euthydemus* 278B; Lucian, *Anacharsis* 1; Pollux 3.155.

Hypsicles, of Sicyon, runner, first century. Hypsicles won DOLICHOS at Olympia in 72, along with Gaius of Rome. Since a DRAW in such a long race is unlikely, and a Roman victor in an athletic competition at this date still more so, the two names may refer to one person, a Greek who was also a Roman citizen (perhaps in recognition of his victory).

Phlegon, *FGrH* 257 F 12.

Hysmon, of Elis, athlete, (?) fourth century. Afflicted with a muscular disease as a boy, Hysmon practised pentathlon to build up his strength, so successfully that he won victories at both Olympia (? 384) and Nemea. His statue at Olympia (which PAUSANIAS saw) depicted his holding old-fashioned HALTĒRES.

Pausanias 6.3.10.

Hysplēx (plural *hysplēges*), portable starting mechanism for Greek races. In the stadium, the *hysplēx* consisted of cord wrapped around wooden rods (*ankōnes*) which were set in bases at either end of the BALBIS. The cord was made taut when the *ankōnes* were turned by a crank and released when they were made to drop forward by the starter (APHETĒS). The *hysplēx* for equestrian events operated on the same principle.

Pausanias 6.20.13; Lucian, *Slander* 12; Heliodorus, *Aethiopica* 4.3; *ID* 1400, 1409 Ba II.

D. J. Bell, "Some neglected passages on the study of the *hysplex* in the hippodrome", *Philologus* 134 (1990) 313–319; P. Valavanis, *Hysplex. The Starting Mechanism in Ancient Stadia. A Contribution to Ancient Greek Technology* (Berkeley and Los Angeles 1999).

Hyssematas, of Argos, equestrian victor, sixth/fifth century. After his death in battle (? against Sparta in 494), Hyssematas's wife Cossina buried him near the HIPPODROME where (as she notes) he had been victorious.

L. W. Daly, "An inscribed Doric capital from the Argive Heraion", *Hesperia* 8 (1939) 165–169; E. McGowan, "Tomb marker and turning post", *AJA* 99 (1995) 615–632 (628).

I

Iaculum (plural *iacula*), the net a RETIAR-
IUS used to entangle a rival GLADIATOR.

Isidore, *Origines* 18.54.

Mosci Sassi (1992) 122.

Ibycus, of Rhegium, Greek poet, sixth
century. Ibycus wrote (among much else)
the earliest known EPINICIANS. Fragments remain of poems for CALLIAS (I)
of Athens, a Spartan victor in games at
Sicyon, a runner from Leontini, perhaps
a wrestler, exemplifying characteristics
of better preserved later works of this
kind.

J. P. Barron, "Ibycus: *Gorgias* and other
poems", *BICS* 31 (1984) 13–24 (20–22); E. A.
B. Jenner, "Further speculations on Ibycus and
the epinician ode: S 220, S 176 and the
'Bellerophon' ode", *BICS* 33 (1986) 59–66.

Iccus, son of Nicolaides, Tarentine pentathlete, fifth century. Iccus won the
Olympic pentathlon competition (perhaps
in 444) and later became (according to
PAUSANIAS) the best TRAINER of his day.
He must have been one of those who
recommended abstention from SEX: during his own periods of training, he never
touched a woman or even a boy.

Plato, *Protagoras* 316D; *Laws* 8.839F-840A;
Pausanias 6.10.5; *SEG* 37.816.

Incitatus, chariot horse of the Green
CIRCUS FACTION. NERO, a fan of the
Greens, is said to have intended to make

Incitatus consul but he died before he
could carry out this plan. Undeterred, we
Canadians appoint horses' asses to the
Senate.

Suetonius, *Nero* 55.3.

Infibulation. Some Greek athletes wound
a cord or thong (*kynodesmē*, "dog
leash"), around the foreskin during exercise and competition, either tying the
penis to the body or curling it around
itself in a snail-like shape. The purpose
was no doubt protective. Depictions of
infibulated men on vase depictions of
parties may be meant to emphasize their
sexual self-control.

Aeschylus fragment 78a Radt; Pollux 2.171;
Phrynichus, *Praeparatio Sophistica* 85B de Bor-
ries.

W. E. Sweet, "Protection of the genitals in
Greek athletics", *AncW* 11 (1985) 43–52.

Introiugus (plural *introiugi*), "under the
yoke", central pair of a Roman four-horse
chariot team, regarded as the most important for success.

ILS 5287; *CIL* 6.37834.

Iphitus, legendary king of ELIS, linked (in
a confusing and inconsistent tradition)
to the early history of the Olympic festival. Troubled by unrest in Greece, Iphitus
is said to have sought advice from
the Delphic oracle, which urged him

(along with Lycurgus, the Spartan lawgiver) to re-establish the Olympic festival (which had been allowed to lapse) or to proclaim the TRUCE and hold the festival for the first time. Aristotle and PAUSANIAS saw Iphitus's discus, inscribed with the terms of the truce and the name of Lycurgus, in the Temple of Hera; a statue in the Temple of Zeus showed Truce (*Ekecheiria*) crowning Iphitus – he was credited with the institution of the olive wreath prize. The date is variously given as 776 or twenty-eight Olympiads before, and some sources (like PHLEGON) place the first award of the olive wreath in 752.

Phlegon, *FGrH* 257 F 1; Pausanias 5.4.5–6, 8.5, 9.4, 10.10, 20.1, 26.2; Plutarch, *Lycurgus* 1.1.

Ischomachus, or Isomachus, of CROTON, runner, sixth century. Ischomachus won the Olympic STADION race twice, in 508 and 504.

Dionysius of Halicarnassus, *Roman Antiquities* 5.1.1, 37.1.

Isidorus 1. or Artemidorus, of Alexandria, runner, second century CE. Isidorus was twice Olympic STADION champion, in 193 and 197.

Eusebius, *Chronicon* 1.217 Schoene.

2. of Alexandria, wrestler, first century. Isidorus, Olympic wrestling champion in 72, became PERIODONIKĒS without suffering a fall.

Phlegon, *FGrH* 257 F 12.

Isolympian, isonemean, isopythian, isoactian, designations for festivals or portions of their programmes which were like (*isos*) those at more famous sites. So the victors in an Alexandrian festival introduced by PTOLEMY II Philadelphus in the early third century were to receive rewards in their home cities like those of Olympic champions, and Pythian honours went to victors at a festival of Artemis at Magnesia on Maeander fifty years later.

At some festivals, musical competitions were isopythian, athletic and equestrian – isolympian or isonemean. Common in later antiquity, even for important foundations like the SEBASTAN games, this practice not only offers evidence for the continued prestige of the original games of the PERIODOS but at times allows us to determine their practices even where direct evidence is lacking.

IvO 56; *SIG*³ 390, 402, 630.

Isthmian games (Greek *Isthmia*), Greek competitive festival. The Isthmian were one of the four crown games of the original circuit (PERIODOS). Their founder was usually said to be Sisyphus, legendary king of Corinth, who first held them as FUNERAL games for his young nephew MELICERTES; a later tradition credited THESEUS either in expiation for the death of the local bandit Sinis or Sciron or in emulation of HERACLES. (Athenians had special privileges at the games.) The historical festival dated from 582, and was held every second year, in spring (April/May) or in early summer (June/July), in the sanctuary of Poseidon at Isthmia. This was on the east side of the Isthmus of Corinth and under Corinthian control. However, during the brief period when Argos incorporated Corinth, the Argives celebrated the Isthmian festival of 390 – it was then repeated by Corinthian exiles under the protection of King AGESILAUS of Sparta – and the games were held at Sicyon for a century or so after the Roman sack of Corinth in 146, before returning to Corinthian control (about 40) and eventually to Isthmia itself (about 40 or 60 CE). Poseidon's sanctuary was on major land and sea routes for much of Greek history – there is evidence for activity on the site as early as the eleventh century – and Corinth was a political centre under Macedonian rule and the capital of the Roman province of Achaea from 27. The festival was therefore thronged, and a convenient occasion for political theatre: PHILIP of Macedon set out his settlement of Greek affairs at the games of 338, and the Roman general Flamininus announced the freedom of Greek cities there in 196.

The Isthmian games included an ambitious programme in music, recitation of poetry, and perhaps a race for rowers. The usual equestrian and athletic events were joined by the HIPPIOS footrace, as at NEMEA. Like Nemea too there was a footrace for girls; and an AGE-CLASS of AGENEIOI as well as adult boys (perhaps defined unusually – we hear of PAIDES Isthmikoi elsewhere) and adult men. Romans could compete (and won) from 228. Eleians, however, were excluded. Or perhaps they boycotted Isthmia: as the story goes, HERACLES had killed the sons of Actor, allies of King Augeas of Elis, on their way to the Isthmian games. Unable to persuade the Corinthians to punish this breach of the sacred TRUCE, their sister Moline cursed any Eleian who took part in the festival. At any rate, none is known to have won an Isthmian crown: pine until the early fifth century, dry celery (selinon) until the second; both pine and dry celery thereafter.

Pindar, Olympians 13.32–34; Thucydides 8.10.1; Xenophon, Greek History 4.5.1–4; Polybius 2.12.8; Strabo 8.6.22; Dio Chrysostom 8.4–6, 9–12; Plutarch, Moral Essays 675D-676F; Pausanias 5.2.1–2; Livy 32.33.

O. Broneer, "The Isthmian victory crown", AJA 66 (1962) 259–263; E. R. Gebhard, "The evolution of a pan-Hellenic sanctuary: from archaeology towards history at Isthmia", in N. Marinatos and R. Hägg (eds) Greek Sanctuaries. New Approaches (London and New York 1993) 154–177; "The Isthmian games and the sanctuary of Poseidon in the early empire", in T. E. Gregory (ed.) The Corinthia in the Roman Period (Ann Arbor 1993) 78–94; M. Kajava, "When did the Isthmian games return to the Isthmus? Rereading Corinth 8.3.153", CP 97 (2002) 168–176.

Iulius Africanus Sextus, Christian philosopher and chronographer, from Aelia Carolina (Jerusalem). His five books of Chronographiae, a compilation of sacred and universal history from the Creation of Adam (5502 BCE) to 221 CE, are usually thought to be the basis of the list of Olympic victors incorporated in the lost Greek Chronicle of Eusebius (325–6 CE), now extant in Latin and Armenian versions. The list includes victors in the STADION race down to the 249th Olympiad (217 CE) as well as occasional comments on the introduction of events and their first winners, noteworthy achievements, and historical events.

J. Rutgers, Sexti Julii Africani Olympiadōn anagraphē adiectis ceteris quae ex Olympionicarum fasti supersunt (Leiden 1862) (reprint Chicago 1980); A. A. Mosshammer, The Chronicle of Eusebius and the Greek Chronographic Tradition (Lewisburg 1979) 138–168.

Iulius Septimius Iulianus, Tiberius, of Smyrna, athlete, ? second century CE. According to an inscription found near Smyrna, Iulianus was a PERIODONIKĒS in an unspecified event.

Année épigraphique (1951) 255.

Iustitiale (plural iustitialia), type of Roman chariot race.

ILS 5283.

Iustius Marcianus Rufus, Marcus, of Sinope, boxer, early second century CE. The winner of many prestigious competitions (Nemea and Isthmia [both twice], the Pythian, CAPITOLINE, SEBASTAN and ACTIAN games among them) and of 150 prizes at TALANTIAIOI and hēmitalantiaioi AGŌNES, Rufus also claimed unique distinctions: he was the first to win as both AGENEIOS and adult on the same day at the Antiochia, the only winner in all three AGE-CLASSES at Nicomedia. Though he lists an Olympic victory, it was not at the most honoured festival of all, in Elis.

SEG 13.540.

Moretti (1953) 191–196.

Iuvenis, GLADIATOR. When he died at twenty-one, commemorated by his wife Pussicina, Iuvenis had been in his LUDUS four years and fought five times as a PROVOCATOR.

ILS 5107.

J

Javelin, Greek *akōn* or *akontion*, one of the three distinctive events of the Greek PENTATHLON. Already attested in Patroclus's FUNERAL GAMES (Achilles awards the prize for throwing the spear to Agamemnon in recognition of his rank as commander of the Greek troops at Troy), the javelin retained its connection with war at the PANATHENAEA, where EPHEBES on horseback threw at a target. Generally, however, the javelin appeared only as one of the events of the pentathlon, where it was thrown for distance. A light shaft of elderwood, five or six feet in length, with a pointed metal-clad tip (to stick in the ground), the javelin was thrown with the aid of a thong (ANKYLĒ) through which competitors inserted their index or first two fingers (long fingers were thought to give an advantage). This lengthened throws, either by increasing leverage or by imparting rotation and so stability to the shaft in flight (champions could reach an estimated 300 feet). Competitors who overstepped the starting line or threw wide of the boundaries of the STADIUM committed fouls – and endangered spectators. An Athenian law-court speech deals with a boy who was struck and killed during javelin practice in the GYMNASIUM.

Homer, *Iliad* 23.884–897; Pindar, *Pythians* 1.42–45; *Nemeans* 7.70–73; Bacchylides 9.33–35; Antiphon, *Tetralogies* 2; Lucian, *Anacharsis* 27; Philostratus, *On Athletic Exercise* 31.

H. M. Lee, "The *terma* and the javelin in Pindar, Nemean vii 70–3 and Greek athletics", *JHS* 96 (1976) 70–79; G. Doblhofer, P. Mauritsch and M. Lavrencic, *Speerwurf* (Vienna 1993).

Jump, Greek *halma*, regular event in Greek competitive festivals. Though found as an event in its own right at some local festivals, the jump was normally one of the distinctive events of the PENTATHLON. Its nature is unclear. An ancient epigram claims that PHAŸLLUS of Croton once jumped 55 feet, and threw the discus 95: his jump was nearly matched by CHIONIS (52 feet). Since such a leap is almost double the modern record for the long jump, it has been explained as the result of a standing or running multiple jump (one such theory was the inspiration for the modern triple jump, meant to mimic Greek practice) or as the total of a series of five standing jumps. It is more likely, however, that the epigram on Phaÿllus is a joke: the 55-foot jump is an exaggeration to match the disappointing discus throw and the combination of short and long mirrors this epigram's form, with its lines of six and five feet. The Greek jump would then be much like the modern, a leap from a hard surface (BATĒR) into a softer pit (SKAMMA), with the addition of jumping weights (HALTĒRES) to improve balance and the music of the AULOS to foster rhythm.

Aristotle, *On the Progression of Animals* 705a16; *Problems* 5.8.881b5; Philostratus, *On Athletic Exercise* 55; Pollux 3.151.

G. Doblhofer, M. Mauritsch and M. Lavrencic, *Weitsprung* (Vienna 1992); Golden (1998) 60–62.

K

Kalpē, an Olympic equestrian event for mares in which riders dismounted and finished by running alongside their horses (cf. ANABATĒS). It was introduced in 496, perhaps in response to the hunger for equestrian victories among Western Greek rulers and their associates – a number of cities in the region minted coins which may illustrate the event. However, the first (and only known) winner was PATAE-CUS of Dyme in the northwest Peloponnese. Like APĒNĒ, it was dropped from the Olympic programme in 444 and goes unmentioned on surviving victor lists on papyrus and stone.

Plutarch, *Moral Essays* 675B; Pausanias 5.9.1–2.

G. C. Brauer Jr, "The *kalpē*: an agonistic reference on several Greek coins", *San* 6 (1974–1975) 6–7; García Romero (1992); Golden (1998) 40–43.

Kamptēr (plural *kamptēres*), or *kampē* (plural *kampai*), post around which runners and horses turned in Greek races. In the shorter footraces (DIAULOS, HO-PLITĒS), runners turned around individual posts; in the longer HIPPIOS and DOLI-CHOS, all used the same one. *Kamptēres*, usually of wood, were inserted into sockets in limestone blocks embedded in the track (DROMOS) of the stadium and were therefore movable.

Aristophanes, *Peace* 905; Aristotle, *Rhetoric* 3.1409a32; Pollux 3.147.

Stephen G. Miller, "Turns and lanes in the ancient stadium", *AJA* 84 (1980) 159–166.

Kelēs (plural *kelētes*), "riding horse", the usual term for the Greek race horse (smaller, swifter and more expensive than the norm), and also for a swift-sailing ship and a sexual position in which the woman rides the man.

Homer, *Odyssey* 5.371; Aristophanes, *Peace* 899–904.

Kērōma (plural *kērōmata*, Latin *ceroma*), mixture of dust, water and oil used as the surface for the wrestling area and as a salve for the skin of those suffering from stiffened joints, paralysis and other ailments.

Plutarch, *Moral Essays* 638E, 790F; Pliny, *Natural History* 28.13.51.

M. B. Poliakoff, "*Pēlōma* and *kērōma*: refinement of the Greco-Roman gymnasium", *ZPE* 79 (1989) 289–291.

Kēryx (plural *kērykes*), "herald", competitor in Greek festivals. Heralds called for silence (with the assistance of trumpeters, SALPINKTAI), announced victors (giving their name, patronymic and native city) and crowned them. At Olympia, heralds were once chosen from among the citizens of ELIS (like other officials), but from 396 the role was made competitive, leading off the series of events on the opening day of the festival. The first victor was CRATES of

Elis; the first outsider to win, ARCHIAS of Hybla (on Sicily), went on to two more triumphs (? 364, ? 360, ? 356). Many years later, this feat was topped by VALERIUS Eclectus of Sinope (in Paphlagonia), who added victories in the other crown games and over forty other festivals to four at Olympia (? 245, ? 253–261). The competition for Olympic heralds (who wore a long robe and carried a staff) took place at an altar in the ALTIS, near the entrance to the stadium. Victors' announcements were to be loud, exalted, extensive, clear, precise, spoken in one breath. This required training – baths of fresh, tepid water were recommended – and perhaps some technical aids: heralds used *anadeigmata*, either mouthpieces for amplification or (more likely) leather thongs which prevented throat strain. Nevertheless, their victories seem to have been valued less than others: they are left off surviving Olympic victory lists and receive smaller prizes at local festivals.

Suetonius, *Nero* 24.1; Plutarch, *Moral Essays* 185A; Pausanias 5.22.1; Lucian, *Demonax* 65; Dio Chrysostom 2.17, 13.11; Philostratus, *On Athletic Exercise* 7; Pollux 4.91–94.

N. B. Crowther, "The role of heralds and trumpeters at Greek athletic festivals", *Nikephoros* 7 (1994) 135–155.

Klimax, "ladder". **1.** A portable object used to bring Greek boxers into contact with each other.

Hesychius, *Etymologicum Magnum s. ek klimakos*; Eustathius 1324.48 (on *Iliad* 23.686).

M. B. Poliakoff, "Melankomas, *ek klimakos* and Greek boxing", *AJP* 108 (1987) 511–518.

2. A move in which a wrestler mounts an opponent's back and wraps his legs around the waist.

Pollux 3.155.

Koina Asias, Greek competitive festival. Originating in a festival, the *Sebasta Romaea*, celebrated in common by the cities of the Roman province of Asia at Pergamum in 29 BCE, independent athletic and musical competitions under the name *Koina Asias* came to be held in eight of the province's major centres, each on a four-year cycle. The festivals at Smyrna (the first to use the name), Ephesus and Pergamum were recognized as more important than those at Cyzicus, Laodicea, Philadelphia, Sardis and Tralles.

Cassius Dio 51.20.9; *IGRom.* 1.445, 4.160, 824.

L. Moretti, "*Koina Asias*", *RFIC* 82 (1954) 276–289; P. Herz, "Addenda agonistica I. Koina Asias in Sardeis", *EA* 30 (1998) 133–136.

Konisalos see PATOS

Konistra (plural *konistrai*), wrestling area (from *konis*, "DUST").

Plutarch, *Moral Essays* 638C.

Kōrykos (plural *kōrykoi*), a leather punching bag. Boxers used a light bag, pancratiasts hit and butted a larger, heavier bag, in part to improve balance. "To exercise against the *kōrykos*" was proverbial for wasting effort or fighting a phantom.

Timocles fragment 31 Kassel-Austin; Philostratus, *On Athletic Exercise* 57; Diogenianus 7.54.

Kylisis, ALINDĒSIS.

Plutarch, *Moral Essays* 638CD.

L. Lomiento, "Semantica agonistica: *kylindein* in Pind. *Nem.* 4, v. 40 e Nonn. *Dionys.* 48, vv. 134;154", *Nikephoros* 3 (1990) 145–155.

L

Lacerta, Roman charioteer, early second century CE. A driver for the red CIRCUS FACTION, Lacerta is said to have earned as much as 100 lawyers.

Juvenal 7.112–114.

Lacrates, of Sparta, Olympic victor in an unknown event, fifth century. Lacrates was one of the notable Spartans killed in 403, fighting against Athenians opposed to the regime of the Thirty Tyrants.

Xenophon, *Greek History* 2.4.33; *IG* 2^2 11678.

Moretti (1987) 69.

Ladas, of (?) Argos, runner, fifth century. The subject of a famous bronze statue by Myron, Ladas won the DOLICHOS at Olympia (perhaps in 460 or 456), fell sick on his way home and was buried near Sparta. His statue (Myron's ?) stood in the Temple of Apollo Lyceius at Argos.

Pausanias 2.19.7, 3.21.1; *Greek Anthology* 16.54.

Lampis, of Sparta, athlete, eighth century. Lampis was the victor in the first Olympic PENTATHLON, in 708.

Pausanias 5.8.7.

Lanista (plural *lanistae*), the owner, manager or trainer of a group (FAMILIA) of GLADIATORS. Senatorial decrees grouped *lanistae* with other undesirables – con-

victs, pimps, actors – but successful ones could become wealthy.

Cicero, *For Roscius of Ameria* 40.118; [Caesar], *African War* 71; Suetonius, *Julius Caesar* 26.3; *ILS* 5163, 6085.

Mosci Sassi (1992) 124–127.

Laquearius (plural *laquearii*), "snarer", type of GLADIATOR, either like a RETIARIUS but bearing a noose instead of a net, or a PAEGNIARIUS.

Isidore, *Etymologies* 18.56.

Mosci Sassi (1992) 129–130.

Lasthenes, of Thebes, runner, fifth century. Lasthenes was Olympic champion in 404 – probably in DOLICHOS, since he also outran a horse in a race from Coroneia to Thebes (about 35km/20 miles).

Diodorus 14.11.5.

Leocrates, son of Stroebus, Athenian boxer, fifth century. Likely honoured in his youth by a victory poem by SIMONIDES, Leocrates later served as general in important Athenian campaigns in 479 and 458.

Thucydides 1.105.2; Plutarch, *Aristides* 20.1; *IG* 1^3 983; Quintilian 11.2.11–16.

J. H. Molyneux, *Simonides. A Historical Study* (Wauconda 1992) 42–45.

Leocreon, of Ceos, boxer, sixth century. Some say that Leocreon, who won in 540, was the first Olympic boxing champion among the boys, but most give this distinction to PHILYTAS, in 616.

Philostratus, *On Athletic Exercise* 13.

Leon, son of Myonides, wrestler, second century. Of uncertain nationality, Leon was PERIODONIKĒS in wrestling in the first half of the second century.

Moretti (1987) 85–87.

Leon, of Ambracia *see* EUPOLEMUS.

Leon, son of Anticleidas, Spartan equestrian victor, fifth century. The winner of the Olympic chariot race in 440 or 424 with Venetian horses, Leon was likely the leader of the Spartan colony at Heracleia in Trachis in 426 (and perhaps also ambassador to Athens in 420 and eponymous ephor in 419).

Thucydides 3.92.5, 5.44.3; Xenophon, *Greek History* 2.3.10; Scholiast on Euripides, *Hippolytus* 231.

Ebert (1972) 99–100.

Leonidas, of Rhodes, runner, second century. Leonidas won all three shorter footraces – *stadion, diaulos*, race in armour – at four successive Olympic festivals (164–152). PAUSANIAS calls him the most famous of ancient runners. PHILOSTRATUS says his versatility made all earlier theories on runners' body types obsolete. It is noteworthy, then, that we know so little about him.

Dio Chrysostom 31.126; Pausanias 6.13.4; Philostratus, *On Athletic Exercise* 33.

Leontiscus, of Messana (Sicily), wrestler, fifth century. Leontiscus used his knack of bending his opponents' fingers to win twice at Olympia (456, 452) and once at the Pythian games; the technique was later used by SOSTRATUS.

Pausanias 6.2.10, 4.3.

Leucarus, of Acarnania, pancratiast, undated. According to Aristotle, Leucarus was the first to make the *pankration* an event requiring skill.

Aristotle fragment 475 Rose.

Leukōma (plural *leukōmata*), white board on which the competitors at Olympia and their AGE-CLASSES were listed.

Cassius Dio 83.10.3.

Lichas, son of ARCESILAUS (3), Spartan leader and chariot victor, died 411. An eminent figure in Spartan public life – he may have been a member of the *gerousia* and led a number of diplomatic missions – Lichas hoped for the Olympic success of his father. Sparta, however, was banned from sacrificing or competing in 420 because of a dispute concerning the Olympic TRUCE. Lichas nevertheless entered a chariot team and, when it won and was announced as an entry by the Boeotians or the Theban state, made its true ownership clear by binding a victory ribbon around the charioteer's head. For this he was whipped (despite his age) by the RHABDOUCHOI. The Spartans did not retaliate at the time, but the incident increased Lichas's political prestige and was one of the major causes of their war with Elis twenty years later.

Thucydides 5.49–50.4; Xenophon, *Greek History* 3.2.21–23; Pausanias 6.2.2.

J. Roy, "Thucydides 5.49.1–50.4: the quarrel between Elis and Sparta in 420 B.C., and Elis' exploitation of Olympia", *Klio* 80 (1998) 360–368; S. Hornblower, "Thucydides, Xenophon and Lichas: Were the Spartans excluded from the Olympic Games from 420 to 400 B.C.?", *Phoenix* 54 (2000) 212–225.

Light events (Greek *koupha*), term used for the Greek footraces, in contrast to HEAVY combat sports.

Euripides, *Alcestis* 1029–1032; Aristotle, *Politics* 8.1338b40; Philostratus, *On Athletic Exercise* 3.

Lot As in other aspects of life – for example, the selection of jurors and officers in democratic Athens – the lot played an important role in Greek sport. It was used to allocate starting positions in equestrian events, to determine the pairings of HEAVY athletes and the make-up of HEATS, and to break DRAWS. The lot preserved equality, prevented foul play by the officials, and provided a way for the gods (in whose honour competitions took place) to influence outcomes.

See also: EPHEDROS, PRAXIDAMAS.

Pindar, *Nemeans* 6.61–63; Posidippus, *P.Mil. Vogl.* 8 309.XI.33–XII.7; Lucian, *Hermotimus* 40; Pausanias 6.13.4, 20.11.

Lucidus, "Full of Light", Roman chariot horse, early second century CE. Lucidus was a member of teams DIOCLES drove to victory 445 times, 103 times in one year.

ILS 5287.

Ludia (plural *ludiae*), a female GLADIATOR or lover of gladiators. Roman sentiment and, sometimes, legislation disapproved and punished women of the Roman elite who fought as gladiators – as they did men of equal status – but slaves and lower-class free women were novelties which might make producers proud and spectators pleased. The emperor Domitian presented female gladiators fighting at night, by torchlight. *Ludiae* frequently took NICKNAMES linked to the Amazons.

Martial 5.24.10; Juvenal 6.104, 266–267; Suetonius, *Domitian* 4.1; Tacitus, *Annals* 15.32; Cassius Dio 76.16.1.

D. Briquel, "Les femmes gladiateurs: examen du dossier", *Ktema* 17 (1992) 47–53; M. Vesley, "Gladiatorial training for girls in the *Collegia Iuvenum* of the Roman Empire", *EMC* 42 (1998) 85–93; K. Coleman, "*Missio* at Halicarnassus", *HSCP* 100 (2000) 487–500.

Ludus (plural *ludi*), "play", "game", the term used for Roman public spectacles, such as chariot races (*ludi circenses*); and also for schools, including training schools for GLADIATORS. Competitions and displays at state religious festivals (*ludi*) were generally authorized by the Senate and presided over by magistrates (usually the aediles), who might supplement public funds with their own in order to enhance their popularity and prestige. *Ludi* were mainly of two types: *ludi circenses*, featuring chariot racing, and *ludi scaenici*, involving theatrical displays (mimes, pantomimes, plays). Either might be augmented by athletic competitions, gladiatorial MUNERA or beast hunts (VENATIONES). The earliest *ludi* were apparently the *ludi maximi* for Jupiter Optimus Maximus. Many others are first (reliably) attested in the third century (*ludi saeculares, Ceriales, Apollinares*). When the dictator CORNELIUS Sulla celebrated his triumphs over Rome's enemies (and his own) with *ludi victoriae Sullanae* in 80, he attracted so many of Greece's best athletes that only the boys' STADION race was held at Olympia; Julius Caesar's *ludi* for his own victories thirty-five years later were similar in scale and purpose. The frequency of *ludi*, already held on fifty-seven days in a year in Caesar's time, increased under the empire until it reached 177 days in the mid-fourth century CE.

During the Republic, gladiatorial *ludi* were private enterprises sometimes owned by a businessman (LANISTA) despised for his trade, sometimes by a member of the elite. (Julius Caesar's *ludi* for 5,000 gladiators at Capua allowed him to cut out middlemen and secure a source of supply for his lavish shows.) Augustus inherited Caesar's property and policy in this respect as others and later emperors dominated the training of gladiators. The emperor Domitian established four *ludi* near the Roman Colosseum, whose construction he had completed: the *Ludus Magnus, Gallicus* and *Dacicus* (for gladiators) and the *Ludus Matutinus* for beast fighters (*venatores*). The manager (*procurator*) of each was a senior official from the equestrian order. There were other *ludi* scattered throughout the empire, with local facilities often supervised by a regional administrator. The staff (FAMILIA) of a *ludus* included trainers, weapons makers and doctors – the famous physician Galen once worked in a gladiatorial *ludus*.

Frontinus, *Aqueducts* 2.97; Caesar, *Civil Wars* 1.14; *ILS* 1397.

F. Bernstein, *Ludi publici: Untersuchungen zur Entstehung und Entwicklung der öffentlichen Spiele im republikanischen Rom* (Stuttgart 1998).

Lusus Troiae, "Troy game", cavalry manoeuvres performed by Roman youth (sometimes divided into two troups, *turmae*, by age), usually to mark a special occasion (a triumph, the dedication of a temple, the celebration of major LUDI). They are attested as early as CORNELIUS Sulla, were institutionalized for the young men of the elite by AUGUSTUS, performed successfully by TIBERIUS and NERO, and survived at least until the end of the second century CE. The etymological connection of the word *troia* with the city of Troy, though accepted in antiquity, is doubtful.

Virgil, *Aeneid* 5.545–603; Suetonius, *Julius Caesar* 39.2; *Augustus* 43.2, *Tiberius* 6.4, *Nero* 7.1; Plutarch, *Cato the Younger* 3.1.

Lycaea, Greek competitive festival for Zeus Lycaeus on Mt Lycaeum in Arcadia. Regarded by PAUSANIAS as one of the oldest of Greek festivals, the Lycaea were held either every two years (perhaps in the summer of the years after and before the Olympics, near the time of the NEMEAN games) or every four. The athletic programme mirrored nearby Olympia's, though the PANKRATION for boys may have been added earlier; there were equestrian events too. PRIZES were bronze objects, perhaps tripods: nevertheless, the Lycaea were listed among athletes' more prestigious triumphs (much like the HERAEA (1) at ARGOS).

Pindar, *Olympians* 9.95–98, 13.107–108; *Nemeans* 10.45–48; Pausanias 8.2.1–2, 38.5; *IG* 5.2 549, 550.

Lyceum, Athenian GYMNASIUM. Set in a sanctuary for Apollo Lyceius just southeast of the city wall, the Lyceum may date to the time of the tyrant PISISTRATUS in the sixth century. It was rebuilt and enlarged by Pericles in the fifth and then again by Lycurgus in the fourth. He added or rebuilt a PALAESTRA, but other modifications may have been meant to accommodate Aristotle, who – like Isocrates and other teachers before him – used the Lyceum and its surroundings as a base for his school from 335 (Plato made similar use of the ACADEMY). The Lyceum's location, close to the city, lent itself to cavalry and infantry exercises, including javelin practice, as well as to athletic training and competition. Its walls were decorated with allegorical scenes by the painter Cleagoras.

Aristophanes, *Peace* 353–356; Xenophon, *Anabasis* 7.8.1; *Greek History* 1.1.33; *Hipparchicus* 3.1, 6–7; Plato, *Lysis* 203AB; Isocrates, *Panathenaicus* 18; Pausanias 1.19.3, 1.29.16; *IG* 1³ 105.

J. P. Lynch, *Aristotle's School* (Berkeley and Los Angeles 1972); Kyle (1987) 77–84.

Lycinus, runner, fifth century. Winner of the race in armour at Olympia in 448, Lycinus has been thought to be the same man as a Spartan victor in a chariot race often dated to 432. However, Pausanias says Lycinus's chariot victory was won only after one of the colts he'd brought to the festival was disqualified and he then decided to run them against full-grown horses. It should therefore date from 384 or later, after the introduction of the chariot race for colts (PŌLOI) at Olympia, and so too late to be the runner's.

Pausanias 6.2.1–2; *Oxyrhynchus Papyri* 222.

S. Hodkinson, *Property and Wealth in Classical Sparta* (London 2000) 330 n15.

Lycomedes, son of Aristodemus, Eleian equestrian victor, first century. An Olympic *SPONDOPHOROS*, Lycomedes won the horse race at the festival (perhaps in 36) as well as a two-horse chariot race at the Pythian games.

IvO 216, 217.

Lygdamis, of Syracuse, pancratiast, seventh century. The winner of the first Olympic wreath for *PANKRATION* in 648, Lygdamis is said to have been as big as Heracles, with a foot one and a half cubits (about 18 inches) in length. He was buried near the quarries at Syracuse.

Pausanias 5.8.8; Philostratus, *On Athletic Exercise* 12.

M

Magic. Ancient competitors relied on innate ability, expended time, effort and money, and prayed to the gods for success. When necessary, they CHEATED. Some, not content to improve their own chances, sought to reduce others' with the help of magicians. These often employed binding spells (Greek *katadesmoi*, Latin *defixiones*), usually inscribed (sometimes with depictions of their intended victims, or symbols) on small, thin pieces of lead, often rolled up or pierced, which called on evil spirits to hinder and harm rivals. Most agonistic binding spells which survive concern chariot races in both the Greek and Roman worlds of the second century CE and after. Naming charioteers and their horses, they ask demons to prevent teams from leaving the starting stalls or, if they do get away, to bring them to ruin on the course. Some have been found buried near the starting area or at turnposts, though points of easy access to the underworld, graves and bodies of water (including drains and wells), are the common sites. (One Egyptian recipe recommends drowning a cat in a bucket of water and stuffing it with tablets. Do not try this at home.) As a defence against such tactics, charioteers commissioned victory charms and bedecked themselves and their horses with gemstones with apotraic devices, necklaces of wolves' teeth, and papyrus sheets covered with magical signs. Spells were also directed at runners – they are to be kept from sleep, food and drink before a race – and wrestlers.

Pausanias 6.20.18; Libanius, *Orations* 1.161–162, 36.20; Ammianus Marcellinus 29.3.5; *Theodosian Code* 9.16.11.

J. G. Gager (ed.) *Curse Tablets and Binding Spells from the Ancient World* (New York 1992) 43–77; F. Heintz, "Circus curses and their archaeological contexts", *JRA* 11 (1998) 337–342; M. W. Dickie, *Magic and Magicians in the Greco-Roman World* (London and New York 2001) 293–300.

Magister (plural *magistri*), a gladiatorial trainer (DOCTOR).

Cicero, *On the Orator* 3.23.86; Quintilian 2.17.33.

Mosci Sassi (1992) 136.

Manica (plural *manicae*), "sleeve", a chain-mail, quilted or padded protection for a GLADIATOR's sword arm.

Juvenal 6.256.

Manicarius (plural *manicarii*), "sleeve-man", a member of a gladiatorial FAMILIA who made and maintained MANICAE.

ILS 5084, 5084a.

Mappa, "napkin", a white cloth dropped from above the *carceres* by the presiding magistrate to start races in the Roman CIRCUS. Though ascribed to NERO – dining late, he signalled the start of racing by having his table napkin tossed out the window – it may be older.

Martial 12.29.9; Suetonius, *Nero* 22.2; Tertullian, *On Spectacles* 16; Cassiodorus, *Variae* 3.51.9.

Marathon, modern long-distance footrace (since 1908, 26 miles, 385 yards), inspired by stories involving the Athenian courier PHEIDIPPIDES.

Marcius, Gnaeus, of Rome, equestrian victor, first century CE. Marcius won at two Olympic festivals in succession, perhaps in 5 and 9. These were likely equestrian victories, following the lead of the future emperor TIBERIUS.

IvO 222.

Marion, son of Marion, Alexandrian HEAVY athlete, first century. Like his compatriot STRATON – and the legendary HERACLES – Marion won wrestling and *pankration* on the same day at Olympia, in 52.

Pausanias 5.21.10; Eusebius, *Chronicon* 1.213 Schoene.

Mastanabal, son of Masinissa, equestrian victor, second century. Son of the king of Numidia in North Africa (and father of Jugurtha, one of Rome's most formidable foes), Mastanabal won the pairs chariot race for colts at the PANATHENAEA in 158. This victory may have prompted his hellenizing father to commission a Greek-style bronze sculpture of Mastanabal.

IG 2² 2316.

D. W. Roller, "A note on the Berber Head in London", *JHS* 122 (2002) 144–146.

Mastigonomos (plural *mastigonomoi*), "whip-wielder", MASTIGOPHOROS.

Pollux 3.145, 153.

Mastigophoros (plural *mastigophoroi*), "whip-bearer", official who maintained order and punished rule-breakers at Greek competitive festivals (and elsewhere). At Olympia, they kept order during the drawing of lots – even NERO was said to

have feared them. At the DEMOSTHENEIA at Oenoanda, twenty citizen *mastigophoroi* chosen by the AGŌNOTHETĒS wore white clothing and carried shields (for crowd control) as well as whips.

See also: RHABDOPHOROS, RHABDOUCHOS.

Xenophon, *Constitution of the Spartans* 2.2; Lucian, *Hermotimus* 40; Pollux 3.153.

Megacles, son of Hippocrates, Athenian chariot victor, born 530–510. Megacles, head of the famous Alcmaeonidae family, was ostracized from Athens in 487/6 and promptly won the chariot race at the Pythian games. A vase painted at the time links this victory with that of Alcmaeon, the family's first prominent member, at Olympia in 592. His son Megacles topped him, winning at Olympia in 436, but was no more popular. His service as secretary to the treasurers of Athena in 428/7 earned him a mention as an embezzler in Aristophanes' comedy *Acharnians*.

Pindar, *Pythians* 7 (with Scholiast); Aristophanes, *Acharnians* 614–616; *IG* 1³ 297–299, 322–324.

Melancomas, of Caria, boxer, first century CE. The son of another Melancomas, an Olympic boxing champion (? 49 CE), Melancomas is said to have surpassed his father despite his lack of so coveted a victory because of his beauty, size and moral qualities: he was so fit and self-controlled that he won at Delphi by outlasting his opponents, holding his arms at the ready but neither hitting or being hit until, exhausted, they gave in. We have very little other information about Melancomas and his manner of fighting seems inconsistent with measures which brought bouts to an end (see KLIMAX (1)). It is therefore possible that he is an invention or at least that his tactics owe much to our sources' desire to portray him as a model of the Cynic sage, master of his passions.

Dio Chrysostom 28, 29.

M. B. Poliakoff, "Melankomas, *ek klimakos* and Greek boxing", *AJP* 108 (1987) 511–518.

Melesias, Athenian pancratiast and trainer, sixth/fifth century. A victor as a boy at Nemea and later as a man, Menander went on to become a famous trainer of pancratiasts and wrestlers, gaining his thirtieth crown in 460; all his athletes whom we can identify were Aeginetan. His son Thucydides, Pericles' main political rival, hired leading trainers of the younger generation, Xanthias and Eudorus, for his boys Melesias and Stephanus, and they became the best wrestlers in Athens.

Pindar, *Olympians* 8.54–66; *Nemeans* 4.93–96, 5.48–49, 6.64–66; Plato, *Meno* 94CD.

Melicertes, legendary boy in whose honour the ISTHMIAN games were founded. Fleeing along the road from Corinth to Megara from her husband Athamas – he was mad or set on revenge for Ino's murder of his son Phrixus – Ino leaped into the sea at the Molurian Rocks with Melicertes in her arms. She was transformed into the sea deity Leucothea; a dolphin brought Melicertes' body ashore, where it was buried by his uncle Sisyphus, king of Corinth. He also established games in Melicertes' honour. These Isthmian games included worship of Melicertes as a HERO under the name Palaemon, "Wrestler", and his image is meant to invoke them on Corinthian coinage under the Romans.

Pindar fragment 6.5(1); Pausanias 1.44.7–8, 2.1.3.

E. R. Gebhard and M. W. Dickie, "Melikertes-Palaimon, hero of the Isthmian games", in R. Hägg (ed.) *Ancient Greek Hero Cult* (Stockholm 1999) 159–165.

Menedemus, son of Protus, Eleian chariot victor, first century. A priest at Olympia, Menedemus won a two-horse chariot race there (perhaps in 60). His son, also named Menedemus, was victor in the two-horse chariot race for colts (*PŌLOI*) at Nemea.

IvO 214.

Menodorus, son of Gnaeus, Athenian wrestler and pancratiast, second century. Two impressive monuments, on Delos and at Athens, recorded Monodorus's accomplishments in crown games: victories in *pankration* (? in 132) and (?) wrestling at Olympia, in *pankration* at the Pythian games, in wrestling (as an AGENEIOS) and wrestling and *pankration* (as an adult) at Nemea, six triumphs at the HERACLEIA of Thebes – thirty-two wins in all. Menodorus also received honours from the people of Athens, Rhodes and Thebes, and from King Ariarathes V of Cappadocia. Oddly, however, though there is no mention of victory at Isthmia, Menodorus is styled PERIODONIKĒS; the festival was perhaps in abeyance after the Roman sack of Corinth (146).

IG 2² 3147, 3149a, 3150; *ID* 1957.

S. Dow, "Greek inscriptions", *Hesperia* 4 (1935) 71–90 (81–90); Moretti (1953) 131–138.

Meson echein, "hold the middle", *meson lambanein* "take the middle", to put a rival wrestler in a waistlock in order to lift him off the ground and then to throw him. Also *dialambanein*.

Pindar, *Nemeans* 4.35–41; Aeschylus, *Eumenides* 155–159; Aristophanes, *Acharnians* 271–275.

Poliakoff (1986) 40–53, 137–142.

Meta (plural *metae*), a turning-post in the Roman CIRCUS. One was placed at either end of the central barrier (EURIPUS). Chariots had to pass on the right side of the near *meta* after leaving the CARCERES. At the CIRCUS MAXIMUS, the *metae* comprised three vertical cones upon a high platform with straight sides. The cones were topped by a short horizontal element, in turn crowned by small egg-like objects. Metae seem to be linked to funerary monuments and to bear other religious associations.

Livy 41.27.6.

J. H. Humphrey, *Roman Circuses. Arenas for Chariot Racing* (London 1986) 255–259.

Miliarius (plural *miliarii*) or *milliarius*, "thousander", Roman CHARIOTEER with 1,000 victories or more.

ILS 5287.

Milon, of Croton, wrestler, sixth century. The most famous of CROTON's great athletes, Milon won once as a boy at Olympia (540) and then five or six times as an adult (536–520 or 516), losing in the end to TIMASITHEUS (1), a younger Crotoniate who knew enough not to come to close quarters with him and so wore him down. He added seven Pythian victories (one as a boy), ten at Isthmia and nine at Nemea in a quarter-century career. Milon was legendary for his size and strength, both owed in part to his appetite. He is said to have eaten twenty pounds of meat and twenty more of bread and washed them down with eight quarts of wine, and to have carried a four-year-old bull a length of the stadium before butchering and eating it in one day. He reputedly also brought his own victory STATUE into the ALTIS. To one element of his DIET, the gizzard-stones of roosters, is credited his virtual invincibility. His strength and reputation served his city well in a battle with Sybaris; bearing HERACLES' lion-skin and club, Milon led an army outnumbered three to one to victory. The story suggests that Milon was well connected at Croton; others make him a disciple of Pythagoras, the philosopher (and even his daughter's husband) and the father-in-law of the famous physician Democedes. Nevertheless, Milon becomes the type of dull gluttony for some hostile writers. Some depict him as bewailing his lost strength in old age. Others recount an end in which physical power is linked to a fatal failure of judgement. Walking in the countryside, he found a tree partially split and, on trying to finish the job bare-handed, was trapped and then eaten by wolves, as large and senseless a victim as the bull he had once consumed.

Herodotus 3.137; Diodorus 12.9.5–6; Pausanias 6.14.5–8; Galen, *Exhortation* 13 (1.34–35 Kühn); Aelian, *Historical Miscellany* 2.24; Athenaeus 10.412F; Cicero, *On Old Age* 9.27, 10.33; Pliny, *Natural History* 37.54.144.

Poliakoff (1987) 117–119; G. Maddoli, "Milone Olimpionico ἑπτάκις ([Simon.] fr. 153 D e Paus. VI 14, 5)", *PdP* 262 (1992) 46–49; V. Visa-Ondarçuhu, "Milon de Croton, personnage exemplaire", in A. Billault (ed.) *Héros et voyageurs grecs dans l'occident romain* (Lyon and Paris 1997) 33–62.

Miltiades, son of Cypselus, Athenian chariot victor, sixth century. Olympic chariot victor sometime in the mid-sixth century (? 560 ? 548), Miltiades became tyrant of the Chersonese and uncle of the Miltiades who was responsible for Athens's victory over the Persians at Marathon. He dedicated an ivory horn of plenty at Olympia.

Herodotus 6.36.1; Pausanias 6.19.6.

Minicius Natalis, Lucius, son of L. Minicius Natalis, Roman politician and chariot victor, second century CE. Son of a Roman consul, Natalis won the Olympic chariot race in 129 CE after serving as praetor, and was himself later consul and proconsul of Africa.

Pausanias 5.20.8; *IvO* 236.

Miscellanea, "mixture", a combination of different kinds of food which made up a GLADIATOR's staple diet.

Juvenal 11.17–20.

Mosci Sassi (1992) 138–139.

Missilia, cloth baskets suspended from pulleys and moved around the AMPHITHEATRE along guide ropes, which were used to distribute gifts (*missilia* or *res missiles*) to the audience at Roman spectacles. These might include coins, fruit, small cakes or tokens; some tokens could be exchanged for valuable prizes – Nero gave away ships, apartment blocks and farms.

Suetonius, *Nero* 11.2; *ILS* 5077.

Missio, "sending away", a GLADIATOR's permission to stop fighting before a victor was determined. Gladiators whose bouts were undecided were said to be *missi*, "let go" – a result indicated by the letter M on reports of gladiatorial shows. Fights *sine missione*, "without reprieve", were banned by Augustus, a sign of his unusual concern for the dignity of public spectacles. They were not uncommon under later emperors.

Livy 41.20.12; Suetonius, *Augustus* 45.3; *ILS* 5088, 5113.

G. Ville, *La gladiature en occident des origines à la mort de Domitien* (Paris 1981) 403–424, Mosci Sassi (1992) 139–140.

Mithradates VI Eupator Dionysus, king of Pontus and equestrian victor, 120–63. Rome's most dangerous enemy in the early first century, Mithradates was defeated by CORNELIUS Sulla and, finally, by Pompey. Eager to cast himself as a worthy successor to ALEXANDER III, Mithradates pursued equestrian victories as eagerly as he did political power, sweeping all the races at a Chian festival except one (won by a woman, Eucleia). And as ruthlessly: he is said to have poisoned Alcaeus of Sardis for outracing him.

Plutarch, *Pompey* 37.1.

Mitra (plural *mitrai*), headband worn by victors at Greek competitive festivals. The *mitra* was often of wool, embroidered so as to be quite stiff.

Pindar, *Olympians* 9.84; *Isthmians* 5.62.

Mnaseas, of Cyrene, runner, fifth century. Known as "the Libyan", Mnaseas was the first Greek from North Africa to become Olympic champion, winning the race in armour in (?) 484. His son Cratisthenes won the chariot race, perhaps in 464.

Pausanias 6.13.7, 18.1.

Mnesibulus, of Elateia (Phocis), runner, second century CE. PERIODONIKĒS in both STADION and the race in armour, Mnesibulus won both at Olympia in 161 and added the hoplite race at the ELEUTHERIA (1) at Plataea and the title, "best of the Greeks", which went with it. He displayed his valour dying in the battle against the Costoboci, "an army of bandits" (as his contemporary PAUSANIAS calls them), and his statue stood in the Street of the Runner at Elateia.

Pausanias 10.34.5; *IG* 9.1 146.

Monokelēs (plural *monokeltes*), "single horse", a race horse.

See also: KELĒS.

Pausanias 8.42.9.

Monomachos (plural *monomachoi*), "single fighter", Greek term for GLADIATOR. Cf. *monomachia*, "single combat", a gladiatorial fight.

Strabo 5.1.7.

Robert (1940).

Morator (plural *moratores*), "delayer", stable staff responsible for steadying chariot horses as they entered the starting gate at the Roman CIRCUS.

ILS 5313.

Moschus, of Colophon, boxer, third/second century. Winner at Olympia in 200, Moschus was the only boy PERIODONIKĒS in boxing.

Eusebius, *Chronicon* 1.209 Schoene.

Munerarius (plural *munerarii*), patron of a GLADIATORIAL show (*munus*). The *munerarii* – a term invented by the emperor AUGUSTUS – dealt with the owner or manager of a troup of gladiators (LA-NISTA). Contracts specified the numbers of fighters, and their types; the amount to be paid increased if a gladiator died. *Munerarii* often commemorated their shows with mosaics in the reception areas of their homes.

Seneca, *Controversies* 4 preface 1; Quintilian 8.3.34; Gaius, *Institutes* 3.146.

Mosci Sassi (1992) 140–141.

Munus (plural *munera*), "gift, obligation", Latin term for display of GLADIATORS. Gladiatorial shows are universally recognized as a symbol of Roman civilization – or savagery. Yet, though they attracted little criticism – their expense aside – Romans themselves regarded them as foreign in origin (ETRUSCAN, Samnite, Campanian) and they became popular in the most Hellenized communities of the eastern empire. The first attested Roman *munera* took place in funeral games put on by the sons of D. Iunius Pera in 264, which featured three gladiatorial pairs. They retained their link, however formal, with the commemoration of dead males for the next two hundred years until Caesar, always the innovator, used the occasion of his daughter's death to mount a particularly elaborate display. They had already begun to play a part in rivalry for political prestige and office among the elite, with the magistrates in charge of public festivals (*LUDI*) supplementing their budget in order to entertain the electorate with ever more extravagant gladiatorial *munera* (until the Senate felt compelled to restrict them). Recognizing their appeal, emperors controlled magistrates' right to give *munera* and monopolized it at Rome itself; their own shows could be spectacular – Trajan celebrated the end of the Dacian War (107 CE) with some 5,000 combats over four months. The first gladiators in the Greek east appeared among the performances of many sorts presented by King Antiochus IV Epiphanes at Antioch in 167. Under the empire, they were offered by members of the same local elite which presided over traditional Greek competitive festivals, often as part of the emperor's cult and certainly with his approval. They were never introduced into traditional AGŌNES, however, just as they were kept distinct from beast hunts (*venationes*) at Rome itself.

The evening before a *munus*, combatants enjoyed a banquet (*cena libera*) open to the public, likely a form of advertising like the hoardings, preserved at Pompeii, which set out the programme and amenities of forthcoming shows. The *munus* itself took place in the afternoon – the morning was reserved for beast hunts, the noon hour for executions of criminals or other forms of entertainment. It began with a parade through the AMPHITHEATRE and then a programme of four or five bouts – ten to thirteen in some lavish displays – each lasting as long as fifteen or twenty minutes. These began with a trumpet blast and ended when one gladiator indicated submission by raising a finger (*ad digitum*) – in the manner of Greek combat athletes – could not continue, or was killed outright. Though the fate of losers was in the hands of the giver of the *munus* (MUNERARIUS), he might refer it to the spectators. They, in turn, could recommend mercy – by pointing two fingers straight down – or death. (Though any movie-goer knows that this was signalled by pointing the thumb downward, the evidence is less clear-cut, and may suggest that any movement of the thumb was fatal.) If the crowd or *munerarius* so decreed – and if the gladiator's owner or manager had agreed beforehand – the final blow was delivered by a dagger driven through the spine. Perhaps only one in every five or six fights ended in death – it was remarkable when eleven at one *munus* all did: gladiators were valuable property. Winners received a palm leaf, a crown if they had distinguished themselves, a victory lap of the amphitheatre, and sometimes more: gold pieces, a mansion, freedom, public acclaim.

Polybius 30.25.5; Livy, *Summaries* 16; Valerius Maximus 2.4.7; Suetonius, *Julius Caesar* 10.2; *Claudius* 21.5; *Nero* 30.3; Juvenal 3.36–37; *Historia Augusta, Hadrian* 3.8; *ILS* 5062, 5145.

Robert (1940); G. Ville, *La gladiature en Occident des origines à la mort de Domitien* (Rome 1981); T. Wiedemann, *Emperors and Gladiators* (London and New York 1992); D. G. Kyle, *Spectacles of Death in Ancient Rome* (London and New York 1998).

Munus assiforanum (Latin *as*, a copper coin, and *forum*), a GLADIATORIAL spectacle meant to profit the sponsor. A second-century CE inscription (our only evidence) limits their cost to 30,000 sesterces.

ILS 5163.

Murmillo (plural *murmillones*) or *mirmillo*, *myrmillo*, a type of GLADIATOR, likely that earlier called *gallus* (though both terms appear in an early imperial inscription). *Murmillones* wore greaves, carried a large oblong shield and a sword, and bore on their head a visored helmet topped with the image of a fish – they usually fought RETIARII. (The emperor Caligula, who favoured *retiarii*, lightened *murmillones*' amour.) The shift in their designation reflects the absorption of Italian Gauls into Roman society.

Cicero, *Philippics* 6.5.13; Martial 8.75.16; Suetonius, *Caligula* 55.2; Quintilian 6.3.61; Juvenal 6.78–81; *ILS* 5083a, 5084, 5084a, 5103.

Mosci Sassi (1992) 144–145.

Musclosus, Roman CHARIOTEER, first/ second century CE. A Tuscan by birth, Musclosus won 672 times for the Red CIRCUS FACTION, thrice as a White, five times as a Green, twice as a Blue, and was commemorated by his wife.

ILS 5281.

Horsmann (1998) 256.

Musclosus, Pompeius, Roman CHARIOTEER, early second century CE. Musclosus won 3,559 races for the Green CHARIOT FACTION, 115 times with a single African horse.

ILS 5287.

Horsmann (1998) 255–256.

Mycenaeans, Bronze Age Greeks known through excavations at Mycenae, Pylos, Tiryns and elsewhere, through the Linear B tablets (written in an early form of Greek) and through the poems of Homer. Though composed during the subsequent Dark Age, these last are set at the end of the Bronze Age (about 1200 BCE) and contain some information likely derived from that period. FUNERAL GAMES like those for Patroclus may be depicted in Mycenaean art (and, it has been suggested, may have provided the first GLADIATORIAL displays, later borrowed by the Romans from Greeks in south Italy) and there is evidence for some of the activities in Homer's account: chariot racing, footraces, the spear throw, boxing (perhaps with a device like the later KLIMAX *(1)* to bring fighters into closer contact). Unlike Homer's, however, Mycenaean athletes (and charioteers) usually appear nude.

J. Mouratidis, "Anachronism in the Homeric games and sports", *Nikephoros* 3 (1990) 11–22; Decker (1995) 21–26.

Mycon, trainer, fourth century. Mycon dedicated a statue of Olympia to one of his pupils, a Samian boxer who won the competition in 380. An epigram claims that the Samians excel other Ionians in athletics and in naval warfare. Mycon himself may have won the Pythian boxing crown for boys some twenty years before.

Ebert (1972) 104–107; Moretti (1987) 69–70.

Myron, of Sicyon, chariot victor, seventh century. Tyrant of Sicyon, among the first of many Greek rulers to seek publicity and prestige at Olympia, Myron won the chariot race in 648 and is said (probably wrongly) to have erected the Sicyonian Treasury there.

Pausanias 6.19.1–2.

Mys, of Tarentum, boxer, fourth century. Mys's Olympic victory in 336 – won against many opponents and at the cost of many blows – gave rise to a proverb for misery, "like a mouse in pitch" – a pun on both Mys/*mys*, "mouse" and PISA/*pissa*, "pitch".

Zenobius 5.46; Diogenianus 1.72; *Suda* μ 1466.

N

Naea, Greek competitive festival. Celebrated (perhaps in the late summer or early autumn of the first year of every Olympiad) in honour of Zeus Naios at Dodona, site of the oldest Greek oracle, the Naea included a full athletic programme, a chariot race (at least), and dramatic competition. Already able to draw competitors such as King PTOLEMY I of Egypt and his wife BERENICE I (chariot victors in the early third century), it was included among the sacred crown games about one hundred years later (? 192).

Athenaeus 5.203A; *IG* 4.1 428.

P. Cabanes, "Les concours des *Naia* de Dodone", *Nikephoros* 1 (1988) 49–84.

Narycidas, or Tharycidas, son of Damaretus, Phigalian wrestler, fourth century. A PERIODONIKĒS, Narycidas won (twice ?) at Delphi and Nemea and three times at Isthmia before his Olympic victory in wrestling (perhaps in 384).

Pausanias 6.6.1; *IvO* 161.

Ebert (1972) 116–118.

Nemean games (Greek *Nemea*), Greek competitive festival. One of the four crown games of the original circuit (PERIODOS), the Nemean games were usually said to have been founded by King Adrastus of ARGOS in memory of the baby OPHELTES/Archemorus, bitten by a snake;

a later tradition credits HERACLES, grateful for the successful completion of his first Labour, the capture of the Nemean Lion. The historical festival dates from 573; it was celebrated every two years, in August or September. Games first took place at Nemea, a sanctuary for Zeus located in an upland valley in the northeast Peloponnese, an international no-man's land between the Argolid to the south and Corinthian territory to the northeast, between Arcadia to the southwest and Achaea to the northwest. At first the sanctuary and festival were under the control of Cleonae, nearby to the northeast. However, the archaeological record reveals traces of a pitched battle in the sanctuary towards the end of the fifth century, after which the festival must have been held elsewhere, probably at Argos. When it returned to Nemea about 340, it was under Argive auspices, and it had moved to Argos itself for good by 250 (except for the celebration of 235; see ARATUS). PAUSANIAS found the sanctuary in ruins. Modern excavations have unearthed evidence for ample "treasuries" or pavilions, constructed by Greek cities for the entertainment of competitors, officials and guests, an athletes' village, apparently organized by event rather than nationality, and a vaulted tunnel leading into the stadium. They have also led to a revival of the Nemean games under the leadership of Stephen G. Miller – in this case, with women competing alongside men, and like them, clothed.

Established at the same time as the Pythian and Isthmian games, the Nemean have many similarities to the Olympics. Zeus and Heracles were linked to both, as were officials called HELLANODIKAI; neither was within a city-state with its own political purposes. The programmes too were alike: at Nemea, as at Olympia, only athletes and equestrian owners competed (apart from heralds and trumpeters), at least until the Hellenistic period. However, the Nemean games included a footrace not run at Olympia (the HIPPIOS), three AGE-CLASSES (PAIDES, AGENEIOI, ANDRES) instead of two, a DOLICHOS for boys and (in the first century CE) a STADION race for girls. The prize was a wreath of fresh celery (selinon).

Posidippus, P.Mil.Vogl. 8 309.XI.27; Pausanias 2.15.2–3.

P. Perlman, "The calendrical position of the Nemean games", Athenaeum 77 (1989) 57–90; Stephen G. Miller (ed.) Nemea. A Guide to the Site and Museum (Berkeley and Los Angeles 1989); "The stadium at Nemea and the Nemean games", in W. Coulson and H. Kyrieleis (eds) Proceedings of an International Symposium on the Olympic Games, 5–9 September 1988 (Athens 1992) 81–86; S. D. Lambert, "Parerga II: the date of the Nemean games", ZPE 139 (2002) 72–74.

Nero, Roman emperor (54–68 CE), competitor and fan, 37–68 CE. Nero was a devotee of chariot racing from childhood. Once, lamenting the death of a Green CIRCUS FACTION driver with a friend, he was rebuked by a teacher, only to respond that he had been misunderstood: the conversation was about Hector, dragged behind ACHILLES' chariot in the Iliad. As emperor, Nero encouraged the addition of extra races and himself rode in the CIRCUS MAXIMUS. (He even drank a cordial made from the dung of wild boars, burnt to ash and mixed with water – a remedy for charioteers' aches and injuries.) He also forced fellow members of the elite to appear in gladiatorial shows and beast hunts. Still more remarkable for a Roman aristocrat was his support for and participation in Greek competitions. In 59, he celebrated the Iuvenalia to mark the first shaving of his beard; these were theatrical and musical performances in which Roman senators and equites took part with considerable reluctance. The next year, Nero instituted a festival on the Greek pattern. The Neronia included athletic and equestrian contests as well, exconsuls as judges, and Vestal Virgins as spectators in the place of Demeter's priestess at Olympia. Members of the elite competed nude like the athletes the emperor brought in from Greece. Nero himself competed (in poetry and rhetoric) at the second celebration, in 65. In the interval, he had built Rome's first permanent GYMNASIUM. Not content with fostering Greek festival competition at Rome, Nero moved onto Greece itself, where in 66–67 he competed in the most prestigious contests (the Olympics, the Pythian, Nemean and Isthmian games, the HERAEA (I) at Argos and the Actian games established by AUGUSTUS). His goal was to become a PERIODONIKĒS. He succeeded, though some festivals had to be rescheduled to accommodate him (the Olympics from 65 to 67) and some events did not run smoothly. Thrown from his ten-horse-chariot at Olympia (an event he had introduced there along with musical contests) he was unable to finish. However, the judges gave him the crown anyway. Nero reciprocated with a gift of money and Roman citizenship, and marked victory at Isthmia by freeing the Greeks from Roman taxes and administration. He was less generous to previous winners, whose statues he had taken down.

On his return to Italy, Nero entered a number of cities through a breach in the wall, setting a style for victors in crown games (see EISELASIS) and at Rome wore his Olympic wreath and carried his Pythian in his right hand. (The report that he won 1,808 crowns, in every Greek city but Athens and Sparta, is unreliable.) Such pursuits and the evident pleasure they brought him did nothing to enhance Nero's position among the Roman elite, generally hostile to Greek athletic competition and contemptuous of its practitioners (in part because they thought public nudity demeaning). They certainly contributed to the revolt which led to his suicide in 68.

Pliny, *Natural History* 28.72.238; Tacitus, *Annals* 14.14, 20, 15.67; Suetonius, *Nero* 22–25, 53; Cassius Dio 63.9.3–21.1; Philostratus, *Life of Apollonius* 4.24, 5.7; SIG^3 814.

J. Mouratidis, "Nero: the artist, the athlete and his downfall", *JSH* 12 (1985) 5–20; N. M. Kennell, "Νέρων Περιοδονίκης", *AJP* 109 (1988) 239–251; Caldelli (1993) 37–43.

Nicagoras, son of Nicon, of Lindus (Rhodes), equestrian victor, fourth century. Nicagoras's Olympic victories, in the two-horse chariot race and the horse race, may have come in 308, about the time of his triumph in the two-horse race at the LYCAEA. He boasted many other victories too, including four-horse chariot races at Delphi, Isthmia and Nemea and the chariot race for colts (*PŌLOI*) at the PANATHENAEA.

ILindos 68; SIG^3 314.

Nicandrus, of Elis, runner, fourth century. Nicandrus won the Olympic *DIAULOS* twice (perhaps in 304 and 300) as well as six footraces of various kinds at Nemea.

Pausanias 6.16.5.

Nicanor, son of Socles, Ephesian wrestler, first century CE. Winners of the boys' wrestling at Olympia in 89 without benefit of a BYE, Nicanor and his victory were commemorated by a dedication by his brother Diodorus.

IvO 227.

Nicasylus, of Rhodes, wrestler, undated. Since he was eighteen, Nicasylus was excluded from the boys' boxing competition at Olympia; he entered the men's and won it, and was later champion at Isthmia and Nemea as well. He died at twenty on his way home to Rhodes.

Pausanias 6.14.2.

Nicknames. Like modern athletes – soccer's Pele, hockey's Rocket Richard, Dr J. in basketball – ancient competitors often attracted nicknames. Sometimes their origins are unknown – why was HELIODORUS (1) of Alexandria, Olympic *STADION* winner in 213 and 217 CE, also called Trosidamas? Sometimes we can guess, as in the case of Heliodorus's contemporary, the long-distance runner known to us only by his nickname GRAUS, "Grey". Most, however, are clear enough; references to great athletes of earlier days or heroes of myth. So HEAVY athletes are called MILON or Atlas or the second Hercules/Heracles, boxers recall Castor or POLLUX/Polydeuces (traditionally the sport's inventor), the SECUTOR Marcianus took the *nom de guerre* of the fratricide Polynices, female GLADIATORS fight under the names Achillia and Amazon to recall ACHILLES' duel with the Amazon Penthesilea. These are likely names bestowed by the gladiators' owner(s). In other cases, the impetus may have come from fans – though we may suspect that NERO himself encouraged his address as Apollo and Heracles on his return from his triumphant tour of Greek festivals.

Cassius Dio 62.20.6; *Greek Anthology* 7.692, 16.52.

W. Ameling, "Maximinus Thrax als Herakles", *Bonner Historia-Augusta-Colloquium 1984/1985* (Bonn 1987) 1–11, K. Coleman, "*Missio* at Halicarnassus", *HSCP* 100 (2000) 487–500.

Nicocles, son of Nicetas, of Acriae (Laconia), runner, second/first century. Nicocles won five races at two Olympic festivals, perhaps *DIAULOS*, *DOLICHOS* and the race in armour in (?) 100 and *DIAULOS* and another in 96. It is clear that he did not win the Olympic *STADION* race. However,

Nicocles did win STADION, DIAULOS and the race in armour at the AMPHIARAEIA at Oropus, as well as two footraces at the ELEUTHERIA (2) at Larisa.

Pausanias 3.22.5; IG 5.1 1108, 7 415+ 417, 9.2 529.

Nicoladas, of Corinth, athlete, fifth century. A likely reading of an epigram ascribed to SIMONIDES reveals that Nicoladas was a successful pentathlete, victorious at Delphi, three times at both Isthmia and Nemea, and elsewhere – including the PANATHENAEA, where his PRIZE was sixty amphoras of olive oil.

Greek Anthology 13.19.

Ebert (1972) 92–96; R. Merkelbach, "Der Fünfkampfer Nikoladas", ZPE 67 (1987) 293–295.

Nicomachus, son of Leonidas, of Messene, pentathlete, second century. Nicomachus was pentathlon champion at two Panathenaic festivals in a row in the early second century. He may also have won at the Pythian games – unless that was his brother Leon.

IG 2² 2314, SEG 24.389.

Ebert (1972) 211–214.

Nicon, of Anthedon (Boeotia), pancratiast, fourth/third century. Olympic *pankration* champion in 300 and 296, Nicon was a PERIODONIKĒS, also winning twice at Delphi and Isthmia and four times at Nemea.

Oxyrhynchus Papyri 2082.

Nicophon, son of Tryphon, Milesian boxer, first century. An epigram by his contemporary Antipater of Thessalonica praises Nicophon's thick bull neck, iron shoulders like Atlas's, and HERACLEAN beard. Not even Zeus could refrain from trembling when Nicophon won the Olympic boxing crown (perhaps in 8).

Greek Anthology 6.256.

Moretti (1987) 74.

Nicostratus, son of Isodotus, of Aegae (Cilicia), HEAVY athlete, first century CE. The child of a noble family of Prymessus in Phrygia, Nicostratus was stolen as a baby and sold at Aegae. His owner dreamed that a lion's whelp slept under Nicostratus's bed. Sure enough, though uglier than his rival and lover Alcaeus of Miletus, Nicostratus grew into a byword for strength, the subject of a mosaic portrait, and the seventh (and last) man to emulate HERACLES by winning both wrestling and pankration on the same day at Olympia (in 37).

Lucian, How to Write History 9; Pausanias 5.21.10; Eusebius, Chronicon 1.213–215 Schoene; Quintilian 2.8.14; Tacitus, Dialogue on Orators 10.

Moretti (1987) 75.

Nomophylax (plural *nomophylakes*), "law guardian", one of a group of Eleian officials who instructed the HELLANODIKAI in their duties.

Pausanias 6.24.3.

Novicius (plural *novicii*), a GLADIATOR who had newly arrived at a training school (LUDUS).

Cicero, For Sestius 36.78.

Nudity, a characteristic of Greek athletes. CHARIOTEERS are usually depicted in a long, close-fitting tunic, jockeys often in a short-sleeved tunic. But artists also show both naked, a representation of the claim of equestrian events to be judged on a par with athletics. The GYMNASIUM, after all, was a place for naked exercise. Though hoplite racers wore armour, HEAVY athletes leather skull-caps and ear guards (AMPHŌTIDES), boxers thongs (HIMANTES), and all practised INFIBULATION, nudity was the norm in Greek athletic competition. Not always: Homer's heroes wore a loincloth (PERIZŌMA). But artists paint athletes naked from the mid-seventh century and the word *gymnazō*, "visit the gymnasium, exercise naked", is attested soon after. Ancient accounts of the custom's origin stress the competitive advantage a runner (usually ORSIPPUS), discovered by chance. Modern explanations invoke prehistoric hunting (the naked body is easier to camouflage), initiations of youth, admiration of the male body (gleaming with OLIVE oil like a bronze STATUE), the (clearly related) wish to demonstrate SEXUAL control even in close quarters with its beauty. Certainly athletic nudity distinguished the Greeks from their neighbours: ETRUSCAN athletes are often shown in the precursors of modern shorts or in loincloths (sometimes painted on Greek pots after firing in respect for the tastes of the Etruscan market). Romans abhorred public nudity. This was one reason for the resistance of the elite to competition on the Greek model. It was NERO who is credited with first presenting naked athletics at Rome (at his Neronia). Perhaps there were examples as early as AUGUSTUS; but athletic nudity did become more accepted after Nero's time.

Theognis 1335–1336; Thucydides 1.6.5–6; Plato, *Republic* 5.452C; Dionysius of Halicarnassus, *Roman Antiquities* 7.72.2–4; Pausanias 1.44.1; Tacitus, *Annals* 14.20.

N. B. Crowther, "Nudity and morality: athletics in Italy", *CJ* 76 (1980–1981) 119–123; Golden (1998) 65–69.

Nyssa (plural *nyssai*), largely poetic term for a turning-post (KAMPTĒR).

Homer, *Iliad* 23.332; Theocritus 24.119; Pausanias 6.13.9, 20.19

O

Oceanus, Roman chariot horse, ? late second century CE. CALPURNIANUS claims to have driven Oceanus to 209 victories for the Green CIRCUS FACTION.

ILS 5288.2.

October Horse, Roman religious ritual. Every 15 October, a two-horse chariot race was held in the Campus Martius and the right-hand horse of the winning team sacrificed to Mars. While its tail and (?) genitals were rushed to the Regia, where they bled onto the altar, residents of two Roman districts, Subura and Sacra Via, fought over the head, severed by a sword. These districts may have participated in the race itself.

Plutarch, *Moral Essays* 287AB; Festus 190 Lindsay.

Octoiugis (plural *octoiuges*), Latin term for eight-horse chariot team or race.

Livy 5.2.10; *ILS* 5286.

Oebotas, son of Oenias, of Dyme, runner, eighth century. According to tradition, Oebotas got no honour from his fellow citizens after winning the Olympic STADION race in 756, and so called on the gods to deny Achaeans victory ever after. Only their dedication of STATUES to him at Olympia and Dyme 300 years later brought the curse to a close with the victory of Sostratus (or Socrates) of Pellene in the boys' *stadion* race of 460. From that time, Achaean competitors sacrificed to Oebotas. However, we know of several Achaean winners before Sostratus, and the story may have arisen to explain the worship Oebotas attracted.

Pausanias 6.3.8, 7.17.6–14.

Ofonius Tigellinus, breeder of Roman chariot horses, first century CE. Sicilian by origin, Tigellinus's expertise as a breeder of chariot champions brought him to the attention of the emperor NERO, who appointed him to the high offices of prefect of the night watch and then praetorian prefect. A leading figure in the terror of Nero's last years, and a companion on his tour of Greek competitive festivals, Tigellinus was forced to commit suicide by the emperor Otho (69).

Tacitus, *Histories* 1.72; Scholiast on Juvenal, 1.155.

Oil *see* OLIVE OIL

Oiokelēs (plural *oiokelētes*), MONOKELĒS.

Posidippus, *P.Mil.Vogl.* 8 309.XIII.28.

Olive oil (Greek *elaion*), a staple of Greek life for food and fuel, was also essential in exercise and athletics. Greeks anointed and dusted themselves before exercise and competition, removed their oil, dust and sweat with a STRIGIL at the end, and applied oil again after a cleansing bath. The two practices may once have been distinguished (*xēraloiphein* being used for oiling before, *aleiphein* after), perhaps when oiling for exercise came into fashion. (Homer's heroes do not oil before competition and the Athenian historian Thucydides refers to it as a fairly recent innovation – like athletic NUDITY.) Over time, however, *aleiphein* came into general use, ALEIPTĒS, "anointer", became synonymous with trainer and *hoi aleiphomenoi*, "the anointed", with athletes. The amounts consumed were significant: daily allotments of oil at a local festival at Roman Sparta were 182 litres for the AGE-CLASS of men, 136 for young men (*neoi*), 91 for boys. Communities brought in oil for their public GYMNASIA and distributed it for a price (often subsidized) or free; this supply was often supplemented or replaced by GYMNASIARCHS or other benefactors among the elite, sometimes through foundations which survived them. (The orator Heraclides had a fountain of oil with a golden roof installed in the gymnasium of Asclepius at Smyrna). The model gymnasium even had a room set aside for oiling, the *elaiothesion*. The Greeks explained their use of oil as an aid to suppleness, a protection against dirt, sun or cold, a means for unscrupulous wrestlers to slip a hold. Modern scholars have added reasons of their own: the magical power of oil to give strength, its ability to hide a prehistoric hunter's smell. Whatever its original purpose, the oil used every day by an athlete in hard training might in the end be repaid by the amphoras filled with olive oil which were the prizes at the PANATHENAEA, or be transformed into glory by the Olympic olive wreath.

See also: *GLOIOS*.

Thucydides 1.6.5; Aristophanes, *Knights* 490–491; Lucian, *Anacharsis* 28; Philostratus, *On Athletic Exercise* 7, 18, 58; *Lives of the Sophists* 2.26.2; Vitruvius, *On Architecture* 5.11.2; *IG* 5.1 20; *OGI* 339, 764.

C. Ulf, "Die Einreibung der griechischer Athleten mit Öl", *Stadion* 5 (1979) 220–238; N. M. Kennell, " 'Most necessary for the bodies of men': Olive oil and its by-products in the later Greek gymnasium", in M. Joyal (ed.) *In Altum. Seventy-five Years of Classical Studies in Newfoundland* (St John's 2001) 119–133.

Olympic games (Greek *Olympia*), oldest and most important Greek competitive festival. Held at the sanctuary of Olympian Zeus, on the Alpheius and Cladeus rivers southeast of ELIS in the northwest Peloponnese, the origins of the festival were subject to debate among the Greeks themselves. Mythical founders included Zeus himself, HERACLES and PELOPS. The traditional date of the first competitions, determined by HIPPIAS of Elis – 776 – was more widely accepted, and is often regarded as our first reliable benchmark in Greek history. But alternatives existed (Eratosthenes preferred 884) and still survive. Modern archaeology reveals both the antiquity of the site (which shows evidence of cult activity as early as the Bronze Age) and an upsurge of interest in it, perhaps linked to the institution of the competitive programme, about 700. A vague Homeric reference to chariot races in Elis need not refer to the festival, so it is even possible that the Olympics, like the other panhellenic games of the original circuit (PERIODOS), were a product of the early sixth century. However old the contests were, Olympia was always dominated by the sacred grove of Zeus (ALTIS), his great Temple, and Phidias's colossal chryselephantine cult statue which stood within it. Facilities for athletes were simple, accommodation for spectators austere (HERODES Atticus endowed the first reliable water supply, in the second century CE); the heat, crowding, noise and lack of shelter were as famous as the festival itself.

Political control of the Olympics was generally less controversial. A persistent if confusing tradition placed nearby PISA at the helm early on. However, the authority of the Eleians was recognized by the mid-sixth century and maintained thereafter (though the Arcadians celebrated the festival under the aegis of Pisa in 364). Organizers, judges and other officials (ALYTARCHAI, HELLANODIKAI) were all Eleians. To some degree, Elis's position was a measure of the community's marginality, politically and militarily as well as in its out-of-the-way location: control of Olympia was too crucial to fall into the hands of one of the great powers. (This was one of the motives for the choice of Ottawa, an isolated lumber town, as Canada's capital over the claims of more qualified communities.) The dynasts and conquerors of the archaic and classical periods – tyrants of Sicily, kings of Cyrene, PHILIP of Macedon – had to content themselves with olive wreaths instead of rule, crowns instead of control, a pattern continued after ALEXANDER III by the PTOLEMIES of Egypt and ATTALIDS of Pergamum. As the Greek world shrunk into an insignificant and impoverished corner of Rome's empire, in the first century, equestrian competition at Olympia became the preserve of the local Eleian elite. But athletics continued to attract competitors from afar (with Alexandria and Asia Minor increasingly prominent among winners' homes). In the early empire, benefactors such as King HEROD of Judaea and the emperor AUGUSTUS himself favoured the festival – a colossal gold and silver statue of Augustus in the likeness of Zeus was erected in the Temple of the Mother Goddess in the Altis – and members of the royal family (TIBERIUS, GERMANICUS, NERO) came to think equestrian victory worthy of their efforts. The peace, prosperity and philhellenism of the age of HADRIAN and the Antonines benefited Olympia's facilities as it did other Greek centres (though our evidence for horse and chariot races is again spotty); the Herulian invasion of 267 CE and an earthquake a generation later interrupted rather than ended its preeminence; and recent excavations suggest that new buildings and old traditions

were visible up to the end of the fourth century CE at least. Until Theodosius I's edict of 393 CE, which banned pagan festivals, Olympia generally headed lists of triumphs in inscriptions.

The Olympics took place every four years, regularly enough that they supplied the hundreds of Greek cities, with their varied calendars, with a panhellenic system for dating years. The first full moon after the summer solstice of an Olympic year signalled the start of the Olympic TRUCE, the safe-conduct for competitors and others travelling to the site. It also (it seems) marked the beginning of the training period at Elis which all athletes had to attend. Whatever the original intent of this unusual requirement – to minimize the impact of different training regimens? – it had the effect of thinning out fields, both by bringing weaker hopefuls into contact with their clear superiors (those who dropped out at this stage went unpunished) and by discouraging those who could not afford to lose a month's earnings from coming at all. At the end of this period, competitors and officials walked from Elis to Olympia, a distance of about 60km (37 miles) – a two-day trek, during which the *Hellanodikai* and the Sixteen Women responsible for the HERAEA (2) may have purified themselves. The festival itself, once confined to one day, grew as the competitive programme expanded (see Table 1). Our account of its development, also derived from Hippias, has invited criticism much like his absolute chronology. PHILOSTRATUS offers a later date – 596 – for the inauguration of boys' events, and modern scholars have questioned the plausibility of the late appearance of chariot racing, so prominent in the FUNERAL GAMES of Patroclus. However delayed, it was the equestrian programme which continued to grow after athletics reached virtually its final form in the late sixth century (an index of the influence of the elite on the festival and of its importance to them). From 468, the Olympics covered five days, with the

Table 1 Development of the Olympic programme

Date	Event	Winner
776	*Stadion*	Coroebus of Elis
724	*Diaulos*	Hypenus of Pisa
720	*Dolichos*	Acanthus of Sparta
708	Pentathlon	Lampis of Sparta
	Wrestling	Eurybatus of Sparta
688	Boxing	Onomastus of Smyrna
680	Chariot race	Pagondas of Thebes
648	*Pankration*	Lygdamis of Syracuse
	Horse race	Crauxidas of Crannon
632	Boys' *stadion*	Polynices of Elis
	Boys' wrestling	Hipposthenes of Sparta
628 (dropped 628)	Boys' pentathlon	Eutelidas of Sparta
616	Boys' boxing	Philytas of Sybaris
520	Hoplite race	Damaretus of Heraea
500 (dropped 444)	*Apēnē*	Thersias of Thessaly
496 (dropped 444)	*Kalpē*	Pataecus of Dyme
408	Pairs chariot race	Euagoras of Elis
396	Trumpeters	Timaeus of Elis
	Heralds	Crates of Elis
384	Chariot race for colts	Eurybiades of Sparta
264	Pairs chariot race for colts	Bilistiche of Macedon
256	Colts' race	Tlepolemus of Lycia
200	Boys' *pankration*	Phaedimus of Alexandria

third, the day of the full moon itself, featuring the great sacrifice to Zeus in the *Altis*. Its age-old ashes from previous celebrations formed the upper part of an altar over twenty feet high in PAUSANIAS's day. Sometime before his visit, an extra day was added (see Table 2). The first day was devoted to the oaths of competitors (and of the fathers or older brothers of boys) and trainers. Over slices of boars' flesh – perhaps testicles – they swore they had trained for ten months before the games and would compete according to the rules. The *Hellanodikai* swore as well, to sort human and equine competitors into AGE-GROUPS fairly (those who disregarded their oaths faced severe penalties, including the hefty fines which paid for the ZANES). This scrutiny (*dokimasia*) was followed (after 396) by the contests for trumpeters (SALPINKTAI) and heralds (KĒR-

YKES). On the last day, there may have been a banquet for the victors at Olympia's Prytaneum.

Though Richard Chandler rediscovered the site of ancient Olympia, Pausanias in hand, in 1766, interest in reviving the games themselves came only two generations later, in the wake of the establishment of the modern Greek state. In 1835, the Romantic poet Panagiotis Soutsos persuaded a Greek government to mount an annual Olympic festival, to rotate among the major Greek cities and to begin on 25 March, the anniversary of the outbreak of the Greek war of independence from the Ottoman Empire. Meanwhile, Gustav Schartau, a Swedish scholar, organized Scandinavian Olympics at Lund. Both initiatives were short-lived: Soutsos's was abandoned when the current government fell, Schartau's was cele-

Table 2   The schedule of the Olympics

---

468 BCE

Day 1	Oath
	Dokimasia
Day 2	Equestrian events
	Pentathlon
Day 3	Rites for Pelops
	Great sacrifice
Day 4	Running (boys and men)
	Heavy events (boys and men)
	Hoplite race
Day 5	Banquet for the victors

---

200 BCE (?)

Day 1	Oath
	Dokimasia
	Trumpeters and heralds (introduced 396)
Day 2	Equestrian events
	Pentathlon
Day 3	Rites for Pelops
	Great sacrifice
	Boys' contests
Day 4	Running
	Heavy events
	Hoplite race
Day 5	Banquet for the victors

---

first century CE (?)

Day 1	Oath
	Dokimasia
	Trumpeters and heralds
Day 2	Pentathlon
Day 3	Equestrian events
Day 4	Rites for Pelops
	Great sacrifice
	Boys' contests
Day 5	Running
	Heavy events
	Hoplite race
Day 6	Banquet for the victors

Source: H.M. Lee, *The Program and Schedule of the Ancient Olympic Games*, *Nikephoros* Beihefte 6 (Hildesheim 2001) 102–103.

brated only twice, in 1833 and 1836. Later movements were more successful. Soutsos's idea was realized by an associate, the millionaire E. Zappas, who funded Greek Olympics (and the refurbishment of the Panathenaic stadium to hold them) in 1859 and (after his death) in 1870, 1875 and 1888. W. P. Brookes, a doctor and local magistrate, held annual Olympic games mixing Greek and medieval elements at his village of Much Wenlock in Shropshire from 1850; these grew

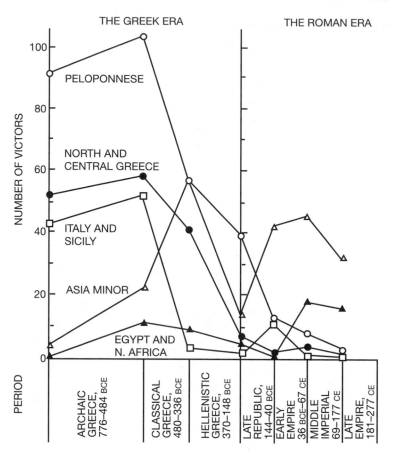

Figure 3 Origins of Olympic victors by region, 776 BCE–277 CE

Source: T. F. Scanlon, *Eros and Greek Athletics* (Oxford 2002) 63. Used by permission of Oxford University Press, Inc.

to become regional in the early 1860s and national a few years later, and were held (at least in their local form) until Brookes's death in 1895. At the same time, the Liverpool Athletic Club sponsored Olympics of its own in 1863, 1864, 1866 and 1867. All these games often attracted first-rate athletes and enthusiastic spectators; all were eclipsed by the success of the French Baron Pierre de Coubertin and his International Olympic Committee. Until recently, Coubertin's was generally believed to be the first and only movement for the revival of the Olympics. Its ability to establish itself (and to purge history of its precursors) was due to three

things: Coubertin's vision and vigour, his insistence on the games' international character, and his ability to attract the support of the royal and the rich to his project. These signed on largely because they were assured that only amateurs, those (like them) free to train and compete without regard for expense or income, would be eligible to boast to be the best. Coubertin believed that this replicated ancient Olympic practice. In fact, the present-day Olympics, in which professionals take part and receive rich rewards on their returns, are a closer match.

Homer, *Iliad* 11.698–702; Pindar, *Olympians* 3.19–22, 5.6; Bacchylides 7.1–11; Plutarch, *Moral Essays* 639A; Pausanias 5, 6; Philostratus, *Life of Apollonius* 5.43.

D. C. Young, *The Modern Olympics: A Struggle for Revival* (Baltimore 1996); U. Sinn, *Olympia: Cult, Sport and Ancient Festival* (Princeton 2001); H. M. Lee, *The Programme and Schedule of the Ancient Olympic Games* (Hildesheim 2001).

Olympio, daughter of Agetor, Spartan chariot victor, second century. Olympio, chariot champion at the PANATHENAEA of 170, was a member of a family in the service of the Ptolemies of Egypt.

Hesperia 60 (1991) 188–189.

Olyntheus, of Sparta, runner, seventh century. Olyntheus won the Olympic STADION race twice, in 628 and 620.

Eusebius, *Chronicon* 1.199 Schoene.

Onasiteles, son of Onasistratus, of Cedreae, runner, second century. Onasiteles won the STADION race for boys three times at Isthmia – he must have started very young – and for AGENEIOI once at Nemea. As an adult, he was successful in the race in armour, DOLICHOS and torch races as well, often at Rhodian festivals.

*SIG*³ 1067.

Moretti (1953) 127–130.

Onomastus, of Smyrna, boxer, seventh century. Onomastus was not only the first Olympic victor in boxing (in 688) but the first in any event from the Greek east. He is sometimes credited with establishing rules for the event – an extraordinary feat, given the Ionian reputation for delicacy and daintiness.

Pausanias 5.8.7; Philostratus, *On Athletic Exercise* 12.

Opheltes, legendary child honoured by the NEMEAN games. In the most common version of the games' origin, Opheltes, the son of King Lycurgus (or Lycus) of Nemea, was placed on a bed of wild celery while his nurse Hypsipyle showed an army on the march from ARGOS to Thebes the way to water. Opheltes was bitten by a snake and died. The child's death presaged defeat for the army and so he was given the name Archemorus, "beginning of doom". Adrastus, king of Argos, then celebrated the first Nemean games in requital – a justification for Argive control of the festival in later antiquity. Opheltes' shrine at Nemea has recently been discovered. His story explains some features of the Nemean games: the celery wreaths, the judges' black robes, cypress trees (linked to mourning) in the grove of Zeus.

Bacchylides 9.1–15; Euripides, *Hypsipyle*; Hyginus, *Stories* 74.

Stephen G. Miller (ed.) *Nemea. A Guide to the Site and Museum* (Berkeley and Los Angeles 1989) 25–29; M.-C. Doffey, "Les mythes de fondation des Concours Néméens", in M. Piérart (ed.) *Polydipsion Argos. Argos de la fin des palais mycéniens à la constitution de l'état classique* (BCH Supplément 22: Paris 1992) 185–193.

Oppidum, early Latin term for the starting-gate of CHARIOT races (*CARCERES*).

Varro, *The Latin Language* 5.153.

Opsōnion (plural *opsōnia*, Latin *obsonium*), "salary", a pension cities paid to victors in Greek competitions.

See also: PRIZES.

PRyl 153.25; Pliny, *Letters* 10.118, 119.

Orsippus, or Orrhippus, of Megara, runner, eighth century. Orsippus, winner of the Oympic STADION race in 720, is said to have been the first athlete to compete nude. The tradition is confused, however, as various sources also report that Orsippus was a Spartan, ran in 724 or 652, and originated nude competition only because he tripped on his loincloth, fell and was killed in a race at Athens. Orsippus is also said to have recovered Megarian territory

from Corinth and to be buried near
COROEBUS.

See also: NUDITY.

IG 7 52; Pausanias 1.44.1; *Etymologicum Magnum s. gymnasia*, Scholia A, B on Homer, *Iliad* 23.683.

W. E. Sweet, *Sport and Recreation in Ancient Greece* (Oxford 1987) 124–129.

P

Pacideianus, GLADIATOR, mid-second century. Pacideianus is called far and away the best gladiator in all history in a fragment of a poem by the Roman satirist Lucilius.

Lucilius, *Satires* 149–158 Marx.

Paegniarius (plural *paegniarii*), a type of GLADIATOR who engaged only in mock combat – perhaps with wooden weapons or whips. One (Secundus) boasted of living to the age of ninety-eight.

Suetonius, *Caligula* 26.5; ILS 5126.

Mosci Sassi (1992) 146–147.

Paeonius, son of Damatrius, of Elis, HEAVY athlete, third century. Paeonius was Olympic wrestling champion in 216 but was defeated by CAPRUS when he tried to repeat. However, after winning the crown for boys' boxing at Delphi, he triumphed there in both men's boxing and wrestling on the same day.

Pausanias 6.15.10, 16.9; IvO 179.

Pagondas, or Pagon, of Thebes, chariot victor, seventh century. Pagondas won the first running of the Olympic chariot race, in 680.

Pausanias 6.8.7.

Paides, AGE-CLASS in Greek athletics. The youngest competitors, *paides* were some-times further divided into subgroups, including *paides Pythikoi* and *Isthmikoi* (first at the ASCLEPIEIA (2) on Cos), *paides* of the first, second and third ages (at the Athenian THESEIA), *pampaides* and *paides presbyteroi* (at the Erotidea at Thespiae) and others, often local or even designed by an individual AGŌNOTHETĒS. Age limits for *paides* were probably from 12 to 17 at Olympia; *paides Pythikoi* may have included those 12 to 14, *Isthmikoi*, 14 to 17. In all cases, a boy's physical development may have influenced officials. *Paides* generally competed in the same events as older athletes, though *pankration* and *dolichos* are less common on their programmes. Variations abound. For example, though *paides* ran only the STADION at Olympia, only competed in pentathlon once (628) and in *pankration* only from 200, the Pythian games included *diaulos*, *dolichos* and pentathlon for boys from their inception and *pankration* from 346. Similarly, the scheduling of boys' events differed at these two most prestigious festivals, preceding all athletic contests (except pentathlon) for men at Olympia, alternating with them at Delphi.

Rules for *paides* were the same in all events – boxing was no safer – with the exceptions that their discus was smaller and their *dolichos* may have been shorter. Aristotle recommends a lighter training regimen up to the age of seventeen on the grounds that boys who are worked too hard rarely go on to successful athletic careers. In fact, we know of many who were champions both as *paides* and later on, in part because inscriptions and EPI-NICIANS boast of such victories. Prizes for *paides* could be considerable. At the PANATHENAEA, the *pais* who won the *stadion* took home fifty amphoras of olive oil, the equivalent of perhaps US$50,000 today, close to the prize of an AGENEIOS (sixty amphoras). However, this was (likely) much less than the prize for men.

It is also striking that boys' events were believed to have joined the programme at Olympia late and at a date which was disputed (? 632 ? 596) at that. Whatever their glory, *paides* were minors; their fathers or older brothers took the Olympic oath on their behalf, and (in keeping with this) it is their fathers we find charged with cheating (or refusing bribes). The separation of younger and older competitors is universal at Greek festivals, where fighters of different sizes and weights regularly faced each other. The motive may have been to prevent a father's defeat by a son – careers in the combat events in particular could cover twenty years, and there were numerous families with champions in several generations. The tendency of events for *paides*, as of subdivisions within the group, to multiply over time probably has a different impulse, the desire for victory and its rewards: local competitors were more likely to triumph among the *paides* than against older athletes.

Aristotle, *Politics* 8.1338b9-a10; Pausanias 5.8.9; Philostratus, *On Athletic Exercise* 13.

A. J. Papalas, "Boy athletes in ancient Greece", *Stadion* 17 (1991) 165–192; M. Lavrencic, "Zu Knabenagonen im antiken Griechenland", in R. Renson, M. Lämmer, J. Riordan and D. Chassiotis (eds) *The Olympic Games through the Ages: Greek Antiquity and its Impact on Modern Sport. Proceedings of the 13th International HISPA Congress, Olympia/Greece, May 22–28, 1989* (Athens 1991) 65–71; Golden (1998) 104–116.

Paidotribēs (plural *paidotribai*), "boyrubber", "boy smoother", physical TRAINER and athletics instructor. The *paidotribēs* usually worked at and often owned a PALAESTRA. In fourth-century Athens, the people elected two *paidotribai* (later reduced to one) to ensure the physical fitness of EPHEBES in military service; on Hellenistic Teos, two were appointed to the local *palaestra* and paid slightly less than instructors in the two other main elements of Greek education, *grammatikē* (reading, writing, literature) and *mousikē* (musical instruments and the poetry sung to them). From Aristotle on, writers often distinguish the *paidotribēs*, concerned above all with athletic skills and techniques, from the GYMNASTĒS, who is said to be more expert in the body's workings and development.

Antiphon 3.3.6; Aristophanes, *Knights* 1238; Isocrates 15.181–185; Plato, *Republic* 3.406A; Aristotle, *Constitution of the Athenians* 42.3; *Nicomachean Ethics* 10.1180b14; *Politics* 4.1288b17, 8.1338b9; Philostratus, *On Athletic Exercise* 14; SIG^3 578.

Jüthner (1909) 3–8; Kyle (1987) 141–145.

Palaemon *see* MELICERTES

Palaestra (Greek *palaistra*, plural *palaistrai*), Greek exercise and training site. *Palaestra* etymologically and perhaps originally referred to an area for wrestling (*palē*), but came to describe a structure with wider functions: an enclosed square or oblong courtyard surrounded by rooms for various activities (e.g. undressing, oiling, dusting). The Roman writer Vitruvius gives two STADIA (about 400m) as a standard circuit; however, no excavated example is so large. *Palaestrae* (from at least the fourth century) might be privately owned and operated, as standalone facilities or as part of a GYMNASIUM, and identified by an individual's name; or public. In some communities, *palaestrae* (like *gymnasia*) were set aside for boys or older users, perhaps in an attempt to prevent undesired SEXUAL activity. Restrictions on SLAVES, non-citizens and tradesmen represent and reinforce ideologies about athletics.

Herodotus 6.26.3; Euripides, *Andromache* 595–600; [Xenophon], *Constitution of the Athenians* 2.10; Plato, *Charmides* 153A; *Lysis* 203A–204A; Antiphanes fragment 298 Kassel-Austin; Theophrastus, *Characters* 5.9; Vitruvius, *On Architecture* 5.11.1–2; Isidore, *Etymologies* 18.23–24.

S. L. Glass, "The Greek gymnasium: some problems", in Raschke (1988) 155–173.

Palaistritēs (plural *palaistritai*, Latin *palaestrita, palaestritae*), "PALAESTRA-goer", an athlete, especially a wrestler, or a slave athlete who trained or entertained a wealthy Roman master. *Palaistritēs* is an epithet of the god HERMES (2), patron of *palaestrae* and GYMNASIA.

Callimachus fragment 554 Pfeiffer; Plutarch, *Moral Essays* 274DE; Cicero, *Against Verres* 2.2.36; Petronius, *Satyricon* 21.4–5; *BE* 1994. 380.

M. W. Dickie, "*Palaistritēs*/'*palaestrita*': callisthenics in the Greek and Roman gymnasium", *Nikephoros* 6 (1993) 105–151.

Palaistrophylax (plural *palaistrophylakes*), "palaestra guard", slave attendant in a PALAESTRA or GYMNASIUM. In Greco-Roman Egypt (and perhaps elsewhere), the term comes to be used for a minor office filled by citizens.

Hippocrates, *Epidemics* 6.8.30; *IG* 5.1 18; *ID* 290, 316, 372A; *Oxyrhynchus Papyri* 390, 1266.

K. J. Rigsby, "Notes sur la Crète hellénistique", *REG* 99 (1986) 350–360 (350–355).

Palē see WRESTLING

Palus (plural *pali*), "stake", term for a wooden stake used in training GLADIATORS and also for their standing. A *primus palus* (or *primuspalus*), "first stake", was a gladiator of the top rank (and so especially expensive). The emperor COMMODUS styled himself *primus palus* of the SECUTORES. Four *pali* were usually recognized, though there is some

evidence for six or even eight at Aphrodisias in Caria.

Historia Augusta, Commodus 15.8; *ILS* 5163.

Mosci Sassi (1992) 147–148.

Pamboeotia, Greek competitive festival, celebrated (at uncertain intervals) in early autumn in honour of Athena Itonia at Coroneia. Though likely older, the Pamboeotia is known by this name only from the third century. As its name suggests, it was primarily reserved for members of the Boeotian confederacy, though some competitions were open to outsiders (and these were encouraged to attend by a sacred TRUCE). It had a markedly military character, including competitions for army contingents (such as *euhoplia* and perhaps *EUTAKTIA*) and horse races which began from a statue of Ares, god of war. Among athletic events were a team TORCH race, *DOLICHOS* for *PAIDES*, and an AGE-CLASS *pampaides*.

Polybius 4.3.5, 9.34.11; *IG* 7 1764, 2871, 3087; *SEG* 18.240.

A. Schachter, "La fête des *Pamboiotia*: le dossier épigraphique", *CEA* 7 (1978) 81–107.

Pammachia, PANKRATION; *pammachos*, pancratiast.

Bacchylides 13.75–76; Aeschylus, *Agamemnon* 168–172; Plato, *Euthydemus* 271C; *IG* 7 2470.

Poliakoff (1986) 64–74.

Panathenaea, Athenian competitive festival. Held in July to mark the birthday of Athena, the city's patron, the Panathenaea was Athens's major festival. The annual celebration included TORCH races (run from the ACADEMY to the Acropolis at night) and competition in PYRRHIC dancing. Every four years from 566 a more elaborate Greater Panathenaea (supervised in the classical period by ten ATHLOTHETAI) added a full programme of literary, musical, dramatic, athletic and equestrian contests – likely a response (by the tyrant PISISTRATUS or his associates) to the contemporary development of the circuit (*PERIODOS*) of panhellenic festivals. Like, them, the Panathenaea sent out *SPONDOPHOROI* to attract competitors (such as *PHAŸLLUS*), from all over the Greek world. Unlike them, the Panathenaea awarded PRIZES of value – oil in distinctive containers, Panathenaic amphoras – for both first and second place in athletic and equestrian events (and as many as five money-prizes in musical contests). In the fourth century, winners received five times as many amphoras as second place finishers; the *STADION* race for men brought the largest number (likely 100) among athletic events (it was double the boys' prize [fifty], nearly that for *AGENEIOI* [sixty]), but less than that for the leading equestrian event for which evidence remains, the chariot race for pairs (140). (Here the second-place finisher too was special, winning forty amphoras rather than twenty-eight.) All three AGE-CLASSES competed in *stadion*, pentathlon, and the HEAVY events; there may have been a race in armour for men as well. Again unlike the games of the circuit, the Panathenaea offered events for citizens only: horse and chariot races (perhaps including *APOBATĒS*, linked to Athens's legendary King Erichthonius in myth, and *APĒNĒ*) with prizes significantly less than in open events, throwing the javelin from horseback at a target (a shield on a post), Pyrrhic dancing in three age-classes (with equal prizes for each), and at least three for teams representing Athens's ten tribes: *EUANDRIA*, a torch race, a boat race. All these, headed "for the warriors", were clearly an adjunct to military training, and team winners did not receive the characteristic amphoras.

Athens's political renaissance after the defeat of Macedon was followed by an expansion of both the athletic and the equestrian programmes of the Panathenaea during the second century; they now took up four days. The boys' programme dropped pentathlon but replaced it with *DIAULOS* and (unusually) *DOLICHOS*; men now raced *diaulos*, HIPPIOS, *dolichos* and

a race in armour as well as *stadion*. Athenians did well in *PANKRATION*, but other events were dominated by outsiders. The equestrian competition was still divided among events for Athenians and for all-comers. The Athenian were held both in the Hippodrome and along the *DROMOS*, the race-course which paralleled the route of the great Panathenaic procession through the *AGORA*. These once again had a military flavour; they featured war-horses (once in a long-distance race), rather than race horses and everyday chariots as well as lightweight sulkies and generally required that competitors rode and drove for themselves. Kings and queens of the Ptolemaic and Attalid dynasties of Egypt and Pergamum – to say nothing of their ministers and retainers – appear prominently among winners of open events, but the local elite were successful too. Evidence suggests that the festival's competitive programme continued to grow: a boys' *hippios* is known from the mid-first century.

Prizes at the Panathenaea

Prizes for the *kithara*-singers

First place: a crown of olive in gold weighing 1,000 drachmas and 500 silver drachmas
    Second place: 1,200 drachmas
    Third place: 600 drachmas
    Fourth place: 400 drachmas
    Fifth place: 300 drachmas

For the *aulos*-singers in the men's category

First place: a crown weighing 300 drachmas
    Second place: 100 drachmas

For the *aulos*-players

First place: a crown weighing [?]

[*several lines missing on the stone*]

For the victor in the *stadion* in the boys' category: 50 amphoras of olive oil
Second place: 10 amphoras of olive oil

For the victor in pentathlon in the boys' category: 30 amphoras of olive oil
Second place: 6 amphoras of olive oil

For the victor in wrestling in the boys' category: 30 amphoras of olive oil
Second place: 6 amphoras of olive oil

For the victor in boxing in the boys' category: 30 amphoras of olive oil
Second place: 6 amphoras of olive oil

For the victor in *pankration* in the boys' category: 40 amphoras of olive oil
Second place: 8 amphoras of olive oil

For the victor in the *stadion* in the *ageneios* category: 60 amphoras of olive oil
Second place: 12 amphoras of olive oil

For the victor in pentathlon in the *ageneios* category: 40 amphoras of olive oil
Second place: 8 amphoras of olive oil

For the victor in wrestling in the *ageneios* category: 40 amphoras of olive oil
Second place: 8 amphoras of olive oil

For the victor in boxing in [the *ageneios* category]: [50 amphoras] of olive oil
[Second place: 10 amphoras of olive oil]

For the victor [in *pankration* in the *ageneios* category]: [50 amphoras of olive oil]
[Second place: 10 amphoras of olive oil]

[*several lines missing on the stone*]

[For the victor in the *stadion* in the men's category: 100 amphoras of olive oil
Second place: 20 amphoras of olive oil

For the victor in pentathlon in the men's category: 60 amphoras of olive oil
Second place: 12 amphoras of olive oil

For the victor in wrestling in the men's category: 60 amphoras of olive oil
Second place: 12 amphoras of olive oil

For the victor in boxing in the men's category: 60 amphoras of olive oil
Second place: 12 amphoras of olive oil

For the victor in *pankration* in the men's category: 80 amphoras of olive oil
Second place: 16 amphoras of olive oil]

[*several lines missing on the stone*]

For the two-horse chariot race in the colts category: 40 amphoras of olive oil
Second place: 8 amphoras of olive oil

For the two-horse chariot race in the full-grown category: 140 amphoras of olive oil
Second place: 40 amphoras of olive oil

Prizes for the warriors

For the victor in the horse race: 16 amphoras of olive oil
Second place: 4 amphoras of olive oil

For the victor in the two-horse chariot race: 30 amphoras of olive oil
Second place: 6 amphoras of olive oil

For the victor in the processional two-horse chariot: 4 amphoras of olive oil
Second place: 1 amphora of olive oil

For the hurler of the javelin from horseback: 5 amphoras of olive oil
Second place: 1 amphora of olive oil

For the pyrrhic dancers in the boys'

category: A bull and 100 drachmas

For the pyrrhic dancers in the *ageneios* category: A bull and 100 drachmas

For the pyrrhic dancers in the men's category: A bull and 100 drachmas

For the winning tribe in *euandria*: A bull and 100 drachmas

For the winning tribe in the torch race: A bull and 100 drachmas

For the individual victor in the Torch race: A water jar and 30 drachmas

Prizes for the boat race

For the winning tribe: 3 bulls and 300 drachmas and 200 free meals
   Second place: 2 bulls and 200 drachmas

[*the rest of the stone is broken away*]

Source: IG 2^2 2311, 400–350.

The programme of the Panathenaea (second century)

Days 1–3: musical and dramatic competitions

Flute playing in the Odeion [?]

Kithara playing in the Odeion [?]

Choral performances in the Odeion [?]

Performances of tragedies in the Theatre of Dionysus

Days 4–7: athletic competitions

Day 4: gymnastic events

Place: the stadium
Open to all comers

A. boys
1 *dolichos*
2 *stadion*

3 *diaulos*
4 wrestling
5 boxing
6 *pankration*

B. *ageneioi*
1 *stadion*
2 pentathlon
3 wrestling
4 boxing
5 *pankration*

Day 5: gymnastic events in the stadium (continued)

C. men
1 *dolichos*
2 *stadion*
3 *diaulos*
4 *hippios*
5 pentathlon
6 wrestling
7 boxing
8 *pankration*
9 race in armour

Day 6: equestrian events

Place: the Agora or Market Square ("in the Eleusinion")
Open only to Athenian citizens, probably only to the cavalry

A. chariot competition
1 driver dismounting race (*hēniochos ekbibazōn*)
2 dismounting race (*apobatēs*)
3 pairs, up and back race
4 pairs, straight race (*akampion*)
5 pairs, parade chariot race
6 pairs, war chariot race

B. horse races for the cavalry commanders
1 race in armour for warhorse
2 up and back race
3 straight race (*akampion*)

C. horse races for cavalrymen

1 race in armour for warhorse

2 up and back race

3 straight race (*akampion*)

Day 7: equestrian events (continued), plus [?] the anthippasia

Place: the Hippodrome

A. open to all comers

1 thoroughbred race for colts

2 thoroughbred race for full-grown horses

3 pairs race for colts

4 pairs race for full-grown horses

5 four-horse chariot race for colts

6 four-horse chariot race for full-grown horses

B. open only to Athenian citizens

1 long-distance horse race

2 four-horse war chariot race

3 pairs parade chariot race

4 pairs, up and back race

5 pairs, war chariot race

6 pairs, up and back race

7 pairs, up and back race

8 pairs, straight race (*akampion*)

9 pairs, straight race (*akampion*)

10 pairs, straight race (*akampion*)

Day 8: tribal competitions

Pyrrhic dances in the stadium [?]

Euandria in the stadium [?]

Boat races at Munychia harbour

Days 1–8: recitations of the Iliad and the Odyssey on the Pnyx [?]

Night of Day 8: all-night celebration with torch races

Day 9: great procession, sacrifice and feast

Days 10–11: rest and clean-up

Source: J. Neils and S. Tracy, *The Games at Athens. Agora Picturebook* (Princeton 2003)

Pindar, *Olympians* 2.82; Aristophanes, *Frogs* 1087–1098; Lysias 21.1,4; Aristotle, *Constitution of the Athenians* 60; IG 2² 2311–2317, 3019, 3022.

S. V. Tracy and C. Habicht, "New and old Panathenaic victor lists", *Hesperia* 60 (1991) 187–236; D. G. Kyle, "The Panathenaic games: sacred and civic athletics", in J. Neils (ed.) *Goddess and Polis. The Panathenaic Festival in Ancient Athens* (Princeton 1992) 77–101; J. Neils (ed.) *Worshipping Athena. Panathenaia and Parthenon* (Madison 1996).

Pancles, son of Pancles, of (?) Tenos, athlete, first century CE. A fragmentary inscription from Tenos, dated to the first century CE, styles Pancles a winner in the Actia and a PERIODONIKĒS.

IG 12.5 909.

Pankration, regular event at Greek competitive festivals. As befits its name – "complete strength" or "total mastery" – *pankration* combined many fighting techniques: boxing (some pancratiasts wore thongs), kicking, wrestling throws, strangleholds, leg scissors. Only biting and gouging were forbidden; even these restrictions were removed at SPARTA and often ignored elsewhere. (We hear of pancratiasts nicknamed "lions" because of their bites.) Successful tactics included kicking the genitals – Galen says donkeys would make the best pancratiasts – tripping and SOSTRATUS's trick, bending back the fingers. Matches did not end until one competitor signalled submission (by raising a finger) or could no longer continue. Pancratiasts needed to be agile as well as strong (they practised with a bigger, heavier bag (KŌRYKOS) to improve balance) and often competed as wrestlers and/or boxers as well. Their event has inspired some recent revivals (Total Fighting, Ultimate Fighting). However, despite its reputation, and the occasional deaths of contestants like ARRICHION, it was regarded in antiquity as less dangerous than boxing.

Provided though it was with a proper mythical pedigree (Athens's Theseus was said to have been a pioneer), *pankration* does not figure in the FUNERAL GAMES of Patroclus, and entered the Olympic programme only after the other HEAVY events, in 648. The boys' *pankration* did not reach Olympia until as late as 200; it is absent from some other games as well. (Not all: Pytheas of Aegina may have won at Nemea as young as age twelve.) However, there is also evidence for the *pankration*'s importance: some fifth-century Olympiads are identified by the winning pancratiast, the prize at the fourth-century PANATHENAEA was second only to the STADION's among athletic events, and *pankration* was later awarded the highest at Aphrodisias (where it may have been called "the most perfect of contests"). In addition, pancratiasts make up by far the majority of XYSTARCHAI under the Roman Empire.

Xenophanes 21 F 2 Diels-Kranz; Thucydides 3.8.1, 5.49.1; Aristotle, *Rhetoric* 1.1361b25; Theocritus 22.66, 24.113–114; Lucian, *Anacharsis* 3, 8; *Demonax* 49; Galen, *Exhortation* 13 (1.36 Kühn); Philostratus, *On Athletic Exercise* 9, 57, 58; *Pictures* 2.6; *SEG* 31.1985; Aulus Gellius 13.28.3–4.

Poliakoff (1987) 54–63; G. Doblhofer and P. Mauritsch, *Pankration* (Vienna 1996).

Pantacles, of Athens, runner, seventh century. Winner of the Olympic STADION in 696 and of *stadion* and probably *diaulos* in 692, Pantacles is the first Athenian victor at Olympia, the first known multiple victor and the first to repeat as champion.

IG 2² 2326.

Pantarces 1. of Elis, equestrian victor, third century. The winner of the Olympic horse race (? in 228), Pantarces earned a statue from the Achaeans for his role in making peace between them and his own city.

Pausanias 6.15.2.

2. of Elis, wrestler, fifth century. Pantarces was boys' wrestling champion at Olympia (436). He was also a boyfriend of the famous sculptor Phidias, who is said to have used him as the model for the figure of a boy binding his head with a victory ribbon (*TAINIA*) which was placed before his gold and ivory statue of Zeus at Olympia.

Pausanias 5.11.3, 6.10.6.

Pantares, son of Menecrates, of Gela, equestrian victor, sixth century. The father of Cleandrus, ruler of Gela in the late sixth century, Pantares was the first of the Sicilian dynasts to win at Olympia, perhaps in the chariot race of 508.

IvO 142.

W. S. Barrett, "The Oligaithidai and their victories (Pindar, *Olympian* 13; *SLG* 339, 340)", in R. D. Dawe, J. Diggle and P. E. Easterling (eds) *Dionysiaca. Nine Studies in Greek Poetry by Former Pupils Presented to Sir Denys Page on his Seventieth Birthday* (Cambridge 1978) 1–20.

Pantonikēs (plural *pantonikai*), "victor in all contests", a term coined to describe NERO's unrivalled accomplishment of winning at all six festivals of the PERIODOS in the same year.

Cassius Dio 63.10.2.

Paraballon, of Elis, runner, third century. Paraballon won DIAULOS (280) and later listed Olympic victors in the gymnasium at Olympia, perhaps as part of anniversary celebrations for the Olympics' first 500 years. His son Lastratidas, a wrestler, won at Olympia (? 248) and Nemea as a boy, at Nemea again as an *ageneios*.

Pausanias 6.6.3.

J. Ebert, "Zur 'Olympischen Chronik, *IG* 11/111² 2326", *APF* 28 (1982) 5–14 (13–14).

Paradoxonikēs (plural *paradoxonikai*), or *paradoxos* (plural *paradoxoi*), "extraordinary victor, victor against the odds", a term originally applied to athletes who won both wrestling and *pankration* on the same day and then to any such winners in two events or two age-classes.

Plutarch, *Comparison of Cimon and Lucullus* 2.1; *IG* 14 747.

R. Merkelbach, "Über ein ephesisches Dekret für einen Athleten aus Aphrodisias und über den Athletentitel *paradoxos*", *ZPE* 14 (1974) 91–96.

Paradromis (plural *paradromides*), "side track", open air practice track in a Greek GYMNASIUM; cf. XYSTOS.

CID 2.139; Vitruvius, *On Architecture* 5.11.4.

Parembolē, "side attack", a wrestling move in which one competitor uses his leg to upset his opponent's balance.

Aeschines 3.205–206; Plutarch, *Moral Essays* 638F; Lucian, *Ocypus* 60–61.

Poliakoff (1986) 28–33.

Parmenides, of Posidonia, runner, fifth century. Parmenides won both STADION and DIAULOS at Olympia in 468.

Dionysius of Halicarnassus, *Roman Antiquities* 9.56.1; *Oxyrhynchus Papyri* 222.

Parmeniscus, son of Philiscus, Corcyraean runner, first century. Parmeniscus won DOLICHOS and DIAULOS for boys at the AMPHIARAEIA at Oropus and went on to be Olympic STADION champion twice as an adult, in 96 and 88.

Eusebius, *Chronicon* 1.211 Schoene; *IG* 7 415+ 417.

Parmularius (plural *parmularii*), "small shield man", a fan (like the emperors Caligula and Titus) of THRAECES, GLADIATORS who carried a small, round shield.

Quintillian 2.11.2; Suetonius, *Domitian* 10.1; Marcus Aurelius, *Meditations* 1.5.

Mosci Sassi (1992) 149–150.

Parthenoi see WOMEN.

Pataecus, of Dyme, equestrian victor, fifth century. Pataecus was the first victor in the KALPĒ at Olympia, in 496, and the only one we can identify.

Pausanias 5.9.2.

Patos, "treading", or *konisalos*, mixture of sweat, OLIVE oil and dust from the wrestling ground of the PALAESTRA, valued for its medicinal properties.

Galen 12.116, 283, 309 Kühn.

N. M. Kennell, " 'Most necessary for the bodies of men': Olive oil and its by-products in the later Greek gymnasium", in M. Joyal (ed.) *In Altum. Seventy-five Years of Classical Studies in Newfoundland* (St John's 2001) 119–133 (128–133).

Pausanias, of Magnesia (? on Sipylus) in Asia Minor, Greek traveller and author, second century CE. Pausanias's *Description of Greece* provides an account of the sites and monuments he saw and thought worth describing on visits to the Greek mainland in the mid-second century CE. (The work was finished by 180.) Like others of his era, Pausanias had a special respect for Olympia, to which he devotes the better part of two (5 and 6) of his ten books (and to a lesser extent for Delphi, in Book 10). Focused though he is on STATUES and other works of art, Pausanias offers enough information, much of it confirmed by modern archaeology, to rank as our most important literary source on the Olympic and Pythian festivals.

C. Habicht, *Pausanias' Guide to Ancient Greece* (Berkeley and Los Angeles 1985); K. Arafat, *Pausanias' Greece* (Cambridge 1996).

Peisidorus, or **Peisirodus** *see* PHERENICE

Pēlōma (plural *pēlōmata*), "mudpit" used in Greek training.

CIG 2 2758.

M. B. Poliakoff, "*Skammatos kai pēlōmatos*: CIG II 2758", *ZPE* 79 (1989) 291–292.

Pelops, son of Tantalus, legendary king of Pisa and founder of the Olympic games.

Once the beloved of Poseidon, Pelops left his native Lydia and came to Pisa, where King Oenomaus required suitors for his daughter Hippodameia ("tamed by horses") to race chariots against him. Though he gave them a head start, Oenomaus invariably caught up before they reached the finish line at the Isthmus of Corinth, killed them and nailed their heads over his palace door. Pelops, however, had a golden chariot and winged horses from Poseidon. He also (according to a darker tradition, hostile to chariot racing) bribed Oenomaus's charioteer Myrtilus. On race day, a wheel fell off Oenomaus's chariot and he died, entangled in the reins. Pelops married Hippodameia and became king. But he and his descendants lay under a curse, pronounced by Myrtilus – Pelops killed him for trying to rape Hippodameia. Pelops later controlled the Peloponnese, which took his name, and (in one tradition) founded the Olympic games to celebrate his victory over Oenomaus or to expiate his death. (Hippodameia too founded a competitive festival, the HERAEA (2) for girls.) Pelops's much venerated shrine in the ALTIS at Olympia likely dates to the early Bronze Age, and his chariot victory was the subject of the sculptures on the east pediment of the Temple of Zeus (about 470).

Pherecydes, *FGrH* 3 F 37a, 37b; Pindar, *Olympians* 1; Baccchylides 8.30–32; Sophocles, *Electra* 504–515; Euripides, *Electra* 988–1006; Phlegon, *FGrH* 257 F 1.1; Pausanias 5.8.2, 13.1–7, 17.7, 8.14.10–12; Apollodorus, *Epitome* 2.3–10.

G. Nagy, *Pindar's Homer. The Lyric Possession of an Epic Poet* (Baltimore and London 1990) 116–135; G. Howie, "Pindar's account of Pelops' contest with Oenomaus", *Nikephoros* 4 (1991) 55–120; W. Hansen, "The winning of Hippodameia", *TAPA* 130 (2000) 19–40.

Pentathlon, regular event in Greek competitive festivals. The pentathlon consisted of five events, DISKOS, JUMP, AKŌN (JAVELIN), *STADION*, WRESTLING, likely in that order. The method of determining the winner is a perennial puzzle of Greek sport history. Three wins were required, but we do not know what happened in the (presumably frequent) cases where no competitor swept the first three or three of the first four events. Our ignorance is the product of Greek familiarity with the procedure: our sources never spell it out. But the Greeks were less sure of the worth of the pentathlon's winner. Some admired him as an all-rounder, the prototype of the decathlete in track and field today. Others noted that he might be second-rate in some events or even in all, as a winner of the Nordic combined will likely lose to specialists in cross-country and ski-jumping. (Of those we know, champion pentathletes tended to be runners rather than wrestlers; an exceptionally versatile athlete known from a new Coan inscription won a *pankration* crown as a boy as well as *stadion* races and fourteen competitions in pentathlon at all ages.) Though it was said to have been added to the Olympic programme at the same time as wrestling, in 708, pentathlon was an event for boys only once (628) and value prizes were less than those for *stadion* or *pankration*.

Xenophon, *Greek History* 4.7.5; Plato, *The Lovers* 135E-136A, 138E; Aristotle, *Rhetoric* 1.1361b10; Philostratus, *On Athletic Exercise* 3, 31; *Suda* ε 2898.

Golden (1998) 69–73.

Periodonikēs (plural *periodonikai*), "circuit winner", winner of all four games of the original PERIODOS or of any four of the games later included in the expanded circuit. The growth of the circuit encouraged further distinctions: a *periodonikēs teleios* won at all and NERO, who won at all within one short trip to Greece, styled himself *periodonikēs* PANTONIKĒS.

Philo 2.438 Cohn-Wendland; Cassius Dio 62.10.1; *Inscr. Magn.* 180.

R. Knab, *Die Periodoniken* (Giessen 1934); E. Maróti, "*Periodonikēs.* Anmerkungen zum Begriff Perioden-Sieger bei den panhellenischen Spielen", *AAntHung* 31 (1985–8) 335–355; P.

Frisch, "Der erste vollkommene Periodonike", *EA* 18 (1991) 71–73.

Periodos, "circuit", the set of the most prestigious Greek competitive festivals. The original *periodos* was made up of the OLYMPIC, PYTHIAN, ISTHMIAN and NEMEAN games. Later, other festivals attained circuit status: the HERAEA (1) at Argos, the ACTIA, the SEBASTA at Naples and the Roman CAPITOLIA (see Table 3).

See also: PERIODONIKĒS.

IvO 186; *ID* 1057.

Perizōma, "girdle" (plural *perizōmata*), *zōma* or *diazōma*, loincloth worn by early Greek athletes (such as Homer's heroes), by some competitors on vases meant for the ETRUSCAN market, and by ATALANTA and other female athletes.

See also: NUDITY.

Homer, *Iliad* 23.683; Thucydides 1.6.5; Pausanias 1.44.1.

Petraites, GLADIATOR, first century CE. The (fictional) *nouveau-riche* freedman Petronius boasted of cups adorned with depictions of the fights of Hermerus and Petraites and planned to have Petraites' contests depicted on his grave monument.

Petronius, *Satyricon* 52.3, 71.6.

Phaedimus, of Alexandra in the Troas (or of Naucratis in Egypt), pancratiast, third/second century. Though his place of origin is disputed, there is no doubt that Phaedimus was the winner of the first *pankration* championship for boys when it was finally introduced to the Olympic programme in 200.

Pausanias 5.8.11; Philostratus, *On Athletic Exercise* 13; Eusebius, *Chronicon* 1.209 Schoene.

Phaininda, a BALL game in which a player tries to intercept a ball thrown between two other players. Also called *harpastum*, "Snatching".

Pollux 9.105; Athenaeus 1.14F–15A; Eustathius 1601.30 (on *Odyssey* 8.372 ff.); *Laus Pisonis* 185–187.

Phanas 1. of Messenia, runner, eighth/seventh century. Winner of the Olympic DOLICHOS sometime between 716 and 684, Phanas died gloriously fighting the Spartans in 683/2.

Pausanias 4.17.9.

2. of Pellene, runner, sixth century. Phanas was the first to win *stadion*, *diaulos* and the race in armour at the same Olympic festival (512).

See also: TRIASTĒS.

Eusebius, *Chronicon* 1.201 Schoene.

Phaÿllus of CROTON, athlete and war hero, sixth/fifth century. A three-time victor at Delphi (twice in the PENTATHLON, once in the STADION), and renowned as a runner in Athenian comedy, Phaÿllus alone among western Greeks brought his own

Table 3   The classical circuit (*periodos*)

Olympiad and year	Place	Date
75.1	Olympia	July/August 480
75.2	Nemea	August/September 479
	Isthmia	April/May or June/July 478
75.3	Pythia	August 478
75.4	Nemea	August/September 477
	Isthmia	April/May or June/July 476
76.1	Olympia	July/August 476

ship to share in the Greek triumph over the Persians at Salamis (480). In recognition, his STATUES were erected at Delphi and on the Athenian Acropolis, and ALEXANDER III the Great sent a share of the spoils of his victory over Persia at the battle of Issus (333) to his home city. Phaÿllus's 55-foot jump, the longest attested, is an important piece of evidence in the debate on the nature of the ancient Greek JUMP.

Herodotus 8.47; Aristophanes, *Acharnians* 214; *Wasps* 1206; Plutarch, *Alexander* 34; Pausanias 10.9.2; *IG* 1³ 823.

Moretti (1953) 25–29; M. Romano, "L'epigrafe ateniese a Phayllos (*IG*, 1³, 2, 823)", *ZPE* 123 (1998) 105–116.

Pheidippides (or Philippides), Athenian courier (*hēmerodromos*), sixth/fifth century. When the Persian invaders landed at Marathon (25 miles from Athens) in 490, Pheidippides ran to Sparta, about 240km (150 miles) away, to ask for help, meeting (so Herodotus says) the god Pan on the way. He arrived the next day only to be told that the Spartans couldn't come because of a festival and returned. According to a later tradition, Pheidippides then fought at Marathon and ran to Athens to announce the result. "Rejoice, we have won", he said, and died on the spot. (Other sources say this was a different runner, Thersippus or Eucles.) Robert Browning's poem *Pheidippides* (1879) first combined the stories and inspired the modern MARATHON.

Herodotus 6.105–106; Plutarch, *Moral Essays* 347C; Lucian, *A Slip of the Tongue* 3.

F. J. Frost, "The dubious origins of the 'marathon'", *AJAH* 4 (1979) 159–163; E. Badian, "The name of the runner", *ibid.* 163–166.

Pheidolas, of Corinth, equestrian victor, sixth century. Pheidolas's horse threw his rider at the start of the Olympic horse race (probably in 512) but finished first and was awarded the crown. The identity of Pheidolas's horse is unclear; it may have been Ourus or a mare, AURA – both meaning "Wind". His sons later won at

Olympia (in 508 and perhaps 504) and at Isthmia with Lycus.

Pausanias 6.13.9–10.

Ebert (1972) 46–49.

Pheidon, king of Argos, (?) early seventh century. The leading power in the Peloponnese after his defeat of Sparta (? 669), Pheidon seized control of Olympia from ELIS and presided over the Olympic festival (? 668), perhaps establishing PISA in authority over it for some time after.

Herodotus 6.127; Pausanias 6.22.2.

Pherenice, daughter of DIAGORAS, of Rhodes. Pherenice accompanied her son Peisidorus (or Peisirodus) to Olympia as his TRAINER (perhaps in 404). When he won the boys' boxing, she leaped over the fence of the trainers' enclosure and, in her excitement, inadvertently revealed her sex, thus becoming the only unauthorized woman to be caught at the Olympic festival. Her pedigree – her father and brothers had been Olympic victors as well as her son – saved her from punishment (this was to be hurled from the peak of Mt Typaeum). From then on, trainers at Olympia had to be as nude as athletes. Pherenice is also called Callipateira, and the unusual nudity of trainers at Olympia – they were clothed at other festivals – otherwise ascribed to the desire to test their endurance in the summer sun.

Pausanias 5.6.7–8, 6.7.2; Aelian, *Historical Miscellany* 10.1; Philostratus, *On Athletic Exercise* 17.

Pherenicus, "bearer of victory", race horse, early fifth century. Chestnut-maned Pherenicus bore victory to HIERON at both Pythian (? 482, 478) and Olympic (476) games. BACCHYLIDES says that he was unsullied by the dust (*konis*) of horses ahead as he rushed towards the finish line, conferring one of an athlete's proudest distinctions, to win AKONITI.

Pindar, *Olympians* 1.18–22; *Pythians* 3.72–76; Bacchylides 5.36–49, 176–186.

Pherias, son of Chares, Aeginetan wrestler, fifth century. Pherias was refused entry to the Olympic wrestling contest for PAIDES in 468 because he was too young. He returned and won at the next festival.

Pausanias 6.14.1; *SEG* 11.1231.

Philammon, of Athens, boxer, fourth century. Philammon won the crown for boxing at Olympia in 364 and remained famous enough later in the century to merit mention in speeches to Athenian juries and a rhetorical treatise by Aristotle. A late tradition says that he was not Greek by origin and could only compete because Aristotle adopted him – and Philammon does look like a NICKNAME – but it also implies that he was a wrestler.

Demosthenes 18.319, Aeschines 3.189, Aristotle, *Rhetoric* 3.1413a14, Themistius, *Orations* 21.249.

Philinus, son of Hegepolis, Coan runner, third century. Philinus figures as a fast runner in a poem by Theocritus, himself a Coan. No wonder: he was twice Olympic champion in the STADION (264, 260), won three other races there (perhaps DIAULOS in the years of his *stadion* victories and also in 256), and four more at Delphi, four at Nemea and eleven at Isthmia.

Theocritus 2.115; Pausanias 6.17.2; Eusebius, *Chronicon* 1.207 Schoene.

Philip II, king of Macedon (359–336) and equestrian victor, 382–336. The man responsible for Macedon's prominence and then pre-eminence in Greece, Philip was acutely sensitive to the value of the major competitive festivals for furthering his prestige and power. He was a two- or three time winner of Olympic races, for horses (356) and for chariots (352, ? 348), commemorating his victories by minting coins in the manner of Sicilian leaders (ANAXILAS, GELON) of the early fifth century. After settling the Sacred War in 346, Philip presided over the Pythian festival; after the Battle of Chaeronea (338), he established a Greek league whose council was to meet at the four festivals of the PERIODOS. His Philippeion, the first structure at Olympia to be named for a mortal benefactor, was situated in the northwest of the ALTIS, conspicuously close to the temples of Zeus and Hera. It was completed by his son ALEXANDER III only after his death: ironically, Philip was assassinated at Aegae while celebrating his daughter's marriage with another Olympic festival, a Macedonian tradition (see ARCHELAUS).

Diodorus 16.60.2; Plutarch, *Alexander* 3.8–9, 4.9; *Moral Essays* 105A; Pausanias 5.20.9; *IG* 4² 1.68.

D. G. Romano, "Philip of Macedon, Alexander the Great, and the ancient Olympic games", in E. C. Danien (ed.) *The World of Philip and Alexander* (Philadelphia 1990) 63–79; T. F. Scanlon, *Olympia and Macedonia: Games, Gymnasia, and Politics* ("Dimitria" Annual Lecture, 3 October 1996: Toronto 1997) 5–7.

Philippides *see* PHEIDIPPIDES

Philippus 1. Arcadian boxer, (?) fifth century. PAUSANIAS saw a statue of a boy boxer named Philippus at Olympia. The sculptor was Myron – which would date Philippus's win to about 436. The Philippus from Arcadia who boasts of defeating four boys from the islands at Olympia about 300 must therefore be a different boxer.

Pausanias 6.8.5; *IvO* 174.

Ebert (1972) 166–169.

2., son of Butacides, of Croton, Olympic victor, sixth century. Forced to leave his native Croton, Philippus contributed a trireme and its crew to the Spartan Dorieus's expedition to Sicily and was killed there along with him in the late sixth century. Though he was an enemy, the Segestans honoured him as a HERO because of his remarkable beauty. The event he won and the date of his victory are uncertain.

Herodotus 5.47.

Philistus, of Elis, second/first century. Philistus was the father and (likely) grandfather of a group of Eleians (Strogien, Telemachus, Praxagoras, Timareta, Philistus, Theodota, Philonicus) whose Olympic victories in chariot and horse races (in about 84 and 76) are commemorated in a now fragmentary monument.

IvO 198–206.

Philombrotus, of Sparta, athlete, seventh century. Philombrotus was the first to win his event three times at Olympia, PENTATHLON champion in 676 and (probably) 672 and 668.

Eusebius, *Chronicon* 1.197 Schoene.

Philon, son of Glaucus, Corcyraean boxer, fifth century. Olympic boxing champion in 500 and 496, Philon may be the boy from Corcyra with the same name who won the STADION race about 504, but this is unlikely.

Pausanias 6.9.9, 6.14.13.

Ebert (1972) 56–57.

Philopoemen, Achaean leader, about 253–182. A promising wrestler in his youth and later an experienced and successful general, Philopoemen doubted that athletes made good soldiers and would not permit his men to compete. Nevertheless, FUNERAL GAMES were established in his honour.

Plutarch, *Philopoemen* 3.2–4; *SIG*³ 624.

Philoponia, "love of effort", a competition in the Greek gymnasium, often associated with EUEXIA and EUTAXIA. A GYMNASIARCH gave a prize (at Beroea and Sestos, a shield) for *philoponia* to the young man or boy who best demonstrated diligence and industry over a period of a month or a year.

*SIG*³ 1061; *SEG* 46.730.

N. B. Crowther, "*Euexia, eutaxia, philoponia*: three contests of the Greek gymnasium", *ZPE* 85 (1991) 301–304.

Philostratus, author of *Gymnastikos*, "On Athletic Exercise", one of the few ancient works to take sport as its theme. There were several intellectuals of the second and third centuries CE called Philostratus. The author of *On Athletic Exercise* is likely Lucius Flavius Philostratus, a well connected Athenian who wrote numerous other works (*Lives of the Sophists*, a biography of Apollonius of Tyana, *Heroïcus*, perhaps *Imagines [Pictures]*) and died about 244–249. *On Athletic Exercise* (written about 220–225) purports to be a technical treatise, but there is no evidence that the author has any experience, let alone expertise, in this area, and his work is marked by sentimental idealization of the good old days of athletic competition (especially at Olympia), denunciation of the modern morals and training regimen which have taken their place, just-so stories on the origins of events and unreliable remarks on their contemporary conduct. It is nonetheless of considerable, if controversial, value.

Jüthner (1909); G. Anderson, *Philostratus* (London 1986) 268–272; A. Billault, "Le *Gymnastikos* de Philostrate: a-t-il une signification littéraire?", *REG* 106 (1993) 142–162; L. De Lannoy, "Le problème des Philostrate: état de la question", *ANRW* 2.34.3 (1997) 2362–2449 (2404–2410).

Philytas, Philetas or Philotas, of Sybaris, boxer, seventh century. Philytas was the first boy to become Olympic champion in boxing, in 616.

Pausanias 5.8.9; *IG* 2² 2326.

Phlegon, of Tralles, Greek author, second century CE. A freed slave and member of the staff of the philhellenic emperor HADRIAN, Phlegon wrote *The Book of Marvels*, *Long-Lived Persons* (both still extant) and *Olympiads*. Surviving fragments of this work deal with the founding of the OLYMPIC festival, the Olympic truce and wreath – first awarded to DAICLES – and the victors of the games of 72.

W. Hansen, *Phlegon of Tralles' Book of Marvels* (Exeter 1996).

Phormion, of Halicarnassus, boxer, fourth century. Phormion won the boxing event at Olympia in 392 but was among those bribed by EUPOLUS of Thessaly at the following festival.

Pausanias 5.21.3.

Photion, son of Barpion, Ephesian boxer, second century CE. Of the many crowns Photion won as an AGENEIOS and an adult, most were at festivals in the east, but he also triumphed at the HERAEA (I) at ARGOS and at Olympia, sometime between 166 and 194.

Ancient Greek Inscriptions in the British Museum 605; *P. London* 1178.

Moretti (1953) 211–215.

Phricias, of Pelinna (Thessaly), runner, sixth century. Phricias won two races in armour at Olympia (perhaps in 508 and 504) and another race, perhaps the DOLICHOS, at the Pythian games (? in 506). His son HIPPOCLEAS was also an Olympic victor.

Pindar, *Pythians* 10.11–16.

Phrynon, of Athens, (?) pancratiast, seventh century. An Olympic victor, in PANKRATION or (less likely) STADION in 628, Phrynon later (? 607/6) was killed in single combat with Pittacus, tyrant of Mytilene, in a struggle over the possession of Sigeum. Sources describe Pittacus as armed with a net and trident, like a later Roman RETIARIUS.

Plutarch, *Moral Essays* 858A; Diogenes Laertius 1.74.

Phyllobolia, "leaf throwing", custom of pelting winners in Greek competitions with leaves or flowers immediately after the event or on their return home.

Pindar, *Pythians* 9.123–125; *Nemeans* 4.13–22; Aristophanes, *Clouds* 1005–1008; Scholiast on Euripides, *Hecuba* 574.

E. K. Borthwick, "A *phyllobolia* in Aristophanes' *Clouds*?", *Nikephoros* 2 (1989) 125–134.

Pil(l)eus, (plural *pil(l)ei)* or *pilleum* (plural *pillea*), a close-fitting felt cap worn by Romans at the Saturnalia and other celebrations and by freed slaves. After five years, a GLADIATOR received the *pil(l)eus* as a mark of his freedom from service and was termed a *pillearius*.

Mosci Sassi (1992) 151.

Pindar, of Cynoscephalae and Thebes in Boeotia, Greek poet, 518–c.438. Ranked first in the ancient canon of nine Greek lyric poets, Pindar wrote hymns, dithyrambs, wedding and dance songs and dirges among other genres, but was best known for his EPINICIANS. It is only these (some forty-five, dated from 498 to 446) which remain extant and intact, collected as they were in four books (*Olympians, Pythians, Isthmians, Nemeans*) by Hellenistic scholars according to the festival where their recipients triumphed. (One celebrated a magistrate on Tenedos, another a champion player of the AULOS, the rest equestrian and athletic victors.) Himself a member of an elite family, Pindar's patrons included rulers of Sicily and Cyrene as well as the merely rich and powerful. His poems offer praise of their families and cities, of the HEROES of old whose deeds they recall (or should beware), of the poetry which will make them live as long in memory – and caution against arrogance or the envy which might malign them. Dense, elaborate, rapid and allusive, Pindar's language is on display every bit as much as the achievements of those who paid for it; he likes to present himself as an athlete and he is as competitive.

E. L. Bundy, *Studia Pindarica* (Berkeley 1986 [1962]); L. Kurke, *The Traffic in Praise. Pindar and the Poetics of Social Economy* (Ithaca NY and London 1991).

Pinnirapus (plural *pinnirapi*), "sleeve-snatcher" or "crest-snatcher", a type of GLADIATOR, probably the RETIARIUS or the SAMNIS.

Juvenal 3.157–158.

Mosci Sassi (1992) 152–155.

Pisa, town and/or district around OLYMPIA. Various (often conflicting) traditions accorded Pisa an important role in the early history of the Olympic festival, ascribing its earliest (Bronze Age) celebrations to Pisus, the community's founder, and to PELOPS, king of Pisa, and its renewal (in 776) to (a group including) Cleisthenes of Pisa. Pisa may have controlled Olympia for about one hundred years in the seventh and early sixth centuries, perhaps installed in the first instance by PHEIDON of Argos; at any rate, the Pisatan tyrant Pantaleon is said to have presided over the Olympiad of 644. Eleian authority is sometimes presented as a consequence of a process of peacemaking involving the Sixteen Women later responsible for the HERAEA (2), about 580. In the classical period, though "Pisa" was sometimes used as a synonym for "Olympia", the Pisatans themselves were thought too rustic and insignificant to manage the sanctuary. In 364, however, when the Arcadians seized it and put on the festival, they took the Pisatans as their partners.

Pindar, *Olympians* 10.43; Xenophon, *Greek History* 3.2.31, 7.4.28–29; Strabo 8.3.30–33; Phlegon, *FGrH* 257 F 1.1, 6; Pausanias 5.16.5–6, 6.22.2–4.

J. Roy, "The *perioikoi* of Elis", in M. H. Hansen (ed.) *The Polis as an Urban Centre and as a Political Community* (Copenhagen 1997) 282–320.

Pisistratus, Athenian tyrant and chariot victor, sixth century. Pisistratus, ruler of Athens for much of the period from 560 to 528, was proclaimed as the victor in the second chariot race won by CIMON in 532 and ended his exile in return.

Herodotus 6.103.2.

Platanistas, "the plane trees", SPARTAN team sport. Each year, two teams of Spartan ephebes, the sons of Lycurgus and the sons of HERACLES, sacrificed a puppy to the war-god Enyalius and next day met in unarmed combat on an artificial island, Platanistas, in the Eurotas river. They drew lots for position and tried to force their rivals into the water by hitting, kicking, biting and gouging.

Pausanias 3.14.8–10, 20.2, 8; Lucian, *Anacharsis* 38; Cicero, *Tusculan Disputations* 5.27.77.

N. M. Kennell, *The Gymnasium of Virtue. Education and Culture in Ancient Sparta* (Chapel Hill 1995) 55–59.

Plato, son of Ariston, Athenian philosopher and wrestler, 428–348. A number of ancient traditions link Plato with wrestling: he trained under Ariston of ARGOS, earned the nickname Plato (from Greek *platys*, "broad") from his physique, competed at Isthmia and Delphi, even won at Olympia and Nemea. In fact, the name was his own, the achievements almost certainly not.

Apuleius, *On Plato's Doctrine* 1.2; Diogenes Laertius 3.14; Cyril of Alexandria, *Against Julian* 6 p. 208; Olympiodorus, *Life of Plato* p. 6.

Pleistonikēs (plural *pleistonikai*), "victor in very many contests", a term used for someone who could boast many triumphs but fell short of sweeping the circuit like a PERIODONIKĒS. In the later Roman Empire, it may be more strictly applied to one who had at least three victories in sacred AGŌNES, one of them in the CAPITOLINE games or the original PERIODOS, and was consequently relieved from civic burdens.

Code of Justinian, 10.54 (53).

R. Merkelbach, "Über ein ephesisches Dekret für einen Athleten aus Aphrodisias und über den Atheletentitel paradoxos", ZPE 14 (1974) 91–96.

Plutarchus, boxer, ? third century CE. Fighting Hermeias of Egypt in the finals at Olympia (? in 205 CE), Plutarchus was parched by the midday sun. Taking advantage of a sudden downpour (he had prayed to the river god Achelous), he refreshed himself from the water which drenched the fleece on his forearms and went on to win.

Philostratus, *Heroicus* 15.4–6 (p. 146.24).

Polites, of Ceramus (Caria), runner, first century CE. Polites won STADION, DIAULOS and DOLICHOS on the same day at Olympia (69), a unique achievement. Since he had to win a preliminary heat in *stadion* as well, he came first in four races.

Pausanias 6.13.3–4; Eusebius, *Chronicon* 1.215 Schoene.

Pollux, or Polydeuces, son of Zeus and Leda and brother of Helen of Troy, legendary Spartan prince sometimes said to be the inventor of boxing. As one of Jason's Argonauts, Pollux taught the savage King AMYCUS a lesson in fisticuffs and hospitality. His half-brother Castor was a noted equestrian, and both brothers (the Dioscuri, "sons of Zeus") were patrons of the Roman cavalry.

Homer, *Iliad* 3.237; *Odyssey* 11.300; Philostratus, *On Athletic Exercise* 9.

Pōloi, "colts", AGE-CLASS at Greek competitive festivals. Elite eagerness for equestrian success eventually led to the addition of events for colts at the leading Greek festivals, at Olympia from 384, at the Pythian games from 378. At each, a colts' chariot race came first; races for pairs and single horses followed. The age division worked much as for athletes; judges had to place horses in the correct category, some colt entries were disqualified (when one of LYCINUS's chariot team was excluded, he promptly entered them in the race for adult horses and won), some horses won as both colts and adults (*teleioi*). The early fourth-century prize list from the PANATHENAEA gives some idea of the relative weight accorded victories with colts. The winner in the pairs event for adult horses took home 140 amphoras of oil, the next finisher, forty amphoras – also the prize for the winning pair of colts. The difference is rather more than that between adult champion athletes and boys (PAIDES).

Pausanias 5.24.10, 6.2.2; *Greek Anthology* 9.20; *IG* 2² 2311.

Polychares, of Messenia runner, eighth century. After winning the STADION race at Olympia (764), Polychares sent cattle to feed on the land of a Spartan, Euaephnus. Euaephnus defrauded him of the cattle and killed his son, and Polychares' revenge is said to have been a cause of the First Messenian War.

Pausanias 4.4.5–5.6.

Polycles, of Sparta, chariot victor, fifth century. Polycles, nicknamed *Polychalkos*, "All Metal", was a PERIODONIKĒS in the chariot race; his Olympic victory may be dated to 440, 428, 424 or even the early fourth century.

Pausanias 6.1.7.

Polycrates, son of Mnasiades, chariot victor, third/second century. Distinguished by the antiquity of his family and his father's reputation as an athlete, Polycrates helped reorganize the Ptolemaic army (220–217), commanded cavalry at the Battle of Raphia (217), governed Cyprus (202–197) and served as chancellor of the Ptolemaic empire, leading an army against rebels in the Delta in 186/5. Chariot victor in the PANATHENAEA of 198, he was joined by his wife Zeuxo (colts' chariot). Their daughters Zeuxo (colts' chariot), Eucrateia (chariot pair) and Hermione (chariot) won in the preceding festival.

Polybius 5.64.6; *IG* 2² 2313.

Polyctor, son of Demonicus, Eleian wrestler, first century. At the Olympic festival of 12, Demonicus bribed Sosander of Smyrna, the father of another boy wrestler, to assure his own son Polyctor's victory. When the bribe came to light, both fathers were fined and two ZANES set up, one in the gymnasium at Elis and the other in the ALTIS.

Pausanias 5.21.16–17.

Polymestor, of Miletus, runner, sixth century. Polymestor, a goatherd fast enough to catch hares, won the Olympic STADION race for boys in 596. A less reliable tradition makes him (rather than POLYNICES) the first winner.

Philostratus, *On Athletic Exercise* 13.

Polynices, of Elis, runner, seventh century. Polynices won the STADION race for boys at Olympia in 632, the first competition for PAIDES, and established a precedent for many Eleian boys who won after him.

Pausanias 5.8.9.

Polynicus, of Thespiae, wrestler, fifth century. Polynicus's Olympic victory, in boys' wrestling in 448, was noted on the list of Thespian casualties at Delion some twenty-five years later.

IG 7 1888; *Oxyrhynchus Papyri* 222.

Polyzalus, son of Deinomenes, Geloan ruler and chariot victor, fifth century. The brother of GELON and HIERON and the father-in-law of THERON, Polyzalus too was a chariot victor. Though his win, at the Pythian games (in 478 or 474) was less prestigious than their Olympic triumphs, it led to a more enduring monument, the famous bronze statue of a charioteer at Delphi.

SEG 3.396.

Ebert (1972) 60–63.

Pompa (plural *pompae*), "procession", the parade which took place at the start of a Roman chariot-racing programme or gladiatorial show. The first race after the *pompa* was generally the most prestigious and best rewarded, perhaps because the track was then in its best shape.

Ovid, *Amores* 3.2.43–62; *ILS* 5287.

Pompeianus, Roman chariot horse, early second century CE. An African paired on the inside with COTYNUS, Pompeianus was part of the teams which won DIOCLES 445 victories. In one year, he took part in 103 triumphs, in another, ninety-nine.

ILS 5287.

Pompeius Eutyches, Publius, or Ninnarus, of Philadelphia (Lydia), Olympic victor, first century CE. A fragmentary inscription from his native city, dated to the first century CE, says Pompeius Eutyches was twice PERIODONIKĒS.

IGRom. 4.1643.

Porta Libitinensis, "gate of Libitina", HARENA entrance through which the bodies of dead GLADIATORS were carried.

Historia Augusta, Commodus 16.7.

Mosci Sassi (1992) 156.

Porta Sanavivaria, gate by which surviving GLADIATORS left the HARENA.

Passion of Perpetua and Felicitas 10.13, 20.7.

Porus, runner, fourth century. Porus was Olympic STADION champion twice, in 364 (as a Cyrenaean), and in 360 (as a Malian).

Diodorus 16.2.1, 15.1; Pausanias 10.2.3; Eusebius, *Chronicon* 1.205 Schoene.

Posidippus, of Pella (Macedonia), epinician poet, third century. A contemporary and rival of CALLIMACHUS, Posidippus too wrote epigrams, some in honour of victors at Greek competitive festivals. A newly discovered papyrus contains eighteen for equestrian winners, many of them members of the Egyptian dynasty of the PTOLEMIES or of their court.

G. Bastianini and C. Gallazzi (with C. Austin), *Posidippo di Pella. Epigrammi (P.Mil.Vogl. 8 309)* (Milan 2001); P. Bernardini and L. Bravi, "Note di lettura al nuovo Posidippo", *QUCC* 70 (2002) 147–163 (154–163).

Praxidamas, son of Socleidas (or Socles), of Aegina, boxer, sixth century. Praxidamas was Olympic boxing champion in 544, not only the first victory by an Aeginetan but the first to be commemorated by a STATUE in the ALTIS; though it was made of cypress, it survived to PAUSANIAS's day. Praxidamas also won three times at Nemea and five at Isthmia. Among other successful athletes in the family, his grandson Alcimidas won the boys' wrestling at Nemea (? 473 ? 465) and twice missed an Olympic wreath by the luck of the draw (cf. LOT).

Pindar, *Nemeans* 6; Pausanias 6.18.7.

Mosci Sassi (1992) 157.

Princeps, GLADIATOR, first century CE. A member of NERO's gladiatorial FAMILIA and likely a SAMNIS, Princeps's gravestone records twelve victories in twelve bouts.

CIL 4 10237.

Prizes. The prize (ATHLON) was an essential element of Greek sport from the outset; the organizer of a contest, the ATHLOTHETĒS, or "prize-giver", provided it – and earned respect from its quantity or quality –, the athlete (*athlētēs*) strove to win it. At the FUNERAL GAMES of Patroclus, many of the participants won prizes (not just winners), valuable items of everyday use (tripods, lumps of iron, oxen, women). There was a tradition that the panhellenic games of the circuit (PER-IODOS) also offered value prizes originally – this is most reliable for the PYTHIAN games – but they soon became crown games, awarding winners (only) distinctive wreaths, of olive (Olympia), laurel

(Delphi), pine or dry celery (Isthmia), fresh celery (Nemea). (The gods might be imagined as *athlothetai*, so that the olive is presented as evidence for Zeus's poverty in comedy.) Other games, however, including some which were almost as prestigious, did offer prizes of value (sometimes as supplements to wreaths), from bronze shields at the ARGIVE HERAEA (1), and silver goblets at Sicyon, to ten drachmas at the Delian APOLLONIA and ten obols – expense money merely – at a minor festival in fifth-century Attica. The most famous were the distinctive amphoras of the PANATHENAEA, filled with olive oil which (exceptionally) could be exported and sold. (Their shape, image of Athena, and legend – "from the contests at Athens" – meant winners advertised the city much as modern athletes do shoe companies.) Whereas other major festivals awarded the same prize for each AGE-CLASS and event, the Panathenaea made distinctions which provide insight into the attitudes and assumptions of fourth-century Athenians. The most lavish prizes (then as now) went to musical performers, up to five winners in one event, a means to attract the Greek world's best singers and players. They, however, did not take away Panathenaic amphoras. Among sporting competitors open to all – who did – the rich got richer: the largest known prize (140 amphoras of olive oil) went for the winning chariot teams. Among athletes, men's prizes were largest, (probably) double boys' and almost as much more than those for AGENEIOI. The STADION race brought the largest prize among their events, 100 amphoras of olive oil, perhaps the equivalent of US$100,000 today. *Pankration* was next, slightly more than pentathlon and the other HEAVY events. Second place earned one-fifth the amount of victory. The Panathenaea also featured team events, in which members got a prize of their own as well as sharing one in common. These and other contests restricted to citizens were significantly less well rewarded than other events. Such implicit judgements varied elsewhere and over time: for example, pancratiasts got the most valuable prizes and pentathletes the least at Aphrodisias in the Roman period. In addition to prizes, victors were often honoured at the site of competition – their names, patronymics and home cities proclaimed by HERALDS, their STATUES allowed admission into the sacred precinct – and rewarded on their return home. At Athens, winners in the *periodos* earned a free meal each day in the public dining room in the Prytaneum and a payment of 500 (for an Olympic victory) and 100 drachmas (for an Isthmian), sums said to have been set by the democracy's founder, SOLON; at SPARTA, they served in the bodyguard of the kings. Similar bonuses go back as early at Sybaris. It is these rewards, and not prizes themselves, which called forth criticism from the poet XENOPHANES. Neither value prizes nor rewards made recipients ineligible for the Olympics or other festivals: ancient Greek amateurism is a nineteenth-century invention, a conspiracy of shoddy scholarship and the desire to exclude working-class athletes from vying with (and perhaps emerging victorious over) their social superiors.

Greek-style festivals founded by the Romans followed their models in offering wreaths as prizes. At the CAPITOLINE games, these were oak – Jupiter's tree; presiding emperors might also award Roman citizenship to winners who did not possess it. Triumphant gladiators bore a victory palm and might get cash bonuses and other gifts – NERO bestowed houses and properties on the MURMILLO SPICULUS. Some emperors sought to limit such rewards (TIBERIUS for actors as well as gladiators). A senatorial decree of Marcus Aurelius (77 CE) imposed restrictions on spectacles in Gaul, setting amounts for prize money which varied according to their overall expense and the status of gladiators. Those of free birth could get up to HS2000, freed slaves – experienced fighters likely to put on a good show –

HS12,000. (The daily wage of a Roman labourer was HS5.) The decree also regulated the prize money available to each class of combatant. Circus factions competed for rich prizes, the largest apparently reserved for races with most horses in each team. The charioteer DIOCLES won purses from HS15,000 to HS60,000 – the annual income of a *procurator*, a senior imperial administrator, in some ten minutes – and a career total of HS35,863,120. His share of these winnings is unknown, but the length of the inscription detailing his successes, and the size and elaboration of other charioteers' tombs, suggest it could be significant, at least at Rome itself.

Homer, *Iliad* 22.158–166, 23.259–261; Aristophanes, *Wealth* 585–589; Lucian, *Anacharsis* 10; Pausanias 6.14.10, 10.7.2, 5; *IG* 1³ 131, 1386, 11.2 203a; *SEG* 35.1053; Suetonius, *Tiberius* 34.1; *ILS* 5163.

M. Blech, *Studien zum Kranz bei den Griechern* (Berlin 1982); N. B. Crowther, "Second-place finishes and lower in Greek athletics (including the pentathlon)", *ZPE* 90 (1992) 97–102; D. G. Kyle, "Gifts and glory. Panathenaic and other Greek athletic prizes", in J. Neils (ed.) *Worshipping Athena. Panathenaia and Parthenon* (Madison 1996) 106–136.

Prohedria, "front seating", the right to a front-row seat at festival competition, *Prohedria* was one of the honours Greek cities awarded festival victors (among others); like others, it came in for criticism from XENOPHANES.

Xenophanes fragment 2 DK.

Prolusio (plural *prolusiones*), "prelude", preliminaries to gladiatorial combat, both mock fights (involving *PAEGNIARII*) and the feinting and verbal abuse of a gladiatorial pair which came to an end with a trumpet blast.

Lucilius, *Satires* 117, 153–158 Marx; Cicero, *On the Orator* 2.80.325.

Mosci Sassi (1992) 158–161.

Promachus, son of Dryon, of Pellene, pancratiast, fifth century. Promachus won the pankration competition at Olympia in 404, defeating the famous PULYDAMAS – a fact (says PAUSANIAS) that Thessalians refused to accept. He also won three times at Isthmia and twice at Nemea and was equally effective as a warrior against the Corinthians. His fellow citizens erected two STATUES of him, bronze at Olympia, stone in the local gymnasium.

Pausanias 7.27.5–7.

Prometheus. Greek Titan and cultural hero. Among the many benefits Prometheus is said to have devised or provided for humankind, he was the first to engage in athletic exercises. The god HERMES (2) then used them to train others.

Philostratus, *On Athletic Exercise* 16.

Pronapes, son of Pronapides, Athenian chariot victor, fifth century. A chariot victor at (at least) Isthmia, Nemea and the Panathenaea, Pronapes may also have been one of the prosecutors of the Athenian politician and hero of the Persian wars Themistocles (around 470).

IG 2² 3123.

Prosgymnastēs (plural *prosgymnastai*), a sparring-partner.

Hyperides, *For Lycophron* 6.

Protophanes, of Magnesia on Maeander, HEAVY athlete, first century. Protophanes won the wrestling and *pankration* competitions on the same day at Olympia in 92, the first to so emulate HERACLES since ARISTOMENES.

Pausanias 5.21.10; Eusebius, *Chronicon* 1.211 Schoene.

Provocator (plural *provocatores*), "challenger", a type of GLADIATOR, perhaps armed much like a *SAMNIS*.

Cicero, *For Sestius* 64.134; *ILS* 5107.

Mosci Sassi (1992) 161.

Proxenides, of Elis, HELLANODIKAS, second century CE. When Aetion showed his painting *The Marriage of Roxane and Alexander* at Olympia, the *hellanodikas* Proxenides admired it so much that he gave Aetion – a stranger – his daughter in marriage.

Lucian, *Herodotus* 4–5.

Psaumis, son of Acron, of Camarina, equestrian victor, fifth century. Psaumis won the Olympic mule-cart race (*APĒNĒ*), likely in 456, and the more prestigious chariot race at the following festival. In the Sicilian fashion, the victories may be commemorated on the coins of Camarina.

Pindar, *Olympians* 4, 5; *Oxyrhynchus Papyri* 222.

M. F. Galiano, "Psaumis en las Olímpicas de Píndaro", *Emérita* 10 (1942) 112–148.

Ptolemaieia, Greek competitive festival at Alexandria (and elsewhere) in Egypt. Founded by PTOLEMY II Philadelphus in honour of his father PTOLEMY I and mother BERENICE I in 282 or 278, the Alexandrian Ptolemaieia was a quadrennial festival modelled on the most prestigious of its kind, the Olympics (ISOLYMPIAN). However, it included musical competitions as well as athletic and equestrian.

Posidippus, *P.Mil.Vogl.* 8 309.XII.14; *SEG* 36.1218.

F. Perpillou-Thomas, *Fêtes d'Égypte ptolémaïque et romaine d'après la documentation papyrologique grecque* (Louvain 1993) 153–154;

R.A. Hazzard, *Imagination of a Monarchy: Studies in Ptolemaic Propaganda* (Toronto 2000) 30–33, 53–57.

Ptolemy II Philadelphus, king of Egypt (285–246) and chariot victor, 308–246. The son of Olympic chariot champions (PTOLEMY I, BERENICE I), Ptolemy married a third (his sister ARSINOE), slept with another (BILISTICHE), and had victors at other festivals in his service (CALLICRATES (2), SOSIBIUS). Ptolemy's own

Olympic victory came in 284. The founder of the PTOLEMAIEIA in honour of his parents, Ptolemy was likely also the driving force behind the addition of a new chariot race, for colt pairs, at Olympia in 264. Our evidence suggests that the most prestigious prizes were reserved for his family, but all might be celebrated by EPINICIAN epigrams commissioned from CALLIMACHUS or POSIDIPPUS.

Posidippus, *P.Mil.Vogl.* 8 309.XIII.35–XIV.1.

Ptolemy I Soter, king of Egypt (305–282) and chariot champion, 367/6–282. One of ALEXANDER III's generals and the founder of Egypt's Ptolemaic dynasty (in 305), Ptolemy also initiated a family tradition of equestrian success by his chariot victory at Olympia.

Posidippus, *P.Mil.Vogl.* 8 309.XIII.35–XIV.1.

Pulvinar, a Roman cult spot raised above ground level. In the CIRCUS MAXIMUS, a procession brought statues and cult objects of the gods to the *pulvinar* by carriage and litter, and they then watched the races. AUGUSTUS built a stone *pulvinar* and used it as a vantage point for himself and (sometimes) his wife and children; later emperors followed his lead.

Augustus, *Achievements* 19, Festus 500 Lindsay.

J. H. Humphrey, *Roman Circuses. Arenas for Chariot Racing* (London 1986) 78–83.

Pulydamas, son of Nicias, of Scotussa (Thessaly), pancratiast, fifth century. Olympic *pankration* champion in 408, Pulydamas (like MILON and THEOGENES) attracted many tales. The type of the strongman for Plato, the tallest of men for Pausanias, he emulated HERACLES by killing a lion unarmed, held a bull by the hoof until it could escape only by leaving it in his hand, halted a speeding chariot from behind, killed three of the king of Persia's Immortals in a single fight. Defeated by PROMACHUS in 404, Pulydamas's strength proved unequal to a later task as well: he was crushed after holding

up the roof of a collapsing cave just long enough to save some friends. His STATUE at Olympia was said to cure fevers.

Plato, *Republic* 1.338C; Pausanias 6.5; Lucian, *Councils of the Gods* 12; Philostratus, *On Athletic Exercise* 22, 43; Tzetzes, *Histories* 2.555–559.

Fontenrose (1968) 87–88; H. Taeuber, "Ein Inschriftenfragment der Pulydamas-Basis von Olympia", *Nikephoros* 10 (1997) 235–243.

Pygmachos see PYKTĒS

Homer, *Odyssey* 8.246.

Pyktēs (plural *pyktai*), "boxer".

Xenophanes fragment 2DK.

Pyrrhic dancing (Greek *pyrrhichē* [*orchēsis*]), event at some Greek competitive festivals. Pyrrhic dancers, naked (like athletes) except for a helmet and sometimes greaves, crouched and leaped to the music of the AULOS. Imitating the defensive and offensive manoeuvres of a warrior, they carried a shield with the left hand and a weapon (sword, spear, javelin) in the right (or pretended to do so). Pyrrhic dancing was a form of physical exercise – vases depict it in PALAESTRA scenes – as well as a means to develop and demonstrate a soldier's skills. Dancers performed both solo and in groups. At Athens, groups competed at a number of festivals, including both the annual and the greater PANATHENAEA. In the quadrennial celebration, all three AGE-CLASSES (boys, AGENEIOI, men), exceptionally, vied for the same prize, an ox (for sacrifice and sharing) and 100 drachmas. Women are shown as pyrrhic dancers on some vases, at private symposia and honouring Artemis – her links with childbirth, as much and as dangerous a mature woman's role as warfare was a man's, must matter here.

Euripides, *Andromache* 1135; Aristophanes, *Clouds* 988–989; Lysias 21.1, 4; Xenophon, *Anabasis* 6.1.1–13; Plato, *Laws* 7.815A; *IG* 2² 2311.

S. H. Lonsdale, *Dance and Ritual Play in Greek Religion* (Baltimore and London 1993) 137–

168; M. H. Delavaud-Roux, *Les danses armées en Grèce ancienne* (Aix-en-Provence 1993); P. Ceccarelli, *La pirrica nell'antichità greco-romana. Studi sulla danza armata* (Pisa 1998).

Pythagoras 1. of Sparta, runner, eighth century. Winner of the STADION race at Olympia in 716, Pythagoras is sometimes said to have brought Spartan practices to Rome through his acquaintance with Numa, the city's second king.

Plutarch, *Numa* 1.3.

2. son of Crates, Samian boxer, sixth century. Refused entry into the wrestling competition for PAIDES at Olympia in 588 – perhaps because he wore his hair long –, Pythagoras won the crown for adult men. He is said to have been the first to box with skill (rather than relying on strength alone), a reputation perhaps linked to his confusion with the famous philosopher.

Diogenes Laertius 8.47–48.

3. of Magnesia on Maeander, runner, fourth/third century. A PERIODONIKĒS, Pythagoras won the STADION race at Olympia twice (in 300 and 296), (?) twice at the Pythian games, five times at Isthmia and (?) six at Nemea. He may also have won the Olympic race in armour at the same festivals as his *stadion* victories.

Eusebius, *Chronicon* 1.207 Schoene; *Oxyrhynchus Papyri* 2082.

Pythian games (Greek *Pythia*), Greek competitive festival. One of the festivals of the original circuit (PERIODOS), the Pythian games at Delphi were second only to the Olympics in antiquity and prestige. (Two ambitious fourth-century outsiders, Jason of Pherae and PHILIP of Macedon, felt control of the festival would legitimate their claims to join Greece's traditional powers.) They owed their status to the sanctity of the site, home to Greece's most influential oracle, and to the fame of their musical competitions in honour of Pythian Apollo. The god himself was said to be the festival's founder, in celebration of his triumph over Python, a dragon who

once guarded the site – they were thus FUNERAL GAMES of an unusual kind. The historical competitions originated in another victory, of the Delphians and a band of neighbouring communities (the Delphic Amphictiony), over Crisa (Cirrha), the city which controlled the area, in the First Sacred War. Held in 591/0 or 586 (PAUSANIAS's date, followed here) under the Amphictiony's auspices, the first games awarded value prizes, but when repeated four years later in August 582 (the subsequent pattern) they offered only a laurel (bay) wreath; apples supplemented this in later antiquity. The importance of musical contests at the Pythian festival, and their standing among such events elsewhere, are beyond doubt: festivals were identified by the winner in singing to the *kithara* (thought to be a contest at the site even before the festival was inaugurated), the champion *aulētēs* accompanied jumpers in the Olympic pentathlon – one was honoured by one of the only Pindaric EPINICIANS not devoted to an athletic or equestrian victor – a festival at Nicephorium (in Mesopotamia) declared itself Isolympian – like the Olympics – in other competitions, but Isopythian in music. (Demetrius Poliorcetes, king of Macedon, established the first Isopythian festival at Athens in 292.) But victory in any Pythian event brought great honour, enough to attract CLEISTHENES, tyrant of Sicyon, to the first chariot race in 582 and, two centuries later, PTOLEMY I, soon to be king of Egypt, to the first pairs race for colts. Rulers of Sicily and Macedon were among equestrian winners in the interval, along with the leading athletes of their times. The programme itself (Pausanias says) was based on Olympia (see Table 4). However, it included a fuller slate for boys, each scheduled before the equivalent event for men; perhaps an additional AGE-GROUP, AGENEIOI, in the Hellenistic period (with a consequent modification in the age of boys to produce the PAIDES *Pythikoi* we hear of elsewhere); a girls' STADION race still later; and equestrian competition from the outset. As at Olympia, the race in armour came later and other new events, mainly equestrian, were likely prompted by the local and neighbouring elite who fancied their chances. The topography of Apollo's sanctuary, as rugged as it is majestic, required the HIPPODROME to be set in the plain of Crisa by the Gulf of Corinth and the stadium to be erected high under Mount Parnassus on one of the few tracts of level land. Excavation has brought to light impressive remains of the temples, treasuries and athletic facilities which testified to Delphi's importance in the Greek world; Pausanias's prejudice for Olympia, and the loss of the Pythian victor list compiled by Aristotle and his nephew Callisthenes, have left the names of most winners in obscurity.

Sophocles, *Electra* 681–756; Xenophon, *Greek History* 6.4.29–30; Demosthenes 9.32; Strabo 9.3.10; Plutarch, *Moral Essays* 639A, 674D–675B; Lucian, *Anacharsis* 9; Pausanias 6.14.9–10, 10.7.2–7; Ovid, *Metamorphoses* 1.445–451; Pliny, *Natural History* 35.35.58; IG 2² 3158; *CID* 2.139.

A. A. Mosshammer, "The date of the first Pythiad – again", *GRBS* 23 (1982) 15–30; J. Fontenrose, "The cult of Apollo and the games at Delphi", in Raschke (1988) 121–140; O. Picard, "Delphi and the Pythian games", in Tzachou-Alexandri (1989) 69–81.

Table 4   Development of the Pythian programme

Date	Event	Winner
586	Singing to the *kithara*	Melampus of Cephallenia
	Singing to the *aulos*	Echembrotus of Arcadia
	Playing the *aulos*	Sacadas of Argos
	Stadion	
	Diaulos	
	Dolichos	
	Pentathlon	
	Wrestling	
	Boxing	
	Pankration	
	Boys' *stadion*	
	Boys' *diaulos*	
	Boys' *dolichos*	
	Boys' pentathlon	
	Boys' wrestling	
	Boys' boxing	
	Horse race	
582	(Singing to the *aulos* dropped)	
	Chariot race	Cleisthenes of Sicyon
558	Playing the *kithara*	Agelaus of Tegea
498	Hoplite race	Timaenetus of Phlius
398	Pairs chariot race	Execestides of Phocis
378	Chariot race for colts	Orphondas of Thebes
346	Boys' *pankration*	Iolaidas of Thebes
338	Colts' race	Lycormas of Larisa
314	Pairs chariot race for colts	Ptolemy of Macedon/Egypt
later	Dithyramb, tragic and comic acting, encomium, pantomime, painting, *stadion* for girls	

Pythion, son of Cleophanes, Rhodian HEAVY athlete, second century. A recently discovered STATUE base records the name of the boxer, pancratiast and wrestler Pythion, who won at all four games of the *PERIODOS* as well as at ten others (including the local HALIEIA) in the early second century.

SEG 45.1066.

Pythodelus, son of Pythodorus, of (?) Athens, HEAVY athlete, fifth century. Winner of two crowns at Delphi, seven at Nemea and five at an unidentifiable festival with his strength in the mid-fifth century, Pythodelus was likely an Athenian.

SEG 24.387.

Ebert (1972) 89–92.

***Pyx** see* BOXING.

Q

Quadriga or *quadrigae*, Latin term for four-horse CHARIOT team.

Livy 1.28.10.

Quadrigarius (plural *quadrigarii*), driver of a QUADRIGA.

Suetonius, *Caligula* 19.2.

R

Record, an unsurpassed achievement. Our sources for Greek sport rarely report quantified records of individual achievements; the jumps of CHIONIS and PHAŸLLUS are unreliable exceptions. This is probably due to local variation – in the lengths of stadia and the weights of *diskoi* – rather than difficulties of measurement. They do, however, take pains to signal original and unique accomplishments: first citizen to win, first to win an event, number of crowns, a combination of events. The desire for records of this kind encouraged both long athletic careers and versatility. The memorials of Roman charioteers (such as DIOCLES) often imitate athletes' in this respect, enumerating victories and highlighting special distinctions.

D. C. Young, "First with the most: Greek athletic records and 'specialization' ", *Nikephoros* 9 (1996) 175–197.

Religion. Among both Greeks and Romans, sporting competitions were usually held as part of regular, recurring festivals in honour of gods and HEROES (AGŌNES, LUDI). In addition, other contexts – FUNERAL GAMES, gladiatorial MUNERA to mark a military victory – often included the characteristic acts of ancient religious observance: processions, sacrifices, prayers. Even in contests as secular and informal as those in Homer's *Odyssey* Athena is present, proclaiming Odysseus victor in the weight-throw in after-dinner games among the Phaeacians, infusing him with strength for his fistfight with Irus. The connection is an old one: Olympia may have been an oracular shrine before it hosted competitions and it lasted as long as ancient sport itself. HERACLES figures in the bronze victor-list which is our latest epigraphic evidence for Olympia, a patron of athletes to the end, and gladiatorial spectacles, like the Olympic festival, were shut down because of the Christian emperors' hostility to pagan piety. As PAUSANIAS puts it, "The Eleusinian rites and the competition at Olympia have the greatest portion of the god's care". Close as this connection is, however, its import is unclear. After all, Greeks and Romans saw their gods everywhere, invoked and propitiated them before any significant act. Is their role in sport in particular any more meaningful than (say) the playing of *O, Canada* before a professional hockey game in Edmonton or Toronto, let alone of *The Star Spangled Banner* when one team is visiting from the US? One school of thought sees a special link in sacrifice, the central act of Greek and Roman worship: athletes dedicated their physical energy to the gods and (in Greek contests) themselves represented sacrificial victims – fit, ribboned and wreathed, willingly come to their fate. Others stress the ancient gods' anthropomorphism; they enjoyed sport like any spectator and even competed in some stories of the first festivals. Consideration of the elements of competitive success may be relevant too. An athlete's hard work or an equestrian's wealth were easy enough to see and account for, and natural ability (in humans as well as horses) might be ascribed to breeding. But the ancients were no more able than we to explain why some competitors rise to the occasion while others stumble at the start, and luck is vital in any competition. The gods explain this as well as anything.

Homer, *Odyssey* 8.189–198, 18.66–74; *Homeric Hymn to Apollo* 146–150; Pausanias 5.10.1.

Golden (1998) 10–23; E. Pemberton, "*Agones hieroi.* Greek athletic contests in their religious context", *Nikephoros* 13 (2000) 111–123; Scanlon (2002) 25–39.

Remissus, "sent back", term in Roman chariot racing. A victor designated *remissus* won a race which was run again after a false start or foul. Also *revocatus*, "recalled".

Ovid, *Amores* 3.2.73–75; Seneca, *Controversiae* 1.3.10; *ILS* 5278, 5288.3.

Retiarius (plural *retiarii*), "netman", type of GLADIATOR. Lightly-clad *retiarii* wore a BALTEUS and carried a dagger, a net and a trident, the better to spear their prey – usually MURMILLONES (with their fish-crested helmets) or SAMNITES. Also unlike other gladiators, they wore the MANICA on their left arm and a metal guard (GALERUS) on their left shoulder. The emperor Claudius is said to have condemned most fallen gladiators to die, but especially *retiarii*, since they wore no helmets and he liked to see their faces.

Suetonius, *Caligula* 30.3; *Claudius* 34.1; *ILS* 5142 d, e.

Mosci Sassi (1992) 162–164.

Revocatus *see* REMISSUS

Rhabdophoros (plural *rhabdophoroi*), "rod-bearer", RHABDOUCHOS. Twenty *rhabdophoroi* who served under an AGŌNOTHETĒS at Athens set up a monument to a member of the family of HERODES ATTICUS in 173/4 CE. Another group of twenty served at Messenia.

Aristophanes, *Peace* 734–735; *IG* 2² 3968, 5.1 1390A.

Rhabdouchos (plural *rhabdouchoi*), "rod-holder", official who maintained order and punished rule-breakers at Greek competitive festivals. It was *rhabdouchoi* who struck LICHAS (on the orders of the HELLANODIKAI) when he flouted the prohibition on Spartan competition at Olympia in 420.

Thucydides 5.50.4; *IG* 9.2 1109.

Rhexibius, of Opus, pancratiast, sixth century. PAUSANIAS thought the statue of Rhexibius (*pankration* champion, 536) the oldest at Olympia after PRAXIDAMAS's.

Pausanias 6.18.7.

Rhypos, "filth", grime scraped from the walls or STATUES of a GYMNASIUM and used for medicinal purposes.

Dioscorides 1.30.6; Pliny, *Natural History* 28.13.53; Galen 12.116 Kühn.

N. M. Kennell, " 'Most necessary for the bodies of men': Olive oil and its by-products in the later Greek gymnasium", in M. Joyal (ed.) *In Altum. Seventy-five Years of Classical Studies in Newfoundland* (St John's 2001) 119–133 (128–133).

Robigalia, Roman agricultural festival in honour of a divinity associated with rust or mildew. Held on 25 April, the Robigalia featured races for younger and older runners (*maioribus minoribusque*), held on the Via Claudia north of Rome.

Fasti Praenestini ad Apr. 25.

Romaea, name of many Greek competitive festivals in the Hellenistic and Roman periods. Romaea were widespread in old

Greece (Delos alone may have had several) but proliferated among the new and reorganized festivals so prevalent in Asia Minor. The name allowed cities to declare friendship and loyalty to Rome at the same time as the traditional AGŌNES trumpeted their Hellenism. Most of these festivals were annual and local, and attracted mainly nearby competitors, but some, such as the Romaea established by the Euboean federation about 194 (one of the earliest) were panhellenic. The designation Romaea was also added to existing festivals, including such important ones as the AMPHIARAEIA at Oropus (as early as the first century) and the Rhodian HALIEIA.

R. Mellor, *Thea Rōmē. The Worship of the Goddess Roma in the Greek World* (Göttingen 1975) 165–180.

Rudis (plural *rudes*), "staff, rod", wooden sword used by GLADIATORS (and soldiers) in training. A gladiator who completed three years' service and retired from combat was given a *rudis* and termed *rudiarius*; such men often trained other gladiators.

Cicero, *Philippics* 2.29.74; Horace, *Epistles* 1.1.1–3; Suetonius, *Tiberius* 7.1.

Mosci Sassi (1992) 164–165.

S

Sagina (plural *saginae*) "stuffing", a coarse mash which was the staple food of Roman GLADIATORS.

Propertius 4.8.25; Tacitus, *Histories* 2.88.

Sagittarius (plural *sagittarii*), "archer", type of GLADIATOR.

ILS 5083a.

Mosci Sassi (1992) 167.

Salpinktēs (plural *salpinktai*), "trumpeter", participant and competitor in Greek festivals. A competition for trumpeters (won by TIMAEUS of Elis) entered the Olympic programme in 396. Like that for KĒRYKES, "heralds", it took place from an altar in the ALTIS, on the way to the stadium, on the first day of the festival. The winner, clad in a short mantle or tunic, a broad-brimmed hat, and sandals, then carried out a trumpeter's duties: attracting attention for the heralds, signalling the start of races and their bell lap, and accompanying officials. They needed to produce a tone which was passionate, piercing, shrill, urgent and above all loud. The most famous, HERODORUS of Megara (a PERIODONIKĒS and ten-time Olympic champion, perhaps from 328 to 292), gave rise to tales worthy of the wrestler MILON: he ate and drank mightily – sitting instead of reclining like others – slept on a lion skin, could blow two trumpets at a time in a military emergency and was so loud that no-one could stand next to him. Another, (?) Epistades, could be heard 50 stades (10km, about 6 miles) away. Despite these feats, there is evidence that trumpeters, like heralds, earned less prestige than other victors: they are omitted on extant Olympic victory lists and drew smaller prizes at local festivals.

Sophocles, *Electra* 709–711; Crinagoras, *Greek Anthology* 6.350; Pausanias 5.22.1, 6.13.9; Athenaeus 10.414F–415A; Philostratus, *Lives of the Sophists* 542; Pollux 4.85–90.

N. B. Crowther, "The role of heralds and trumpeters at Greek athletic festivals", *Nikephoros* 7 (1994) 135–155.

Samnis (plural *Samnites*), "Samnite", type of GLADIATOR. Samnites, the earliest attested gladiatorial type, represented one of the Italian peoples conquered by Rome as it gained control of Italy. They were heavily armed with a visored helmet, a large oblong shield, a greave on the left leg and a short sword, and often fought RETIARII. The term *secutor*, "pursuer", may have replaced *Samnis* over time, as the Romans grew less eager to draw attention to divisions within their home territory. Cf. HOPLOMACHUS, MURMILLO.

Lucilius, *Satires* 149–152, 1273–1274 Marx; Livy 9.40.17; Suetonius, *Caligula* 30.3; Isidore, *Etymologies* 18.56; *ILS* 5113.

Mosci Sassi (1992) 168–169, 171–172.

Sarapammon *see* DIDAS

Sarapion, of Alexandria, pancratiast, first century CE. Sarapion became the only Olympic competitor known by PAUSANIAS to have been fined for cowardice: he ran off the day before the *pankration* event in 25 CE. Two other Alexandrians of the same name had more glorious careers in Olympia. One was STADION winner in 37, the other, boy boxing champion in 89 CE, supplied the Eleians with food during a famine and had his statue erected at the Maltho gymnasium at Elis.

Pausanias 5.21.18, 6.23.6; Eusebius, *Chronicon* 1.213 Schoene.

Satyrus, son of Lysianax, of Elis, boxer, fourth century. A member of the prophetic clan of the Iamidae, Satyrus won two boxing crowns at Olympia (? 332, ? 328), two at Delphi and five at Nemea, as well as one at the AMPHIARAEIA at Oropus. His brother Andromachus, also a boxer, was victor at the Arcadian LYCAEA.

Pausanias 6.4.5; *IG* 5.2 549.

Scirtus, Roman charioteer, first century CE. A freed slave, Scirtus drove for the White CIRCUS FACTION, winning eleven times with four-horse teams between 13 and 25 CE – including four times after false starts –, placing second thirty-nine times and third on sixty occasions. Scirtus also won with a six-horse team. His is our earliest datable victory catalogue for a Roman charioteer. Its relatively few victories may reflect less frequent and less crowded race cards of the day.

ILS 5283.

Horsmann (1998) 283–284.

Scissor (plural *scissores*), "carver", type of GLADIATOR, or an attendant who cut the bodies of fallen gladiators to ensure that they were not feigning death.

ILS 5083a.

Mosci Sassi (1992) 170–171.

Scorpus, Flavius, Roman CHARIOTEER, late first century CE. A driver for the Green CHARIOT FACTION, Scorpus won 2,048 races and (according to the poet Martial) a fortune in an hour. He died at 25, 26 or 27, perhaps in a chariot crash.

Martial 4.67, 5.25, 10.50, 53, 74; *ILS* 5287, 5289.

Horsmann (1998) 286–288.

Scutarius (plural *scutarii*), "shield man", fan of MURMILLONES.

Marcus Aurelius, *Meditations* 1.5.

Mosci Sassi (1992) 171.

Sebasta, "Sebastan games", name of several competitive festivals of the Roman Empire. The most important, the Italica Romaea Sebasta Isolympia at Naples (Neapolis), was founded for AUGUSTUS in 2 CE on the model of the Olympic games – *sebasta* is Greek for Latin *augustus* – and soon joined it among the most prestigious festivals. Its status may be gauged from the eighty-seven athletes who entered an event involving running in the third century CE, and its survival well into the fourth. Though it retained its Isolympian designation and its quadrennial schedule (in August) – and much of our information on the Sebasta comes from an inscription set up at Olympia to advertise the festival there – it grew larger and more dissimilar after Augustus's death, adding other AGE-CLASSES (*paides Klaudianoi*, AGENEIOI), musical and dramatic competitions with cash prizes (as well as the APOBATĒS), and restricting some boys' events to citizens. It also included a footrace for girls. Though the Sebasta, like the Olympics, imposed a thirty-day residency at the site on competitors, it was the only festival we know to pay their living expenses, one drachma per day for the first half of the period and 2 or 3 drachmas for the remainder.

Strabo 5.4.7; Velleius Paterculus 2.123.1; Suetonius, *Augustus* 98.5; *Claudius* 11.2; *IvO* 56; *IG* 14 746–748.

R. M. Geer, "The Greek games at Naples", *TAPA* 66 (1935) 208–221; N. B. Crowther,

"The Sebastan games at Naples (IvOl. 56)", *ZPE* 79 (1989) 100–102; Caldelli (1993) 28–37; E. Maróti, "Zur Regelung der Sportwettkämpfe der *Sebasta* in Neapel", *AAntHung.* 38 (1998) 211–213.

Secundus, GLADIATOR, A PAEGNIARIUS, Secundus lived until 98 BCE and was commemorated by his gladiatorial FAMILIA.

ILS 5126.

Secutor see SAMNIS

Seiraphoros (plural *seiraphoroi*), or *seirophoros*, "trace horse", member of a Greek four-horse chariot team (TETHRIPPON) who drew by lines (*seirai*) rather than from under a yoke. The trace horse carried a lighter load in the straights, but the right-hand *seiraphoros* (DEXIOSEIROS) had furthest to run in the counterclockwise turns and so became proverbial for a helping hand in an emergency. Cf. ZYGIOS.

Aeschylus, *Agamemnon* 842, 1640; Euripides, *Iphigenia in Aulis* 223.

Seiugis (plural *seiuges*) or *seiugae*, Latin term for six-horse chariot team and race.

Livy 38.35.4; *ILS* 5283.

Sellarius (plural *sellarii*), perhaps misspelling of *cellarius*, "storekeeper", member of a Roman chariot-racing FAMILIA.

ILS 5313.

Septimius Aurelius (?) Serapion, Lucius, of Alexandria, athlete, third century CE. A PERIODONIKĒS, Serapion (if that was his name) was likely a runner, perhaps one of the many Alexandrian sprinters who won at Olympia from the mid-second century CE on.

Moretti (1987) 90–91; W. Decker, "Olympiasieger aus Ägypten", in U. Verhoeven and E. Graefe (eds) *Religion und Philosophie im alten Ägypten. Festgabe für Philippe Derchain* ... (Louvain 1991) 93–105.

Sex. Some Greek athletes abstained from sex while preparing for competition. In training, ICCUS of Tarentum (winner of the Olympic pentathlon, 444) never touched a woman or a boy (less tiring); CLITOMACHUS of Thebes is said to have left a symposium if anyone so much as mentioned sex. Their self-control was all the greater (and the more exceptional) in that equestrian and athletic competition took place in a sexually charged environment. Greek athletes competed nude in a culture which admired the male body and regarded sex with attractive males and females alike as one of life's great pleasures; the PALAESTRA and GYMNASIUM were well known pick-up spots, and vases with an athletic ambience often bore *kalos* names, graffiti or inscriptions attesting the charm of one youth or another; girls daydreamed about present and future champions; at night, victory parties might turn into drunken orgies – the famous call-girl Neaera took on all-comers at the celebration for CHABRIAS's chariot win at Delphi in 374. Among the Romans, GLADIATORS were usually SLAVES and shared the social and legal disabilities of prostitutes, who also sold their bodies for others' pleasure. Yet they enjoyed a reputation for virility, intensified by their fame and familiarity with death. The RETIARIUS CRESCENS (1) is called "the netter of girls by night"; Juvenal's Eppia, a senator's wife, runs off with Sergius, scarred, wounded – but a gladiator; the emperor COMMODUS's enthusiasm for the arena was explained by his mother's alleged liaison with a gladiator.

Pindar, *Pythians* 9.97–99, 10.56–60; Aristophanes, *Wasps* 1023–1028; Plato, *Laws* 8.839E–840A; Demosthenes 59.33–34; Aeschines 1.135; Plutarch, *Moral Essays* 720D; Juvenal 6.82–114, *Historia Augusta, Marcus* 19.7; *CIL* 4.4353, 4356.

W. Fiedler, "Sexuelle Enthaltsamkeit griechischer Athleten und ihre medizinische Begründung", *Stadion* 11 (1985) 137–175; H. Aigner, "Hinweis auf sexuelle Abstinenz von Athleten in einer Inschrift aus Thuburbo Maius in Afrika?", in R. Renson, M. Lämmer,

J. Riordan and D. Chassiotis (eds) *The Olympic Games Through the Ages: Greek Antiquity and its Impact on Modern Sport. Proceedings of the 13th International HISPA Congress Olympia/Greece, May 22–28, 1989* (Athens 1991) 73–83; Scanlon (2002).

Shield race *see* HOPLITĒS

Silicius Firmus Mandrogenes, Lucius, of Magnesia on Maeander, pancratiast, third century CE. A PERIODONIKĒS, Mandrogenes' Olympic win may date to 213 CE.

IMagn. 199.

Silvanus, "Woody", Roman chariot horse, ? late second century CE. While driving for the Blue CIRCUS FACTION, CALPURNIANUS drove Silvanus, an African chestnut, to 105 victories.

ILS 5288.1.

Simonides, son of Leoprepes, of Iulis (on Ceos), Greek poet, sixth/fifth century. Reputed to be the first poet to write for pay, Simonides nevertheless (or consequently) is linked with many of the leading figures of the Greek world of his day, as guest of the tyrant Hipparchus of Athens, adviser of the Spartan regent Pausanias, friend of HIERON of Syracuse (at whose court he finished his career). As versatile as other writers of EPINICIANS, Simonides may have written an epigram for MILON as well as (now fragmentary) poems for such victors as ASTYLUS of CROTON, ANAXILAS of Rhegium, and (like PINDAR) Xenocrates of Acragas and the Corinthian Oligaethidae. Later tradition regarded him as a sage (though rather a cynical one) and credited him with discoveries in music and mnemonics.

Simonides fragments 506–519, *PMG*.

J. H. Molyneux, *Simonides. A Historical Study* (Wauconda 1992).

Sitēsis, "feeding", reward for (among others) victors in Greek competitions. At Athens, lifetime *sitēsis* in the Prytaneum was granted to victors at the four major festivals of the PERIODOS. Socrates suggested that the jurors provide him *sitēsis* in recognition of his activities, but they opted for a diet of hemlock instead.

Plato, *Apology* 36D; Plutarch, *Moral Essays* 970B; IG 1³ 131.

P. Schmitt Pantel, *La Cité au banquet. Histoire des repas publics dans les cités grecques* (Rome 1992) 147–163.

Skamma (plural *skammata*), "dugout, pit", soft landing area for the Greek JUMP or for wrestling. "Over the *skamma*" was proverbial for anything extraordinary or excessive ("over the top"); "in the *skamma*" for a decisive event.

Plato, *Cratylus* 413A; Polybius 38.18.5.

E. N. Gardiner, "Phayllus and his record jump", *JHS* 24 (1904) 70–80 (70–74).

Slaves underpinned sport as they did so much else in Greek society, working as guards and attendants in PALAESTRAE and GYMNASIA, preparing STADIA for competition, helping athletes with their equipment and acting as their sparring partners. They might even be prizes (as in the FUNERAL GAMES for Patroclus) or spectators – a slave is threatened with a trip to Olympia, hot, dusty and packed, as a punishment. But they were excluded from exercise in public facilities in many parts of the Greek world (for example, at Athens, Beroea in Macedonia, Crete and Sparta), though some cities admitted them from the Hellenistic period. (In 41/2 CE, a female benefactor at Gytheum in Laconia funded slaves' admission and access to oil for six days a year, apparently against some opposition.) Competition was still rarer; a local festival in second-century CE Pisidia envisaged slaves winning money prizes but was unusual in other respects too. Slaves certainly appear in equestrian events, boys as jockeys, older slaves as charioteers, but it was of course the owners who were proclaimed as victors. It is remarkable, then, that competitors had to put themselves under the authority of a festival's judges and suffer the slavish indignity of corporal punishment at the hands of MAS-TIGOPHOROI and RHABDOUCHOI if they broke the rules. The whipping demeaned them at the same time as fortitude gave them the chance to reclaim their status.

Private *palaestrae*, not unknown in Greece, were more common at Rome, rich as it was, and troupes of slave athletes (*PALAESTRITAE*) trained in them and entertained their owners. However, slaves and freed slaves were most prominent in gladiatorial and circus spectacles. Here they not only staffed the gladiatorial schools (*LUDI*) and CIRCUS FACTIONS but took centre stage: most GLADIATORS and CHARIOTEERS were slaves or freedmen. Fame, fortune and freedom awaited the most successful; so we know many more Roman charioteers by name than Greek, and their careers are detailed in long and costly inscriptions. But violent death was a more likely outcome.

Hippocrates, *Epidemics* 6.8.30; Aeschines 1.138; Demosthenes 61.23; Aristotle, *Politics* 2.1264a21; Dionysius of Halicarnassus, *Rhetoric* 7.6; *SEG* 46.730.

N. B. Crowther, "Slaves in Greek athletics", *QUCC* 40 (1992) 35–42; Crowther and M. Frass, "Flogging as a punishment in the ancient games", *Nikephoros* 11 (1998) 51–82.

Socrates, son of Socrates, Epidauran runner, second/first century. Socrates won the *HIPPIOS* race at the Nemean and ASCLE-PIEIAN games as a boy, and many others of middle distance as an adult including *hippios*, DIAULOS and the race in armour.

IG 4².1 629.

Moretti (1953) 140–141.

Sogenes, son of Thearion, Aeginetan pentathlete, fifth century. Though there was no pentathlon competition for boys at Nemea, Sogenes won there against older competitors (in the earlier fifth century) when he was still a minor.

Pindar, *Nemeans* 7.

Stephen G. Miller, "The pentathlon for boys at Nemea", *CSCA* 8 (1975) 199–201.

Solon, Athenian lawgiver, seventh/sixth century. Generally regarded by the Athenians as the founder of their democracy, Solon is said to have passed a number of laws related to sport. One limited Athenians' civic rewards for victory at Olympia to 500 drachmas, at Isthmia to 100. Solon also figures as an admirer of the Argive athletes CLEOBIS and Biton in Herodotus, and as an exponent of Greek athletics in Lucian's *ANACHARSIS*. Such accounts are of doubtful reliability – Athens likely did not issue coins as early as 594, Solon's year in office – but do testify to the central place of competition in Athenians' ideas of their community.

Herodotus 1.30–32; Plutarch, *Solon* 23.3; Diogenes Laertius 1.55–56.

I. Weiler, "Einige Bemerkungen zu Solons Olympionikengesetz", in P. Händel and W. Meid (eds) *Festschrift für Robert Muth* (Innsbruck 1983) 573–582; D. G. Kyle, "Solon and Athletics", *AncW* 9 (1984) 91–105; C. Mann, *Athlet und Polis im archaischen und frühklassischen Griechenland* (Göttingen 2001) 70–81.

Sosibius, son of Dioscurides, Alexandrian athletic and equestrian victor, third century. Sosibius's competitive career is the subject of one of our last Greek EPINI-CIANS, written by CALLIMACHUS in the late 240s. It was as versatile as that poet, including a victory in DIAULOS for boys in a festival for one of the Ptolemies, in wrestling for *AGENEIOI* at the PANATHE-NAEA, and in chariot races at Isthmia and Nemea. Sosibius was a major political figure at the courts of the Ptolemies at Alexandria, an advisor to Ptolemy IV, and allegedly complicit in the murders of his mother (BERENICE II) and widow.

Callimachus 384, 384a Pfeiffer.

Sostratus, son of Sosistratus, Sicyonian pancratiast, fourth century. Sostratus was nicknamed *Akrochersitēs*, "Finger-tips", for his trick of grabbing rivals' fingers and bending them. It worked (as it had for LEONTISCUS): he was a *PERIODONIKĒS*, *pankration* champion three times at

Olympia (364, 360, 356), twice in the Pythian games, a total of twelve times at Isthmia and Nemea, and his image appeared on Sicyon's coins.

Pausanias 6.4.1–2; SEG 23.325.

Ebert (1972) 129–132; Moretti (1987) 70.

Sotades, of Crete, runner, fourth century. Winner of the DOLICHOS at Olympia in 384, and mentioned as the standard for running a lot in an Athenian comedy shortly thereafter, Sotades took a bribe to declare himself a native of Ephesus after he repeated at the next festival and was banished by his Cretan fellow citizens.

Philetaerus fragment 3 Kassel-Austin; Pausanias 6.18.6.

Moretti (1987) 69.

Soteria, name of a number of Greek competitive festivals. The best known, at Delphi, was established as an annual celebration with musical and dramatic contests to thank Zeus Soter ("the saviour") and Pythian Apollo for deliverance from the Gauls in 279/8. It was reorganized as a quadrennial crown games with athletic and equestrian competitions as well sometime soon after 246/5, a pioneer in the Hellenistic trend to enhance the status of local festivals. The quadrennial Soteria followed immediately after the Pythia, in September. An annual Soteria with musical contests continued to be held (unusually) during the winter. Sicyon was another city with both a Pythia and a Soteria, in this case, a memorial to the hometown hero ARATUS.

Plutarch, Aratus 53.4–6; IG 2^2 680, 3150; Delph. 3.1 481–483.

G. Nachtergael, Les Galates en Grèce et les Sôtêria de Delphes (Brussels 1977).

Sparsio (plural *sparsiones*), "scattering", the distribution of gifts by MISSILIA or the sprinkling of scented water on spectators (to cool them) and on sand (to cover the smell of blood) in the Roman AMPHITHEATRE.

Seneca, Natural Questions 2.9.2; Statius, Silvae 1.6.65–66.

Sparsor (plural *sparsores*) or *spartor* (plural *spartores*), "sprinkler", stable hand who cooled Roman chariot horses with water.

ILS 5313.

Sparta, Greek city in Laconia in the Peloponnese, a major military and political power in the archaic and classical periods and an influential ideological force long after. Sparta's unique internal challenges – the Spartans controlled a large and self-conscious subject population, the Messenians – and internal ambitions combined to produce a competitive culture which diverged in some respects from the Greek norm. But its importance to antidemocratic and aristocratic activists and writers makes accounts difficult to evaluate. Thus one tradition makes boxing a Spartan discovery and the need to avoid and endure blows a part of Sparta's constant preparation for war, and claims that *pankration* at Sparta alone permitted biting and gouging. Another denies that Spartans practised these events at all, since they were unwilling to signal submission in any context. Our controls on these strains – the story that the Spartan ephor CHILON (2) died happy when his son became boxing champion at Olympia, the lack of known Spartan victors in the *pankration* there – are inadequate to resolve or reject them. At any rate, it is clear that the *agōgē*, as the unusual state-organized and run upbringing of Spartan boys is called, focused on building physical fitness, group solidarity, and (however inconsistently) leadership. It therefore included a number of TEAM sports, a hand-to-hand combat on a man-made island called The Plane Trees (PLATANISTAS) and BALL games for five teams (of fourteen or so twenty-year-olds) in an annual tournament at the city's theatre. These were meant to produce good soldiers, as were the equally unusual physical activities of girls, themselves subject to a state-supervised education involving aerobic jumping (*BIBASIS*), wrestling and running (including the mysterious *TRIŌLAX* race) in the same places as men and oiled like them. The footraces at least are well attested for unmarried girls all over the Greek world. What differentiates Sparta is their conduct in plain view and as part of everyday life, rather than just in an isolated sanctuary and a cult context.

This interest in competitions was also exhibited in a rich calendar of local festivals – DAMONON's column records no fewer than nine – including the Gymnopaediae (in which boys competed in their distinctive Spartan age-groups) and the Leonidea in honour of the Spartan king who fell at Thermopylae. As well as the *DOLICHOS*, they ran the *pentē dolichos* and *makros dromos*, perhaps more demanding footraces in the Spartan mould – the *makros dromos* a torch race – and kept lists of victors. Only with the revival of festival culture during the Roman empire – and the contemporary desire to explore and exploit Sparta's glorious past – did games attract athletes from outside (Classical Sparta was notoriously unwelcoming to visitors.) The first, the Caesarea in honour of Augustus, was soon supplanted by the quadrennial Urania (97/98 CE), which offered money prizes as well as wreaths to bring in leading competitors, Euryclea and COMMODEIA Olympia (one of only two *AGŌNES* in Greece to gain the designation "eiselastic" at this time).

Their fitness in itself afforded Spartan athletes an advantage, and they are prominent among early victors at nearby Olympia. The wrestlers HIPPOSTHENES and Hippocleides, father and son, won eleven times, and Hipposthenes was worshipped as a HERO. Victors in the major crown games became members of the kings' bodyguards in battle. But the Spartans prided themselves on strength rather than skill – they disdained trainers – and the increased interest in competition which accompanied the expansion of the circuit (*PERIODOS*) in the early sixth century reduced their prominence. Other cities' champions (who did not appear at Sparta) might not get the recognition they expected: the Athenians freed DORIEUS when he fell into their hands; the Spartans put him to death. However, athletic preeminence was replaced a century later by equestrian excellence. EUAGORAS (2) won three Olympic chariot races with the same team in the mid-sixth century, King Demaretus won once some fifty years later, and Spartans then came first in seven of the eight races from 448 to 420 (LICHAS), a record likely interrupted only by their exclusion from the festival as a result of conflict with Elis for as long as twenty years during the Peloponnesian war, and in four more after the war was over. Like victors elsewhere, Sparta's equestrians might gain political preferment as well as prestige. Demaretus risked defeat – a possibility that kept future kings out of the competitive *agōgē* – because of rivalry with Cleomenes, his colleague in Sparta's unique dual monarchy. But at Sparta, unlike other cities, the ethos of equality which coexisted with significant disparities in wealth prohibited the public presentation of EPINICIANS. Spartan women played a part here too. CYNISCA became the first woman to keep and perhaps breed horses to win a chariot race at Olympia, and was followed by EURYLEONIS and (PAUSANIAS says) others.

See also: OLYMPIO.

Euripides, *Andromache* 595–601; Xenophon, *Spartan Constitution* 1.4, 9.5; Theocritus 18.22–25; Plutarch, *Lycurgus* 14.2–15.1, 19.4, 22.4; *Moral Essays* 189E, 227D, 228D, 233E, 639E; Pausanias 3.8.1, 13.7, 14.1, 15.7; Philostratus, *On Athletic Exercise* 9, 58; *Greek Anthology* 16.1; Seneca, *On Kindnesses* 5.3; *IG* 5.1 18–20, 213, 222, 1120; *SEG* 11.830.

A. Spawforth in P. A. Cartledge and A. Spawforth, *Hellenistic and Roman Sparta* (London and New York 1989) 184–189; S. Hodkinson, "An agonistic culture? Athletic competition in archaic and classical Spartan society", in S. Hodkinson and A. Powell (eds) *Sparta: New Perspectives* (London 1999) 147–187; *Property and Wealth in Classical Sparta* (London 2000) 303–333; Scanlon (2002) 121–138.

Spartacus, GLADIATOR and rebel, first century. A Thracian by origin and once a soldier in the Roman auxiliary, Spartacus was later sold as a slave and trained as a gladiator in the *LUDUS* of Cn. Lentulus Batiatus at Capua in southern Italy – a centre of gladiatorial activity. In 73, he led an outbreak of perhaps seventy gladiators; other slaves and rural labourers joined him until he had an army of as many as 120,000. This fought its way to northern Italy (perhaps with the intention of escaping into Gaul, the home of many of Spartacus's followers), defeating a series of Roman commanders (including two consuls), before turning south and contemplating an invasion of Sicily (in ships to be supplied by pirates). In 71, the army was defeated, and Spartacus killed, by a large force under M. Licinius Crassus; its remnants were mopped up by Pompey, who lined the road from Capua to Rome with 6,000 crucified prisoners. Spartacus's success, and the courage, charisma and humanity which helped him achieve it, made him a legendary figure even in a tradition dominated by slaveholders who regarded Thracians as savages.

Livy, *Summaries* 95–97; Plutarch, *Crassus* 8–11.

K. R. Bradley, *Slavery and Rebellion in the Roman World 140 B.C.–70 B.C.* (Bloomington 1989) 83–101.

Speudusa, "Hasty", Roman chariot horse, uncertain date. "Speedy as the wind", Speudusa was an African mare commemorated by a tombstone and grave epigram.

CIL 6.10082.

Sphairai, "balls", or *episphairai*, padded hand coverings used for training or sparring (*sphairomakhia*) by Greek boxers.

Plato, *Republic* 8.830B; Menander, *Dyscolus* 517; Plutarch, *Moral Essays* 80B, 825E.

Poliakoff (1986) 88–100; T. F. Scanlon, "Boxing gloves and the games of Gallienus", *AJP*

107 (1986) 110–114; P. Angeli Bernardini, "*Sfairai* e *kylikes* nel simposio: un'immagine agonistica in Dionisio Calco, fr. 2.3–4 Gent.-Pr.", *Nikephoros* 3 (1990) 127–132.

Sphairistērion (plural *sphairistēria*), area (likely) for BALL play in a Greek *PALAESTRA* or GYMNASIUM.

Theophrastus, *Characters* 5.9; *CID* 2.139.

Spiculus, GLADIATOR, first century CE. The emperor NERO gave Spiculus, a *MURMILLO*, properties and residences like those of conquering commanders and called on him to return the favour by helping him commit suicide in 68 CE – in vain.

Suetonius, *Nero* 30.2, 47.3.

Spina see EURIPUS

Spoliarium (plural *spoliaria*), a place in the AMPHITHEATRE where dead GLADIATORS were stripped of their arms and clothing.

Seneca, *Letters* 93.12; *Historia Augusta, Commodus* 18.3–19.3.

Mosci Sassi (1992) 173–174.

Spondophoros (plural *spondophoroi*), "truce bearer", emissary who proclaimed a festival TRUCE.

Pindar, *Isthmians* 2.23–24; Aeschines 2.133.

Spongia (plural *spongiae*), part of the equipment of the *RETIARIUS*.

Tertullian, *On Spectacles* 25.4.

Mosci Sassi (1992) 174–176.

Stadion (plural *stadia*), Greek term for (1) a distance of 600 Greek feet; (2) a footrace of that length at Greek competitive festivals; and (3) the venue for that and other athletic contests. A *stadion* was a distance of 600 Greek feet. Since the foot varied from place to place and over time, the length of a *stadion* also differed. The shortest known, at Corinth, was 165m (based on a foot of 0.275m), the longest, that at Olympia in the classical period, was

192.28m (based on a foot of 0.320m). The length of a *stadion* (600 Greek feet) at some Greek sites was as follows:

Corinth	165m
Halieis	166.50m
Delphi	177.55m
Nemea	178m
Isthmia (later stadium)	181.20m
Epidaurus	181.30m
Delos	182m
Athens	(?) 178 or 184.30 or 184.96m
Priene	(?) 191.39m
Miletus	(?) 177.36 or 191.39m
Olympia (stadium III)	192.28m
Isthmia (early stadium)	192.28m

The *stadion* race was a regular and especially important event at Greek competitive festivals. The shortest of the footraces at 600 Greek feet (one length of the stadium), it was also usually regarded as the most prestigious athletic event, much like the 100m dash today. According to the traditional account of early Olympic history, the *stadion* race was the first event on the programme (in 776), the only event until 724, and the only footrace for boys after its introduction in 632. The winner of the men's *stadion* race earned the honour of lighting the fire for the holocaust of 100 bulls which was the festival's central religious rite; his name was used to identify Olympiads from at least the third century and heads lists of Olympic victors on papyri. (As a result, we know of many more *stadion* champions than other athletes.) In addition, the *stadion* race (like wrestling) was part of the pentathlon as well as a stand-alone event (and runners tended to be the most successful pentathletes), brought the largest reward among athletic events at the PANATHENAEA in the early fourth century, and was the race usually won by girls

such as the daughters of HERMESIANAX (2). (However, prizes for HEAVY events are larger at some festivals in late antiquity, and girls at the HERAEA (2) ran a shorter race of 500 Greek feet.) PHILOSTRATUS, who regards the *stadion* as the least strenuous of races, says specialists at the distance need a slightly elongated build, with a smaller chest than normal, moderate muscles (bulk cuts down speed) and large hands – they stir the light, slender legs into the race like wings. Many runners did not specialize: we hear of those who won *stadion* as boys and the DOLICHOS as men or reversed that trajectory and POLITES of Ceramus won *stadion*, DIAULOS and *dolichos* at the same Olympic festival. Victories in both *stadion* and one of the heavy events were much less common; examples (as at the Meleagreia at Balboura) may result from small fields. (Were some good athletes unwilling to take on members of the local elite?) The *stadion*'s prestige seems to have attracted large fields, so a winner likely needed to prevail in preliminary HEATS – an extra demand which may have enhanced his reputation. Those who won at three Olympic festivals in succession (like ASTYLUS and LEONIDAS) deserved theirs.

A *stadion*, "stadium", was the main site of athletic competition at Greek festivals. (Equestrian events required a HIPPODROME, athletes exercised and trained in the PALAESTRA and GYMNASIUM.) A stadium was a track (DROMOS) and playing field bordered on (at least) one side by an embankment, terrace or grandstand for spectators. Originally rectangular, later stadia had one semi-circular end. Seating was usually simple, with designated spots for only judges, priests and other dignitaries – *stadion* is linked to Greek *histēmi*, "I stand" – and many *stadia* got permanent seats only in the Hellenistic period or later. Estimated capacities ranged from 1,500 at Halieis (this in a town of about 2,500) to 21,000 at Hellenistic Isthmia and 40,000 or more at Nemea and Olympia. These last two sites were among

those which featured a vaulted tunnel to
bring athletes and officials from the sanctuary to the stadium. The tunnel also gave
athletes a place to prepare for their
events, an opportunity many at Nemea
took to write graffiti on the walls. The
track itself was some 200m in length (see
above) and much narrower, a challenge
for pentathletes, whose discus and javelin
throws had to land within it, and for
spectators (death by discus is a motif of
Greek myth). Starting mechanisms (see
BALBIS, HYSPLĒX) at both ends could
accommodate from eight to twenty athletes. The track was surfaced with hard-
packed clay (which was dug up, levelled
and rolled periodically), divided into lanes
by lime and gypsum and lengthwise by
100-foot markers (at rather less precise
intervals). It was bordered by ditches and
sloped lengthwise for drainage.

Herodotus 2.149; Philostratus, *On Athletic
Exercise* 5, 32–33; *CID* 2.139.

O. Broneer, *Isthmia I. The Temple of Poseidon*
(Princeton 1971) 174–181; Stephen G. Miller,
"Turns and lanes in the ancient stadium", *AJA*
84 (1980) 159–166; D. G. Romano, *Athletics
and Mathematics in Archaic Corinth: The
Origins of the Greek Stadion* (Philadelphia
1993); T. Aigner, B. Mauritsch-Bein and W.
Petermandl, *Laufen* (Vienna 2002).

Statues. Athletes were a major subject of
Greek sculpture, focused as it was on
depicting the naked male body. From at
least the sixth century, winners at major
games earned the right to erect a statue
commemorating their victory at the site
(PAUSANIAS mentions over 200 in the ALTIS
at Olympia) and in public spaces, such as
the AGORA, in their native city. Life-size
images of wood and then of marble and
bronze, they bore an inscription in prose,
verse or both indicating the victor, his
ancestry and his native city; this reflected
the HERALD's victory announcement much
as the image (which generally showed a
moment of the competition or the athlete
at rest after it) did the victory itself. And
just as the epigrams inscribed on the base,
and the EPINICIANS which celebrated the

victory, were the work of the Greek
world's leading poets, so too victory statues were commissioned from such prominent sculptors as Myron, Naucydes and
Polyclitus. They are therefore important in
the history of Greek art, though less valuable in illustrating competitive technique.
Materials were intractable, movement difficult to imitate, and absolute accuracy in
any case not always an aim. (It may be
relevant in this context that only three-
time winners were allowed portrait statues.) Like praise poetry too, statues were
expensive, and so often underwritten by
the victor's community. The *polis*'s pride in
such achievements sometimes led to the
erection of statues for long-dead champions – the SPARTANS did this for CHIONIS
– and resentment at rejection caused the
Crotoniates to pull down ASTYLUS's when
he ran for Syracuse.

Pausanias 5.21.1, 25.1, 6.13.1; Lucian, *For
Images* 11; *Greek Anthology* 9.588; Pliny,
Natural History 34.9.16.

W. W. Hyde, *Olympic Victor Monuments and
Greek Athletic Art* (Washington 1921); H.-V.
Herrmann, "Die Siegerstatuen von Olympia",
Nikephoros 1 (1988) 119–183; F. Rausa, *L'im-
magine del vincitore. L'atleta nella statuaria
greca dall'età arcaica all'ellenismo* (Treviso and
Rome 1994).

Stephanitēs see AGŌN

Stomius, of Elis, athlete, fourth century.
Victor in pentathlon at Olympia (? 376)
and three times at Nemea, Stromius later
commanded Elis's cavalry and killed a
Sicyonian general who challenged him to
single combat.

Pausanias 6.3.2.

Straton, son of Corrhagus, of Alexandria,
HEAVY athlete, first century. Though privileged by birth and wealth, Straton was
afflicted with an ailment of the spleen. He
exercised to treat it – perhaps in a portico
built for this purpose near Aegium – and
succeeded so well that he became a
PERIODONIKĒS, winning four crowns on

the same day at Nemea (wrestling and *pankration* for both boys and AGENEIOI) and two at Olympia twice, in both 68 and 64. He was the first successor of HERACLES since PROTOPHANES.

Pausanias 5.21.9, 7.23.5; Aelian, *Historical Miscellany* 4.15; Eusebius, *Chronicon* 1.211 Schoene.

Strigil (Latin *strigilis*, plural *strigiles*; Greek *stlengis*, plural *stlengides*), a curved tool used to scrape oil, sweat and dust off an athlete's body after exercise. Most strigils were metal, usually bronze, but the SPARTANS' were made of reed and those at wealthy Acragas, of silver and gold. The strigil marks the athlete in classical Greek sculpture (as the ARYBALLOS had earlier).

Diodorus 13.82.8; Plutarch, *Moral Essays* 239B; Philostratus, *On Athletic Exercise* 18.

D. Sansone, *Greek Athletics and the Genesis of Sport* (Berkeley and Los Angeles 1988) 122–128; E. Kotera-Feyer, *Die Strigil* (Frankfurt am Main 1993); "Die Strigilis in der attisch-rotfigurigen Vasenmalerei: Bildformeln und ihre Deutung", *Nikephoros* 11 (1998) 107–136.

Sulla *see* CORNELIUS SULLA

Suppositicius (plural *suppositicii*), "substitute", or *tertiarius*, GLADIATOR who fought the winner of the previous bout.

Martial 5.24.8.

Mosci Sassi (1992) 176–177.

Swimming. Though Greeks and Romans swam for recreation and (in the case of sponge-divers) livelihood, the only evidence for competitive swimming is linked to Dionysus. An annual festival for Dionysus Melanaegis at Hermione in the Peloponnese included a musical competition, a BOAT race and a contest in swimming (perhaps underwater as well as on top), and swimming races (one between Dionysus and a boyfriend) feature in Nonnus's epic account of the god's career.

Pausanias 2.35.1; Nonnus, *Dionysiaca* 11.43–55, 400–430.

D. Larmour, "Boat-races and swimming contests at Hermione", *Aethlon* 7.2 (1990) 127–138.

Symmachus, of Messana (Sicily), runner, fifth century. Symmachus won the STADION race at two Olympic festivals in succession, 428 and 424.

Diodorus 12.49.1, 65.1; Pausanias 6.2.10.

Syngymnastēs (plural *syngymnastai*), a sparring partner.

Xenophon, *Constitution of the Lacedaemonians* 9.4.

Synōris (plural *synōrides*), Greek term for two-horse CHARIOT team.

Aristophanes, *Clouds* 1302.

Syzygos (plural *syzygoi*), "yoke-fellow", a CHARIOTEER of a Roman CIRCUS FACTION who raced as a partner of a different faction's team; Latin COLLEGA.

D. R. Jordan, "New defixiones from Carthage", in J. H. Humphrey (ed.) *The Circus and a Byzantine Cemetery at Carthage* 1 (Ann Arbor 1989) 117–134 (124).

T

Tagma, "order, rank", a competition known only from the SEBASTA at Naples, perhaps a form of mock combat.

IG 14 748.

Tainia (plural *tainiai*), "ribbon, fillet", wound around a Greek victor's forehead, or limbs.

Eubulus fragment 3 Kassel-Austin; Xenophon, *Symposium* 5.9.

Talantiaioi *see* AGŌN

Taraxippos, "horse-scarer", dangerous part of the Greek HIPPODROME. Several Greek hippodromes featured a place – generally near the first turn – where crashes were especially frequent. At Olympia, it had the shape of a round altar, explained (among other ways) as a mound made by PELOPS to propitiate the murdered charioteer Myrtilus. At Isthmia, the *taraxippos* was Glaucus, who had been killed and eaten by his horses at funeral games for Pelias; at Nemea, it was red-coloured rock. (There was no *taraxippos* at Delphi, it seems – crashes could happen anywhere.) Charioteers would sacrifice and pray to propitiate the *taraxippos*.

Dio Chrysostom 32.76; Pausanias 6.20.15–19, 10.37.4.

Taurosthenes, of Aegina, wrestler, fifth century. After losing to CHIMON in 448, Taurosthenes became Olympic wrestling champion at the next festival. The story goes that the victory was announced at Aegina on the same day, either by an apparition of Taurosthenes himself or by a pigeon he outfitted with a purple flag.

Pausanias 6.9.3; Aelian, *Historical Miscellany* 9.2.

Taurothēria, "bull-hunting", a rodeo event in Greek games. A mounted rider pursued a bull, leaped off his horse to grapple with it, subdued it and wrestled it to the ground. *Taurothēria* (also called *taurokathapsia*) is attested for the ELEUTHERIA (2) at Larisa in Thessaly, at Smyrna and Sinope, and at Rome.

Philip of Thessalonica, *Greek Anthology* 9.543; Heliodorus, *Aethiopica* 10.28–30; *IG* 9.2 531.

L. Robert, "Deux épigrammes de Philippe de Thessalonique", *Journal des Savants* (1982) 139–162 (148–162); K. Gallis, "The games in ancient Larisa. An example of provincial Olympic games", in Raschke (1988) 217–235 (221–225).

Teams. Greek sport stressed the achievements of individuals. As often, equestrian competition provides exceptions – not just the chariot teams which raced in its marquee events, but the group entries by communities such as ARGOS, DYSPONTIUM and ELIS, the large-scale cavalry contests like the ANTHIPPASIA, and the teamwork required between charioteer and runner in APOBATĒS. (Chariot-racing stables, the CIRCUS FACTIONS, are Roman.) Otherwise, team competitions had little place in the prestigious circuit (PERIODOS) of panhellenic festivals. (BOAT RACES were held at Actium and perhaps Isthmia.) They occur in local games: though the PANATHENAEA attracted the best and most ambitious athletes to Athens, its group competitions – boat races, TORCH races, the EUANDRIA – involved teams made up from the ten civic tribes only and their prizes did not include the distinctive Panathenaic amphoras. Here and elsewhere group events were primarily preparations for the real team sport of the Greeks, WAR – something which explains the relative richness of evidence for team BALL games (EPISKYROS) and combat (PLATANISTAS) for young men at SPARTA.

N. B. Crowther, "Team sports in ancient Greece: some observations", *International Journal of the History of Sport* 12 (1995) 127–136.

Telemachus *see* HAGIAS

Telemachus, son of Telemachus, Eleian equestrian victor, third century. Telemachus won the chariot race at Olympia (perhaps in 292) and also the horse race at the Pythian games.

Pausanias 6.13.11; *IvO* 177.

Telestas, of Messene, runner, fourth century. Winner of the boys' STADION race at Olympia in the late fourth century, Telestas may have inscribed his name next to the word *nikō*, "I win", in the tunnel athletes used to enter the stadium at Nemea.

Pausanias 6.14.4.

Stephen G. Miller, "Excavations at Nemea, 1978", *Hesperia* 48 (1979) 73–103 (100).

Tēnella kallinike, or *tēnella kallinikos*, "Hurrah, fair victor", a chant which greeted victors in Greek competitive festivals. It was sung three times (perhaps with *kallinike* or *kallinikos* alone) for victors at Olympia. The word *tēnella* is said to imitate the sound of the AULOS or the lyre.

Archilochus fragment 324 West; Pindar, *Olympians* 9.1–4; Aristophanes, *Acharnians* 1227; *Birds* 1765.

Tentor (plural *tentores*), "holder", attendant involved in start of Roman chariot races.

ILS 5313.

Terma (plural *termata*), "boundary, limit", Greek word used for the start, turning-point or finish of a race.

Homer, *Iliad* 23.309; Pindar, *Nemeans* 7.71; Pollux 3.147.

H. M. Lee, "The *terma* and the javelin in Pindar, Nemean vii 70–3, and Greek athletics", *JHS* 96 (1976) 70–79.

Tertiarius *see* SUPPOSITICIUS

Petronius, *Satyricon* 45.11.

Tethrippon (plural *tethrippa*), Greek term for four-horse CHARIOT team.

Pindar, *Olympians* 2.48–51; Herodotus 6.103. 2.

Thaliarchus, son of Soterichus, Eleian boxer, first century. Thaliarchus was boys' boxing champion at Olympia (perhaps in 40) and repeated as an adult (perhaps in 32). His father may have been Olympic champion in boxing among boys before him, in 72.

Phlegon, *FGrH* 257 F 12; *IvO* 213.

Thallus, Roman charioteer, early second century CE. Thallus, a famous driver for the Red CHARIOT FACTION, was a slave freed by L. Avilius Planta.

ILS 3532, 5287.

Theagenes *see* THEOGENES

Themis see AGŌN

Theochrestus, of Cyrene, chariot victor, fourth century. Theochrestus won the Olympic chariot race (perhaps in 360), a feat repeated by his son's son, another Theochrestus (perhaps in 300). As for his son, he was chariot victor at Isthmia.

Pausanias 6.12.7.

Theodorus, of Messenia, runner, first century. Theodorus won the Olympic STADION race twice, in 48 and 44.

Eusebius, *Chronicon* 1.213 Schoene.

Theodota, daughter of Antiphanes and TIMARETA, Eleian chariot victor, first century. A member of the family of PHILISTUS, Theodota won the chariot race for colts (*PŌLOI*) at Olympia in about 84.

IvO 198–204.

Theogenes, or Theagenes, son of Timoxenus, of Thasos, boxer, early fifth century. One of the most famous of all ancient athletes, Theogenes won 1,200, 1,300 or 1,400 crowns (perhaps counting preliminary bouts). Two came at Olympia, where he was the first to triumph in both boxing (480) and *pankration* (476); he named a son Diolympius, "twice Olympian", as a result. He also won three Pythian crowns as a boxer (once AKONITI), and nine at each of Nemea and Isthmia, where he was also the victor in *pankration* at one festival. He tried for the same double at Olympia in 480, but was so drained after defeating EUTHYMUS in boxing that he withdrew from *pankration*. The HELLANODIKAI fined him one talent for failing to fight and ordered him to pay another to Euthymus, on the grounds that he had entered the context only to spite him. He paid the fine at the next Olympiad, and left the field open for Euthymus, the eventual champion in boxing. Undefeated in boxing for twenty-two years, Theogenes also won *DOLICHOS* at the Hecatombaea at ARGOS and at Phthia in

Thessaly – in emulation of a hometown hero, ACHILLES. Theogenes first came to prominence as a boy when he walked home with a bronze STATUE he'd picked up in the AGORA. A similar story is told of MILON; like him as well, Theogenes had a prodigious appetite – he could eat an ox – and apparently played a distinguished part in community life. That part was prolonged even after his death. One of Theogenes' statues (it is said), vandalized by an enemy, fell and killed him. According to Greek custom, the Thasians hurled it into the sea. Afflicted afterwards by famine, they sent to the Delphic oracle, which advised them to honour Theogenes. A fisherman retrieved the statue and the Thasians established a cult to Theogenes as a healing divinity; he apparently drew honours as a HERO elsewhere as well. Rumoured to be the son of HERACLES – his father was a priest of Heracles – he too was worshipped after his athletic career was over.

Dio Chrysostom 31.95–97; Plutarch, *Moral Essays* 811DE; Lucian, *Council of the Gods* 12; Pausanias 6.6.5–6, 11.2–9, 15.3; Athenaeus 10.412DE; *SIG*[3] 36A.

J. Pouilloux, *Recherches sur l'histoire et les cultes de Thasos* (Paris 1954) 62–105; Ebert (1972) 118–126; O. Masson, "À propos de Théogenès, athlète et héro", *REG* 107 (1994) 694–697; Pouilloux, "Théogenès de Thasos – quarante ans après", *BCH* 118 (1994) 199–206.

Theognetus, of Aegina, wrestler, fifth century. Winner of the boys' wrestling at Olympia, perhaps in 480, Theognetus may have won at the Pythian and Isthmian games as well. His brother Cleitomachus won at Isthmia, his nephew Aristomenes at Delphi (in 446) – wrestlers both.

Pindar, *Pythians* 8.35–37; Pausanias 6.9.1; *Greek Anthology* 16.2.

Ebert (1972) 58–59.

Theopompus 1. of Thessaly, runner, fifth century. The winner of the Olympic

STADION race in 436, Theopompus is probably the same man as the Diopompus mentioned in Plato among the famous athletes who abstained from SEX during training.

Plato, *Laws* 8.840A; Diodorus 12.33.1.

2. son of DAMARETUS, of Heraea (Arcadia), pentathlete, fifth century. Theopompus won the Olympic pentathlon (perhaps in 484 and 480), following in the footsteps of his father and setting a standard matched by his son, another Theopompus, who was Olympic wrestling champion in (perhaps) 440 and 436.

Pausanias 6.10.4–5.

Theōros (plural *theōroi*), "viewer", a state's official representative on an embassy, to an oracle, or at a panhellenic festival. *Theōroi* announced the beginning of a festival TRUCE (cf. SPONDOPHOROS). Their persons were inviolable.

Thucydides 5.50.2, 8.10.1; Demosthenes 19. 128; Diodorus 14.109; Pausanias 5.2.1–2.

Theotimus, son of Moschion, Eleian boxer, fourth century. Theotimus won the boys' boxing at Olympia, perhaps in 308. His father took part in ALEXANDER III's campaigns in Asia, his brother Hippomachus also became Olympic boxing champion among the boys (? in 300) winning three bouts without receiving a blow. This HIPPOMACHUS may be the same man as the TRAINER who said he could recognize his athletes at a distance even if they were just carrying meat from the market.

Plutarch, *Dion* 1.2; Pausanias 6.12.6; Aelian, *Historical Miscellany* 2.6.

Theron, son of Aensidamus, tyrant of Acragas and chariot champion, died about 473. An ally of GELON (who married his daughter) and of HIERON (his niece's husband), Theron ruled Acragas from about 489 to 473. Like theirs, his equestrian success (in the Olympic chariot race, 476) was meant to bring him the same prestige among Greeks elsewhere that he could command on Sicily, an aim furthered by the two poems he commissioned from PINDAR. Theron's brother Xenocrates used the same CHARIOTEER, Nicomachus, in winning at Delphi (490) and Isthmia.

Pindar, *Olympians* 2, 3; *Pythians* 6; *Isthmians* 2.

Thersias, of Thessaly, equestrian victor, fifth century. Thersias was the first victor in the mule-cart race (APĒNĒ) at Olympia, in 500.

Pausanias 5.9.1.

Theseia, Athenian competitive festival. Established to mark Cimon's seizure of the island of Scyrus and the return of the legendary King THESEUS's bones for burial sometime soon after 476/5, the Theseia was reorganized some 300 years later to mark the Romans' return of Scyrus, Imbrus and Lemnus to Athenian control. At that time, it became a biennial festival celebrated in late September in the second and fourth years of each Olympiad (or perhaps quadrennially, in the fourth year only), with some events open to all-comers (though most known victors even in these are Athenian). In addition to the usual athletic events, the Hellenistic Theseia featured military displays, trumpeters and heralds, armed combat (with shield and sword or spear), contests in APOBATĒS and javelin throwing, horse and chariot races for cavalry, and TORCH races. These last were for teams of PAIDES from the city's PALAESTRAE, EPHEBES (age eighteen), ex-*ephebes* representing GYMNASIA (nineteen) and those of twenty and over. In athletic events (besides DOLICHOS, which they did not run) citizen *paides* were divided into three classes, aged perhaps 12/13, 14/15 and 16/17. They might also compete in a class of *paides* of all ages (*ek pantōn*) against non-citizens. This segregation of competitors in a single event by citizenship is unusual, as too the inclusion

of mercenaries in Athens's pay in EUAN-
DRIA and EUOPLIA.

Plutarch, Cimon 8.6; Theseus 36.4; IG 2² 956–
965, 1014.

G. R. Bugh, "The Theseia in late Hellenistic
Athens", ZPE 83 (1990) 20–37; N. M. Kennell,
"Age categories and chronology in the Helle-
nistic Theseia", Phoenix 53 (1999) 249–262.

Theseus, son of the god Poseidon and a
mortal woman, legendary Athenian HERO
and king. Like HERACLES, whose statues
often joined his in GYMNASIA and PALAES-
TRAE, Theseus used expertise in HEAVY
events to aid humankind. Sometimes regarded as the inventor of PANKRATION, he
is more usually linked with wrestling.
When Cercyon forced travellers on the
road to Megara to wrestle with him and
killed all those who complied, Theseus
alone was able to overcome him with
superior skill (Cercyon relied on size and
strength) or by developing upper-body
techniques (Cercyon went for the legs).
The victory was depicted on the Athenian
Treasury at Delphi, the place itself ("The
Palaestra of Cercyon") pointed out to
PAUSANIAS. Said to be the king who first
unified Attica, Theseus was commemorated by the THESEIA. Like Heracles again
– and in emulation of him – he was a
founder of festivals too, the PANATHENAEA
and especially the ISTHMIAN games in
honour of his father Poseidon (as Heracles
had honoured Zeus at Olympia). At
competitions on Delos celebrating his
victory over the Minotaur, Theseus gave
the first palm leaf crowns to the victors.

Isocrates 10.33; Pausanias 1.39.3, 4.32.1;
Apollodorus, Epitome 1.3; Plutarch, Theseus
11, 21.2, 24.3–5.

Thessalus, son of Ptoeodorus and father
of XENOPHON, Corinthian runner, sixth
century. Thessalus won a footrace at
Olympia (probably DIAULOS) in 504, STA-
DION and diaulos on the same day at the
Pythian games, both races as well as the
race in armour on the same day at the

Panathenaea, and the torch race at the
Hellotia at Corinth.

Pindar, Olympians 13.35–40.

Thraex (plural Thraeces) or Threx,
"Thracian", type of GLADIATOR. Moder-
ately armed – less heavily than a SAMNITE,
more than a MURMILLO – Thraeces carried a small, round shield and a short
curved sword, reminiscent of Thracian
warriors, and wore high greaves on both
legs. They often fought MURMILLONES.
The emperor Caligula, a fan of Thraeces,
made some officers of his bodyguard.

Cicero, Philippics 6.5.13; Horace, Satires
2.6.44; ILS 5142a, b.

Mosci Sassi (1992) 177–178.

Tiberius Claudius Nero, chariot victor
and Roman emperor (14–37 CE), 42 BCE–
37 CE. Like his adopted son GERMANICUS
and the emperor NERO after him, Tiberius
could boast an Olympic chariot victory,
perhaps in 4 BCE. He also won at Thespiae, with a chariot for colts (PŌLOI).
Unlike his predecessor AUGUSTUS or some
later emperors, Tiberius nevertheless did
nothing to promote Greek-style festival
competition in the West.

IvO 220; SEG 22.385.

Moretti (1987) 74; L. Santi Amantini, "Olim-
piadi e imperatori romani", in C. Stella and A.
Valvo (eds) Studi in onore di Albino Garzetti
(Brescia 1996) 361–375.

Tie see DRAW

Timaeus, of Elis, trumpeter, fourth century. Timaeus won the first competition
for trumpeters (see SALPINKTĒS) at Olympia, in 396.

Eusebius, Chronicon 1.203 Schoene.

Timanthes, of Cleonae, pancratiast, fifth
century. After defeating all other pancratiasts at Olympia (in 456), Timanthes
continued to test his strength by drawing
a great bow every day, and threw himself

into a fire when he was no longer able (to PAUSANIAS's disgust).

Pausanias 6.8.4; *Oxyrhynchus Papyri* 222.

Timareta, daughter of PHILISTUS, Eleian chariot victor, second century. Like others of her family, Timareta was successful at the Olympic festival in about 84; she shared the winning two-horse chariot entry with her son Philistus.

IvO 198–204.

Timasitheus 1. of Croton, wrestler, sixth century. It was Timasitheus – a younger man who refused to come to close quarters with him – who put an end to MILON's long reign as Olympic wrestling champion in 512.

Pausanias 6.14.5.

2. of Delphi, pancratiast, sixth century. Twice victor at Olympia (perhaps in 516 and 512) and three times at Delphi, Timasitheus was renowned for his strength and daring in battle. He was one of those captured on the Athenian Acropolis and later killed in the aftermath of Isagoras's unsuccessful attempt to establish a tyranny (507).

Herodotus 5.72.4; Pausanias 6.8.6.

Timocrates, son of Antiphon, Athenian politician and chariot victor, fourth century. Olympic champion in the two-horse chariot race, perhaps in 352, Timocrates helped outfit an Athenian warship in the 360s – a duty of the wealthiest Athenians – and attracted an attack in a speech by Demosthenes in 353/2. He repaid him by testifying for the orator's enemy Midias in 348.

Demosthenes 21.139, 24; *IG* 2^2 3127.

Timodemus, son of Timonous, Athenian pancratiast, fifth century. Timodemus won *pankration* at Nemea and later (? 460) at Olympia. The family boasted four Pythian victories, eight at Isthmia and seven at Nemea, as well as many at home

in Athens, and may have included men of wealth and distinction well into the fourth century.

Pindar, *Nemeans* 2.

Timon 1. of Elis, athlete, (?) third/second century. Timon won pentathlon at Olympia (? 200), Delphi and Nemea. An ally of the Aetolians, he later led the garrison at Naupactus.

Pausanias 5.2.5, 6.16.2.

2. son of Aegyptus, Eleian chariot victor, fifth/fourth century. Timon won the chariot race and his own son Aegyptus (or Aesypus) the horse race at Olympia, perhaps in the same year (? 400). Aegyptus's statue showed a mounted boy, the earliest depiction of a jockey at Olympia. Perhaps, unusually, he rode for himself – but we cannot assume that his victory came when he was so young.

Pausanias 6.2.8.

Tiro (plural *tirones*), "recruit", novice GLADIATORS, so designated at their first fight.

[Caesar], *African War* 71.1; Suetonius, *Julius Caesar* 26.3; *ILS* 5084, 5084a, 5088, 5107.

Mosci Sassi (1992) 179–180.

Tisamenus, son of Antiochus, Eleian athlete and seer, fifth century. A member of the Iamidae, a famous clan of diviners and seers, Tisamenus was told by the Delphic oracle that he would prevail in five great contests (AGŌNES). He thought that this presaged athletic success, so he trained and came within one fall of winning the Olympic pentathlon (in ? 492), winning the race and the jump but losing the wrestling match and the competition as a whole to Hieronymus of Andros. The Spartans correctly concluded that Tisamenus's triumphs would come in war. They therefore made him and his brother citizens, an extraordinary honour, in order to put him on their side. In the event, Tisamenus served on five victorious campaigns, from Plataea (479) to Tanagra (457).

Herodotus 9.33–36; Pausanias 3.11.6–8, 6.14.13.

Tisandrus, son of Cleocritus, of Naxus on Sicily, boxer, sixth century. As difficult to date as he was to beat, Tisandrus was boxing champion at Olympia four times (perhaps from 572 through 560) and four times at the Pythian games as well. He is said (by a source which confuses his homeland with the island of Naxos) to have trained by swimming in the sea.

Pindar fragment 23; Pausanias 6.13.8; Philostratus, *On Athletic Exercise* 43.

Tisias, trainer, sixth century. When GLAUCUS (2) of Carystus was in danger of losing his boys' boxing match at Olympia in 520, Tisias urged him to "hit him like you did the plough". Inspired by this reference to the hammer-like right hand which could shape metal, Glaucus went on to win. Another version of this story credits his father with the timely advice.

Philostratus, *On Athletic Exercise* 20.

Tisicrates, of Croton, runner, fifth century. Tisicrates was part of CROTON's remarkable success in the Olympic STADION race, winning in 496 and 492.

Dionysius of Halicarnassus, *Roman Antiquities* 6.1.1, 34.1, 49.1.

Titeia, Greek competitive festival. At the NEMEAN festival of 195, the Roman commander Titus Quinctius Flamininus announced the freedom of ARGOS from Spartan domination. The grateful Argives founded the Titeia, the first occasion on which a Roman was honoured with a competitive festival in his name.

Livy 34.41.3.

G. Daux, "Concours des *Titeia* dans un décret d'Argos", *BCH* 88 (1964) 569–576.

Tlasimachus, of Ambracia, chariot victor, third century. Tlasimachus won both the two-horse and four-horse chariot race for colts (*PŌLOI*) at Olympia in 292.

Oxyrhynchus Papyri 2082.

Tlepolemus, of Lycia, equestrian victor, third century. Likely the son of Artapates who held high office under the Ptolemies of Egypt, Tlepolemus (like HIPPOCRATES) is said to have been the winner of the first Olympic race for colts (*PŌLOI*), in 256.

Pausanias 5.8.11.

Moretti (1987) 71.

Torch race (Greek *lampas*, *lampadēdromia*), event at Greek competitive festivals. Torch races were generally relay races, run by teams (of *lampadēphoroi*), often from one altar to another; the first finisher might kindle the fire for a sacrifice. At Athens, torch races (under the supervision of the King Archon) were crowd-pleasers attested at a number of major festivals (including the PANATHENAEA and THESEIA). Each of the ten civic tribes entered a team (perhaps of ten), sponsored by a GYMNASIARCH and likely made up of the well-off young men who appeared in other athletic events. At the Panathenaea, the course led from the altar of Eros in the ACADEMY to the Acropolis, a distance of some two miles and uphill; there were prizes for both the winning tribe and for an individual runner, perhaps (on the analogy of races on Delos and Samos) the fastest of those who ran the first leg for each team. There were many variations: the Athenian Prometheia featured a race for individual runners who had to keep the torch lit to qualify (a reflection of Prometheus's successful theft of fire), foreign teams competed at the Alexandrian Basileia, there were preliminary HEATS (*prolampades*) at the ALSEIA on Cos, the course at Didyma required a return to the altar at the start, some torch races were mounted (see APHIPPOLAMPAS). That at the festival of Bendis of Athens, a night-time event, must have been especially spectacular.

Aeschylus, *Agamemnon* 312–314; Aristophanes, *Frogs* 129–133, 1087–1098; *Wasps* 1202–1205; Plato, *Republic* 328A; Xenophon, *Ways and Means* 4.52; Aristotle, *Constitution of the Athenians* 54.7, 57.1; Pausanias 1.30.2; *ID* 1956; *SIG*³ 671A.

G. Dünst, "Die Siegerliste der samischen Heraia", *ZPE* 1 (1967) 225–240; Kyle (1987) 190–193; N. V. Sekunda, "*IG* ii² 1250: a decree concerning the *lampadephoroi* of the tribe Aiantis", *ZPE* 83 (1990) 149–182.

Trainers. Nestor offers his son Antilochus advice before the chariot race at the FUNERAL GAMES of Patroclus, and coaches, instructors and trainers were a constant of Greek sport, especially athletics, ever after. The first (like Nestor) were likely family or friends, but others (often ex-athletes such as MELESIAS) are attested for as early as the mid-sixth century (see ERYXIAS). (It is perhaps symptomatic that sources credit either a coach (TISIAS) or his father with the Olympic victory of GLAUCUS (2) of Carystus.) Trainers supervised athletes' physical well-being, including DIET, taught specific skills, and acted as sport psychologists, building endurance and instilling the desire for victory (and a horror of defeat). Their encouragement could continue during an event as well as in preparation for it. Some might even fundraise: in about 300, a coach (EPISTATĒS) asked the council of Ephesus to subsidize a young athlete's training and travel to a festival. Such services might not come cheap. At about the same time, access to HIPPOMACHUS cost 100 drachmas (two or three months' wages for a working man). Some athletes would therefore settle for group instruction. Trainers could be tough; they are identified by a forked rod (much like referees) on vases. One is said to have used a STRIGIL to stab an athlete who failed to do his best at Olympia, another to have worked an Olympic champion to death. This trainer inflexibly followed the tetrad, the four-day cycle, much criticized by PHILOSTRATUS: preparation (short, brisk workouts), concentration (all-out effort), relaxation, moderation (specialized exercises). Others recommended weight training or suited their approach to athletes' physique and temperament. (Colder phlegmatic athletes needed to be driven, hotter choleric ones needed restraint.) Though we hear more of trainers for young and HEAVY athletes – a papyrus fragment describes a set of wrestling drills – it is likely that their use was also widespread among older competitors, including runners and pentathletes. At Olympia, they swore oaths and appeared naked like their athletes and watched competitions from a special enclosure. Their evident importance posed a problem for aristocratic ideology in the archaic and classical periods, which preferred to stress innate ability, the inheritance of elite ancestors, over tactics and techniques taught for pay. Later athletes, however, often named their trainers on inscriptions listing their achievements.

See also: ALEIPTĒS, GYMNASTĒS, GYMNASTIKOS.

Homer, *Iliad* 23.301–350; Pindar, *Olympians* 8.54–66, 10.17; Plato, *Meno* 94AD; *Statesman* 294DE; Philostratus, *On Athletic Exercise* 14–58; *Oxyrhynchus Papyri* 466.

Jüthner (1909) 3–60; Harris (1964) 170–178; L. Robert, "Sur des inscriptions d'Éphèse", *RPh* 41 (1967) 7–84 (14–32); N. Nicholson, "Pindar, *Nemean* 4.57–58 and the arts of poets, trainers, and wrestlers", *Arethusa* 34 (2001) 31–59.

Triastēs (plural *triastai*), honorific term for the winner of three events in a single festival. Known Olympic *triastai* are all runners: PHANAS (2) of Pellene (512), ASTYLUS of Croton, LEONIDAS of Rhodes (164–152), NICOCLES of Acriae (Laconia, ?100), HECATOMNUS of Miletus (72), POLITES of Ceramus (Caria) (69 CE), HERMOGENES of Xanthus (81), AELIUS Granianus of Sicyon (137). HEAVY athletes such as CLITOMACHUS were *triastai* at other festivals.

Eusebius, *Chronicon* 1.210 Schoene; *SEG* 27.843, 39.1596d.

P. Frisch, *Zehn agonistische Papyri* (Opladen 1986) 140.

Triga (Greek *tripōlon harma*), three-horse racing chariot of the Etruscans and Romans. The horse furthest left was a trace-horse, left unyoked. The *triga* gave its name to the Trigarium, the equestrian training area in the northwest of the Campus Martius at Rome where the chariot race of the OCTOBER HORSE was run.

Dionysius of Halicarnassus, *Roman Antiquities* 7.73.2.

Trigon, "triangle", a BALL game in which players formed a triangle to throw and catch or to strike the ball with their hands in turn.

Herodianus 1.23 Lentz; Horace, *Satires* 1.6.126; Martial 7.72, 12.82.

V. J. Matthews, "*Suram dare*: a gesture in Roman ball playing", *Nikephoros* 3 (1990) 185–187.

Triōlax, "three furlongs", a race for (? SPARTAN) girls, likely three lengths of the STADION.

Hesychius *s. triōlax.*

Triumphus, GLADIATOR, first century CE. In retirement, the MURMILLO Triumphus is said to have longed for the good old days of gladiatorial spectacles of his prime.

Seneca, *On Providence* 4.4.

Troilus, son of Alcinous, of Elis, HELLA-NODIKAS and equestrian victor, fourth century. In 372, Troilus won chariot races for full-grown pairs and four colts while serving as HELLANODIKAS. The Eleians then excluded HELLANODIKAI in office from entering chariot events. (Prince Albert of Monaco, a member of the International Olympic Committee, competed in the four-man bobsleigh at the Salt Lake City games, but was tactful enough not to

pose similar problems.) Troilus may have won again in 368 when his term of office was over.

Pausanias 6.1.4–6; *IvO* 166.

Ebert (1972) 127–129.

Truce (Greek *ekecheiria*, *hieromēnia*, *spondai*), a period before and after Greek festivals during which the territory of the host city was inviolate and competitors, spectators and others had safe passage to and from it. The beginning of the truce was proclaimed by emissaries (SPONDO-PHOROI, THEŌROI) to the major centres of the Greek world. The period of the truce varied. For the Olympics, it grew from one to two months on either side of the festival; for the Pythian games, it extended for a full year. In these cases and others, violations occurred. A writer on tactics even recommends attack during a festival and the ALTIS at Olympia was the site of a pitched battle during the festival in 364. It was sufficiently well known by the mid-fifth century to be used to schedule sacrifices on far-off Selinus on Sicily.

Isocrates 4.43; Aeneas Tacticus 4.8; Plutarch, *Aratus* 28.3–4; *Lycurgus* 1.1; *Moral Essays* 413D; Pausanias 5.2.1, 20.1; Lucian, *Icaromenippus* 33.

G. Rougemont, "La hiéroménie des Pythia et les 'trèves sacrées' d'Eleusis, de Delphes et d'Olympie", *BCH* 97 (1973) 75–106; M. Lämmer, "Der sogenannte Olympische Friede in der griechischen Antike", *Stadion* 8/9 (1982–1983) 47–83.

Trumpeter *see* SALPINKTĒS

Tryphosa *see* HERMESIANAX (2)

Tullius, Marcus, of Apamea (Bithynia), boxer, second century CE. Tullius won thirty-five crowns, including two at Olympia (perhaps in 141 and 145 CE) and others at Isthmia, Nemea, the Panathenaea, the CAPITOLINE games and the SEBASTA at Naples, before dying at thirty-two. His brother erected his monument at

Athens, where he was an honorary citizen.

IG 2² 3163.

Tuscus, Roman chariot horse, early second century CE. Owned by the Green CHARIOT FACTION, Tuscus was part of FORTUNATUS's winning team 386 times.

ILS 5287.

Tyrtaeus, Spartan poet, seventh century. Exhorting his fellow citizens to do battle, Tyrtaeus ranks all other achievements – including excellence in running and wrestling – below valour in war.

Tyrtaeus fragment 12 West.

U

Ulpius Domesticus, Marcus, of Ephesus, pancratiast, second century CE. A *PERIOD-ONIKĒS*, Domesticus's Olympic victory may date to 129 CE. It was followed by a life of achievement as an honorary citizen of Antinoopolis and Athens, superintendent of the Imperial baths, life president of the athletes' GUILD and its (successful) representative in obtaining a permanent site in Rome under the emperors HADRIAN (134) and Antoninus Pius (143).

IG 5.1 669, 14 1052, 1054, 1055, 1100, 1109, 1110.

Moretti (1987) 77; W. C. West, "M. Oulpius Domestikos and the athletic synod at Ephesus", *AHB* 4 (1990) 84–89.

Unctor (plural *unctores*), "anointer", member of a gladiatorial *FAMILIA*.

ILS 5084, 5084a.

Urania, "Sky ball", a BALL game in which one player throws a ball high in the air and others try to catch it before it falls to the ground. A similar game is played by Phaeacian youths in the *Odyssey*.

Homer, *Odyssey* 8.360–370; Pollux 9.106.

Urbicus, GLADIATOR. A left-handed *SECUTOR*, Urbicus died at twenty-two, having fought thirteen times. He left his wife of seven years, a five-month-old daughter, and her nurse. According to his wife (who erected his tombstone), everyone he defeated, died.

ILS 5115.

V

Valerius Eclectus, of Sinope, herald (*KĒRYX*), third century CE. No herald won more often at Olympia then Valerius Eclectus, victor in 245, 253, 257, 261 CE. He was also champion three times at the Pythian and Nemean games and four at the Isthmian among many other triumphs.

IG 2² 3169/70; *IvO* 243.

Moretti (1953) 263–268.

Varazdat, son of Anop, king of Armenia (374–378 CE) and boxer, fourth century CE. Varazdat, a boxer, is one of the latest Olympic victors we can identify by name.

Moses Chorenaçi 3.40.

Veles (plural *velites*), "flyer", type of lightly-armed GLADIATOR, who used spears as weapons.

Isidore, *Etymologies* 18.57; *ILS* 5083a.

Mosci Sassi (1992) 181–182.

Venustus, Roman CHARIOTEER, early second century CE. A *MILIARIUS* – winner of 1,000 races – for the Blue CIRCUS FACTION, Venustus was one of the rivals of DIOCLES.

ILS 5287.

Horsmann (1998) 302.

Veteranus (plural *veterani*), "veteran", GLADIATOR who had had his first fight, and was no longer a *TIRO*.

ILS 5084, 5084a.

Victor, Roman chariot horse, ? late second century CE. In the memorial he had erected for himself, the famous CHARIOTEER CALPURNIANUS says he drove the chestnut horse Victor to 429 wins for the Green CHARIOT FACTION, but the number is inconsistent with other information on the monument.

ILS 5288.2.

Vindex, "Protector, Avenger", Roman chariot horse, ? late second century CE. Vindex, a bay, was part of a team owned by the Green CIRCUS FACTION in 157 victories by CALPURNIANUS.

ILS 5288.2.

Volucer, "Flyer", Roman chariot horse, second century CE. Owned by the Green CHARIOT FACTION, Volucer was a favourite of the emperor Lucius Verus (161–169). Verus is said to have carried about a golden statue of Volucer, fed him with nuts and raisins, entertained him in his palace at Rome – Volucer wore a purple blanket – and built him a tomb when he died.

Historia Augusta, Verus 6.3–6.

W

Warfare. Homer's heroes rode to battle on chariots, dismounted to throw spears, and, when things went against them, ran for their lives. The most famous competed in the FUNERAL GAMES for their fallen fellow Patroclus (the programme included chariots, a fight in armour, a spear throw, a footrace); the best among them, swift-footed ACHILLES, stayed out of the contests as he had once retired from battle, a mark of his pre-eminence as much as of his special tie to Patroclus. Later Greek sport continued to echo warfare – images of Ares and AGŌN stood side by side on the table for winners' wreaths at Olympia – but with a more distorted and indistinct voice. Cavalry officers rode their mounts at the PANATHENAEA and THESEIA, joined by war chariots which had long since disappeared from the battlefield. As for athletes, the GYMNASIUM arose at the same time as the circuit (PERIODOS) of panhellenic games in the early sixth century, and served as a site for the training of young men (EPHEBES) (as well as for cavalry manoeuvres) for several centuries. (It was such young men who took part in most ancient Greek TEAM sports.) Its impetus, however, is uncertain. Some regard the gymnasium as the invention of the heavy infantrymen (HOPLITĒS) who replaced aristocratic champions as the ideal type of the warrior in the archaic period; these needed to be fit enough to march in heavy armour under the hot summer sun before charging an enemy and fighting hand to hand. Others, as the response of the elite, who sought a new sphere to demonstrate their courage (the HEAVY events might involve injury, even death) and merit. The late introduction of the race in armour (*hoplitēs*) into the festivals of the *periodos*, and the absence of PYRRHIC dancing, tell for this alternative. In any case, though Greek armies often exercised and competed on campaign – and SPARTAN law required it – it did not escape critics that some athletic skills, such as throwing the discus, were of limited use in a hoplite battle line. Plato therefore preferred the soldiers of his model Cretan city to conduct mock battles, and such successful commanders as Epaminondas and PHILOPOEMEN – himself a wrestler – discouraged or forbade their men to train as athletes. Modern soldiers have reached similar conclusions. "A boxer, eh, a fighter? Good show, good man. Though I never saw how having a good left hook helped you dig a recoil pit" (Lenny, in Graham Swift, *Last Orders* (1996) 44).

Plutarch describes the elder Cato, stern upholder of Roman tradition, taking his son's education in hand himself. Acting as his own athletic trainer (GYMNASTĒS), Cato taught how to throw a javelin, fight in armour, ride a horse, box, endure heat and cold, swim the Tiber: all activities, unlike Greek sport, of practical application to warfare. As if to underline the contrast, Plutarch adds that Cato refused to bathe with his son: such NUDITY – the hallmark of Greek sport – was unseemly. A Greek, Plutarch might not favour such fanaticism – he elsewhere criticizes Crassus for failing to organize athletic competitions on his disastrous Parthian campaign – but the very different role active competition played in the lives of Roman citizens necessarily affected its links with warfare. These are closest where the Romans served as spectators, especially in gladiatorial spectacles (MUNERA). GLADIATORS' arms and armour recalled Rome's conquered enemies: Gauls (MURMILLONES), SAMNITES, Thracians (see THRAEX). Though this equipment was mostly obsolete, the qualities required of those who wielded it were not. Roman commanders used LANISTAE to train recruits as early as 105, and SPARTACUS's success soon after confirmed their credentials. On a more ideological level, a leading justification for gladiatorial spectacles was the model they provided of bravery and endurance even on the part of slaves and social outcasts. The Roman audience was to become inured to danger and aroused by its rewards – valuable virtues in a soldier.

Euripides fragment 282 N.²; Xenophon, *Constitution of the Lacedaemonians* 12.5–6; Plato, *Laws* 7.796A; Plutarch, *Agesilaus* 34.7–8; *Cato the Elder* 20.4–7; *Crassus* 17.5; *Philopoemen* 3.2–4; Pausanias 5.20.3; Cicero, *Tusculan Disputations* 2.17.41; Pliny, *Panegyric* 33.1; *Historia Augusta, Maximinus and Balbinus* 8.7; *ILS* 6635.

S. Müller, " 'Herrlicher Ruhm im Sport oder Krieg' – der *Apobates* und die Funktion des Sports in der griechischen Polis", *Nikephoros* 9 (1996) 41–69; Golden (1998) 23–28; Reed (1998).

Women played a number of parts in Greek competition. Among the Minoans of Bronze Age Crete, they appear in scenes of BULL-LEAPING, though their precise role (like the nature of the activity itself) is unclear. A slave woman is one of the prizes at the FUNERAL GAMES of Patroclus. In the Hellenistic and Roman periods, women figure as founders of games (a mother in Asia Minor so honoured her three sons), as GYMNASIARCHS (both with their husbands and alone), and as AGŌNOTHETAI. Women also attended competitions as spectators. (The Olympic festival was unusual in excluding married women, with the exception of the priestess of Demeter Chamyne. Those found on the wrong side of the Alpheius river were supposed to be thrown from the steep cliffs of Mt Typaeum, though family connections spared PHERENICE, the one woman who was caught, this fate.) Footraces for girls (*parthenoi*) before marriage were widespread throughout the Greek world at all times. The most famous venue was the HERAEA (2) at Olympia, the best known runners, Athens's "bears", ARKTOI. At Sparta, girls used the same PALAESTRA and running tracks as men and trained in their presence – not running only, but doing jumping exercises (BIBASIS), wrestling and even (according to unreliable sources) throwing the discus and javelin and fighting as pancratiasts. The Hellenistic period provides evidence for races for girls (such as the daughters of HERMESIANAX (2)) at panhellenic festivals too, at the Pythian, Isthmian and Nemean games, the ASCLEPIEIA (1) at Epidaurus, the SEBASTA at Naples. Here too Olympia is anomalous, but girls did run and wrestle at the Olympic festival at ANTIOCH in the Roman period – winners became priestesses and swore to be chaste for life. In none of these festivals did females compete as athletes against males: The legendary ATALANTA had no imitators. However, women (married or not) could enter equestrian competition even where they were forbidden to attend, winning at Olympia from the time of CYNISCA in the early fourth century. Later victors here and elsewhere included other SPARTANS, the wives and girlfriends of Hellenistic rulers, queens in their own right. For some observers, their victories demonstrated the wealth and merit of the families to which they belonged; for others, they devalued a pursuit in which even women could prevail. Only Cynisca has left a record of her own feelings, a victory monument which sounds as proud as any man's.

Roman women could not serve among the magistrates who presided over LUDI, and we know of no female CHARIOTEERS for the CIRCUS FACTIONS, though some (surely slaves) did fight as GLADIATORS (LUDIAE). Women were, however, prominent among the audiences at CIRCUSES and AMPHITHEATRES. The Roman poet Ovid recommends the race track as a place to meet women, and Valeria's pick-up of the dictator CORNELIUS Sulla at a gladiatorial spectacle indicates that this was a game where women could compete as equals. (Sulla, says Plutarch, was "clearly a little excited" when Valeria plucked some lint from his clothes – a state readily revealed when sitting in a toga.) It was perhaps to prevent such encounters that AUGUSTUS took care to keep women away from athletic competitions – nudity might give them ideas – and to separate their seats from men's at gladiatorial shows. Only the Vestal Virgins sat close to the action.

Thucydides 3.104.4–5; Plutarch, *Sulla* 35.3–5; Pausanias 5.6.7, 13.10, 6.20.9; Ovid, *Amores* 3.2; Suetonius, *Augustus* 44.2–3.

Golden (1998) 123–140; R. Frei-Stolba, "Frauen als Stifterinnen von Spielen", *Stadion* 24 (1998) 115–128; A. Bielman, "Femmes et jeux dans le monde grec hellénistique et impérial", *Étude de Lettres* (Lausanne) 1 (1998) 33–50; M. P. J. Dillon, "Did parthenoi attend the Olympic games? Girls and women competing, spectating and carrying out cult roles at Greek religious festivals", *Historia* 128 (2000) 457–480.

Wrestling, Greek *palē*, sometimes *mouno-palē*, regular event in Greek competitive festivals. Along with the STADION race, wrestling was the central sport in Greek athletics. Like the *stadion*, it was etymo-logically linked with a fundamental athletic facility – in the case of wrestling, the PALAESTRA (from *palē*), – part of the PENTATHLON as well as an event on its own, and one of the areas where ATALANTA challenged men in myth. According to tradition, wrestling was the first event admitted to the Olympic programme after the footraces (with pentathlon, in 708); it was frequently depicted on vases (where it is often associated with major figures such as HERACLES and THESEUS); and, in texts, it often figures metaphorically in references to mainstays of Greek culture, sex and warfare, and was the subject of training manuals. Though classified among the HEAVY events, wrestling required skills as well as strength, agility no less than endurance: Galen mocks the pretensions of other athletes by pointing to animals who would surpass them in their specialties, but he is silent about wrestlers.

BOXING and *PANKRATION* matches did not end until one competitor was unwilling or unable to go on. So too wrestlers might attempt to immobilize, to strangle or to incapacitate opponents. (LEONTISCUS of Messana won twice at Olympia by bending back his rivals' fingers until they conceded.) Usually, however, a wrestling match was settled by falls, touches of the back or shoulder to the ground (Greek wrestlers did not need to pin their opponents). Since wrestlers who were thrown or tripped might touch only a knee, matches could continue on the ground much as in *pankration* until a fall was recorded. Victory usually required three falls. Olympic rules once sought to ban Leontiscus's tactics, and tripping was sometimes regarded as unsporting. (While Theseus was said to have invented wrestling with the arms, the use of the legs was ascribed to his outlaw opponent Cercyon.) In general, however, any means of achieving a fall was permitted – wrestlers were recognizable by their hair, shorn short so as to prevent a rival grabbing it – and injuries were not unknown. (The young Heracles is supposed to have broken an opponent's ribs with a waistlock.) But wrestling was less dangerous than either *pankration* or (especially) boxing. This may afford another reason for its important place in the life of Greek men.

Homer, *Iliad* 23.700–739; Aeschylus, *Agamemnon* 167–173; *Libation Bearers* 338–339; Herodotus 6.27; Aristophanes, *Knights* 571–573; Plato, *Euthydemus* 277C; *Laws* 7.796AB; Theocritus 24.111–114; Lucian, *Anacharsis* 1, 24; *Ocypus* 60–61; Philostratus, *On Athletic Exercise* 35; *Greek Anthology* 12.206, 222; *Oxyrhynchus Papyri* 466.

Poliakoff (1986) 128–142, 149–172; (1987) 23–53; J. Ebert, "Eine archaische Bronzeurkunde aus Olympia mit Vorschriften für Ringkämpfer und Kampfrichter", in Ebert, *Agonismata* (Stuttgart 1997) 200–236 (200–211).

X

Xenarches, son of (?) Philandridas, Spartan chariot victor, fifth century. A PERI-ODONIKĒS, Xenarches' chariot victory at Olympia likely dates to 432.

Pausanias 6.2.1–2.

S. Hodkinson, *Property and Wealth in Classical Sparta* (London 2000) 329 n13.

Xenocles, son of Euthyphron, Maenalian wrestler, fourth century. Xenocles won the boys' wrestling competition at Olympia in the early fourth century (perhaps 372), defeating four rivals without being thrown once.

Pausanias 6.9.2; *IvO* 164.

Ebert (1972) 107–110.

Xenodamus, of Anticyra (Phocis), pancratiast, first century CE. The gymnasium of Anticyra held a STATUE of Xenodamus, who won *pankration* at the Olympic festival rescheduled and dominated by NERO in 67. Perhaps the Eleians, who did not recognize the legitimacy of Nero's celebration, did not permit Xenodamus the usual statue in the ALTIS.

Pausanias 10.36.9.

Xenombrotus, son of Xenodicus, of Cos, equestrian victor, fifth century. Xenombrotus, the first Coan victor, won the horse race at Olympia (? 420); his son Xenodicus, boys' boxing (? 400).

Pausanias 6.14.12; *IvO* 170.

Ebert (1972) 154–157.

Xenophanes, of Colophon, poet and philosopher, about 570–475. An independent thinker (sometimes said to be the first satirist), Xenophanes mocked anthropomorphic conceptions of divinity and criticized the honours cities paid to athletic and equestrian victors.

Xenophanes 21 F 2 DK.

M. Marcovich, "Xenophanes on drinking-parties and Olympic games", *ICS* 3 (1978) 1–26.

Xenophon, son of THESSALUS, Corinthian runner, fifth century. In 464, Xenophon became the only athlete to win STADION and PENTATHLON at the same Olympic festival; he dedicated 100 *hetairai* to Aphrodite's temple on Acrocorinth in gratitude for the victories. Xenophon also won at Isthmia (twice) and Nemea. His father THESSALUS was also an Olympic victor (? DIAULOS, 504), who won *stadion* and *diaulos* on the same day at Delphi and these along with the race in armour on the same day at the PANATHENAEA. Their family, the Oligaethidae, could also claim four other victories at Delphi and no less than sixty at each of Isthmia and Nemea.

Pindar, *Olympians* 13; Pausanias 4.24.5; Athenaeus 13.573E–574B.

W. S. Barrett, "The Oligaithidai and their

victories (Pindar, *Olympian* 13; *SLG* 339, 340)", in R. D. Dawe, J. Diggle and P. E. Easterling (eds) *Dionysiaca. Nine Studies in Greek Poetry by Former Pupils Presented to Sir Denys Page on his Seventieth Birthday* (Cambridge 1978) 1–20.

Xenothemis, son of Cleostratus, Milesian boxer, second century. The Olympic victory of Xenothemis – a *PERIODONIKĒS* – may date to 144.

Ancient Greek Inscriptions in the British Museum 929.

Moretti (1953) 126–127.

Xystarchēs (plural *xystarchai*), "leader of the *XYSTOS*", the president of a Greek athletes' GUILD. Roman emperors often named distinguished athletes (usually pancratiasts) *xystarchēs* for life, and made them responsible (at least in theory) for the management of festivals or all the festivals in a city or region. *Xystarchai*, decked out with a wreath and a purple robe, played the role of the AGŌNOTHETAI in many new festivals and (like them) often supplemented their funds.

IG 14 1102; *IGRom.* 4.1215.

Xystos (plural *xystoi*) or *xyston* (plural *xysta*), "scraped, raked (track)", covered practice track in a Greek GYMNASIUM, used for winter exercise; cf. *PARADROMIS*. The term also referred to the enclosure which included the gymnasium at Elis where athletes trained – HERACLES used to scrape up (*anaxyein*) thistles there for exercise. This gave rise to the term *hē sympas xystos*, "the entire portico", for the group of athletes who participated at the Olympic and then any other festival. It was eventually employed in connection with the international GUILD of athletes.

Pausanias 6.23.1; Vitruvius, *On Architecture* 5.11.5; *IG* 14 747.

C. A. Forbes, "Ancient athletic guilds", *CP* 50 (1955) 238–252.

Z

Zanes, bronze statues of Zeus at Olympia paid for by fines collected from athletes and others who broke the festival's rules. The first such fine was levied in 388.

See also: APOLLONIUS RHANTES, CALIPPUS, DIDAS, EUPOLUS, HERACLIDES.

Pausanias 5.21.2–18.

H.-V. Herrmann, "Zanes", *RE Supplementband* 14 (1974) 977–981.

Zōma see PERIZŌMA

Zygios (plural *zygioi*), "draught horse", member of a Greek four-horse chariot team (TETHRIPPON) harnessed to the yoke (*zygon, zygos*), cf. SEIRAPHOROS.

Euripides, *Iphigenia in Aulis* 221; Aristophanes, *Clouds* 122.

Index

Main entries are indicated by bold type. *Periodonikai* are not included in the entries for winners at the Isthmian, Nemean and Pythian festivals. Some items appear more than once on a page.